MANPOWER
RESEARCH
and
LABOR
ECONOMICS

Committee on Department of Labor Manpower Research and Development

edited by
GORDON I. SWANSON
JON MICHAELSON

MANPOWER RESEARCH and LABOR ECONOMICS

Prepared for the Committee on Department of Labor
Manpower Research and Development

National Research Council / National Academy of Sciences

SAGE Publications Beverly Hills London

For information address:

SAGE Publications, Inc.
275 South Beverly Drive
Beverly Hills, California 90212

SAGE Publications Ltd
28 Banner Street
London EC1Y 8QE, England

Printed in the United States of America

Library of Congress Cataloging in Publication Data
Main entry under title:

Manpower research and labor economics.

"Papers prepared for the Committee on Department of Labor Manpower Research and Development of the National Research Council (National Academy of Sciences)."

Includes index.

1. Labor supply—Research—United States—Addresses, essays, lectures. 2. Manpower policy—Research—United States—Addresses, essays, lectures.
I. Swanson, Gordon Ira. II. Michaelson, Jon. III. National Research Council.
HD5724.M243 331.1'1'072073 79-11162
ISBN 0-8039-1268-4
ISBN 0-8039-1269-2 pbk.

FIRST PRINTING

NOTICE

The project that is the subject of this report was approved by the Governing Board of the National Research Council, whose members are drawn from the Councils of the National Academy of Sciences, the National Academy of Engineering, and the Institute of Medicine. The members of the Committee responsible for the report were chosen for their special competences and with regard for appropriate balance.

This report has been reviewed by a group other than the authors according to procedures approved by a Report Review Committee consisting of members of the National Academy of Sciences, the National Academy of Engineering, and the Institute of Medicine.

CONTENTS

Preface

This volume concerns the problems of the American work force and the role of the government in supporting research on those problems. It grew out of an independent review and assessment of the U.S. Department of Labor's manpower research and development effort since 1962. The review was undertaken by a committee of the Assembly of Behavioral and Social Sciences of the National Research Council; its resulting report, entitled *Knowledge and Policy in Manpower: A Study of the Manpower Research and Development Program in the Department of Labor,* was published by the National Academy of Sciences in 1975.

In the course of its assessment, the committee commissioned leading scholars to consider the state of knowledge in the field and its relationship to policy and to inquiry. Their papers provided background information for the committee report. With selection and editing, they now constitute the chapters of the volume.

A useful anthology is always more than the sum of its parts. Just how useful such an anthology can be is related to the purposes of its creation. The scholars whose work appears in this volume were asked to examine research conducted over the past 15 years relating to the American work force and to offer a structure for thinking about employment issues and study in the future.

In addition to the efforts of these authors, the contributions of several others must be acknowledged. Dr. Howard Rosen, Director of the Department of Labor's Office of Employment and Training Research and Development, has been a pioneer in the management of social science inquiry focused on the mission-defined problems of a government agency. He has demonstrated an uncanny ability to assume simultaneously the role of central figure in the flow of events and detached observer offering and inviting criticism. Much that has been added to the base of knowledge relating to manpower is a product of his creative exercise of this dual role. We are most grateful for his support and encouragement of this volume.

The principal officers of the Assembly of Behavioral and Social Sciences, of the National Research Council, particularly Dr. Henry David, its executive director at the beginning of the work of the Committee on Department of Labor Manpower R&D, and his successor, Dr. David A. Goslin, provided stimulating and careful direction. The work of other members of the Assembly staff, especially that of editor Eugenia Grohman, has been of unfailing assistance. Finally, both individually and collectively, the members of the Committee on Department of Labor Manpower R&D offered valuable insights in helping to plan for this volume and in reviewing the papers presented in it.

Gordon I. Swanson
Jon Michaelson

Introduction

Gordon I. Swanson and Jon Michaelson

Since the passage of the Manpower Training and Development Act in 1962 and its successor, the Comprehensive Employment and Training Act, in 1973, the federal government through the Department of Labor has invested approximately $350 million in manpower research and development (R&D). The investment itself was and continues to be an experiment to test whether scientific study can clarify, illuminate, or inform employment-related issues.

This manpower R&D investment can be assessed in several ways. These ways are not mutually exclusive, and no one is readily accepted as a more powerful tool of analysis than any other. All are employed to varying degrees in the papers contained in this volume.

First, the manpower R&D investment can be regarded as an overall map with explored and unexplored, or at least unfamiliar, territory. Assessment thus poses questions of coverage and of relative emphasis among domains of interest within the larger setting.

Second, the investment can be regarded as an attempt to address an array of problems within some system of priorities. The problems may have been solved, more fully understood, or redefined. Over time, the problems will have changed in relation to policies, to programs, and to each other. Assessment is therefore a matter of both how well problems were analyzed and how well R&D activities anticipated or adjusted to changing concerns.

Third, the investment can be viewed as helping to prompt a series of discoveries, which may take many forms. They may take the form of unexpected interactions among variables, tending to enhance the development of theory, or they may take the form of validated processes for achieving program goals. The value of any such contribution may become apparent only over a long period of time.

Finally, one can assess the federal R&D investment in the light of its catalytic effect on other investors. It can alter the contexts (social, economic, political, etc.) in which investment decisions are made, and it can expand the capacity of public and private institutions, and of individuals, for absorbing or undertaking various types of investments. Assessment of R&D efforts from this perspective demands not only a long-term view, but also an appreciation of means of and capabilities for generating and using new knowledge.

In examining manpower R&D, a few observations are critical. First, the issues addressed by manpower researchers are central to the economy and to the problems of its governance. Employment, inflation, labor markets, income distribution, and training are major concerns at all levels of government and for all society's institutions. The domain of manpower research is therefore immense. By comparison, the federal investment in manpower R&D ($350 million) is miniscule, sufficient only to illustrate the mere existence of a federal interest.

Second, the federal investment in manpower research began in the early 1960s at a very rudimentary level. The nation's institutional capacity to address employment problems was then very limited. After a decade and a half, the research has become more highly sophisticated, but the institutional commitment and capacity remain limited. Unlike the health sciences, agriculture, or education, manpower research is still a matter of limited concern in the nation's institutional structure.

Third, government manpower programs have expanded and changed, almost explosively, since the early 1960s. Most of the expansion has occurred by congressional mandate, with program additions conceived as short-term remedies to immediate problems. It is not surprising, therefore, that the federal R&D effort in manpower, which is managed side-by-side with manpower programs by the Department of Labor, also appears to have been responding constantly to forces of rapid change.

These observations about coverage, institutional development, and varying emphasis help explain and justify the use of the term "manpower," with its obvious sexist connotations. It came into popular use in the early 1960s with the passage of the Manpower Training and Development Act. To administer this legislation, the Department of Labor created its Manpower Administration with a research arm ultimately designated as the Office of Manpower Research and Development (OMRD). With the growth of services and programs, there was need for a generic designator. The meaning of the term "manpower" evolved to describe an array of services and programs provided largely by government to affect employment, job acquisition, training, income maintenance, labor market functions, employment problems of the disadvantaged, and a myriad of related concerns, including family services, health care, and counseling. While the term was not descriptive, it had a derived meaning by common agreement and use.

After the passage of the Comprehensive Employment and Training Act (CETA) in 1973, the program services of the Department of Labor again adopted nomenclature taken directly from the authorizing legislation. The Manpower Administration became the Employment and Training Administration, and its research arm also adopted the employment and training (E&T) designation. But taken alone, the term "employment and training" is descriptive and not synonymous with the concepts ascribed by common agreement and use to the term "manpower." What thus appears to be a confusion of terminology is also a measure of the growing complexity of the field. Both the term "manpower" and the term "employment and training" will be used in the subsequent chapters of this volume, but their use will not always be interchangeable. Where "employment and training" might be descriptively narrow, excluding many of the concepts embraced in the broader context of "manpower," the latter term will be used.

The Realms of Manpower Research

The papers in this volume concern a body of thought having a number of dimensions. First, manpower research has a global or macrodimension, described largely by traditional estimates or aggregate measures of such phenomena as migration, immigration, labor force participation, unemployment, and the demand-supply relationships of the labor market. Such measures have always reflected a concern for human resources, although usually expressed in quantitative terms. This is no longer sufficient: measures of this kind are now seen as having equally or more important qualitative aspects.

A second dimension of manpower research is a precursor to the first, but without direct lines of influence. It includes the micro-dimension, such as the training site, job content, the workplace, and the public and private institutions designed to assist individuals with their access to and interactions with the work setting. In this dimension, measures are less precise or more conditional. It is in this area, however, that much new thought is emerging.

A third dimension of manpower research, related to individual or group values, threatens to defy measurement and to confound inquiry. It includes such phenomena as work satisfaction, mobility within the occupational structure, influence of voluntary institutions such as the family, and various interpretations of equality of opportunity. The interrelations of these issues with other areas of manpower research continue to attract a great deal of scholarly attention.

Finally, there are dimensions of manpower research defined by certain nonsubstantive distinctions. Scholars in any field have a tendency to attribute different degrees of importance to different areas and methods of inquiry; they also tend to develop semantic habits that reflect such judgments. For example, among manpower researchers a clear differentiation has evolved between experimental and demonstration (E&D) projects and research projects. At its core, this distinction is unrelated to the methodology of inquiry; rather, it is more a matter of differences in interactions between research participants and the style as well as loci of agency management. The E&D project style was less rigorous than other research efforts and more enmeshed in manpower program operations. Although this approach has been discontinued for the most part, references to it are continued in the literature and in the chapters of this volume.

Recurring Themes in Manpower Research

Theory has never been expressly identified as a main aspect of manpower research. Indeed, academically oriented research, from which theory development is often expected, has always received a small proportion of federal investment in manpower. Yet upon review, theory development emerges as an important theme in a decade and a half of manpower research.

The task of measurement is central to all science. The meaning of a measure is interpreted or evolves from its pattern of relationships with other measures and its operation in different settings, across different cultural groups, and in different time periods. The extent to which a measure displays the same properties under different conditions is an important empirical question. Gathering evidence to support an inferential leap from such observed consistencies in the empirical world to an idea or model that will explain them is the task of theory development.

The chapters in this volume are theory-oriented. There is a search for theories to explain the consistencies and inconsistencies in the empirical world of manpower phenomena. There is also criticism of existing constructs involving neoclassical theory and the Phillips curve.

These new and existing academic theories, however, are not the only ideas influencing manpower programs and manpower research. There are also theories resulting from a continuing reinterpretation of the concepts of equality, freedom, and justice. Problems of poverty, unemployment, income distribution, migration, and the segmentation of labor markets are not independent of the problems of discrimination and inequality of opportunity. Here, as elsewhere, there is a far-from-perfect correlation between knowing how to describe the problems and knowing how they are best resolved. Understanding and attempting to invent ways to bridge these disjunctures has been a main theme in manpower programs and in much of manpower research.

Recurring Premises in Manpower Research

Sooner or later any mission-oriented agency becomes preoccupied with organizing various categories of knowledge and information. In any plan for organizing knowledge there is a tendency to include some information at the expense of other information or to emphasize some categories of knowledge at the expense of others. Manpower research tends to deal with highly conventional forms of knowledge and highly conventional approaches to dealing with it, mostly deriving from the discipline of economics. There are patterns of inclusion and exclusion and of emphasis and subordination. Eventually, such patterns acquire the status of premises reappearing as accepted elements of natural phenomena in the real world.

The chapters in this volume reflect a number of recurring premises that have characterized all or most of manpower research.

- The concept of structural unemployment has been widely accepted in the field. Briefly, it describes a mismatch between the available jobs and those who are searching for work. The premise offers a convenient explanation of why unemployment is both high and unresponsive to traditional fiscal and monetary remedies. It further provides the most important basis of programs intended to diminish the mismatch. Although rarely mentioned by researchers, a structural theory also leads to the notion that progress is hampered by rather loosely defined "bottlenecks," which can be alleviated by rather selective program activities.
- An astonishing aura surrounds the neoclassical or "orthodox" explanation of market behavior. Although it is no longer an article of faith among serious researchers, alternatives to this view are most often described as deviations from orthodoxy. Discussions, for example, of the dual labor market (which tend to strain the premises of neoclassical analysis) are not couched in the language of an alternative religion, but in language that shows a new accommodation within a traditional framework. In a great deal of manpower research, orthodox theory has the status of a premise even when used only as a referent to describe significant departures from it.
- There is continuing reliance on the concept of the market as the point of convergence for the demand behavior of potential employers and the supply behavior of potential employees. The market continues to be regarded as the available mechanism for allocating human resources, although manpower research, which has been very instructive in illuminating the concept of labor markets, has diminished the hegemony and usefulness of the market concept. The description of internal and dual markets (see

Piore) and the existence of labor market "imperfections," "intermediaries," and "transaction costs" (see Barth) are examples of the growing complexity of the idea of the labor market. These examples help demonstrate the growing risk in predicting the behavior of the labor market.

Chapter 1

Implications of Labor Market Theory for Employment Policy

Ray Marshall
Secretary of Labor

Theory is a useful guide to manpower policy study—imperfect yet necessary. It can provide a means to order and interpret workers' employment experiences, to explain and assess labor market operations, and to identify possible avenues of appropriate and effective government manpower activity. However, theory takes on new and often conflicting forms as scholars seek to integrate observations of changing behavior patterns with their understanding of similar phenomena in the past. This is especially true in an area as broadly defined as manpower. In this context, Ray Marshall examines several important formulations of labor market theory and analyzes their explanatory capacities with particular references to problems of racial discrimination in the employment context.

On the basis of Marshall's survey, we can point to some of the inherent dilemmas faced in organizing a program of government-supported R&D in the behavioral and social sciences. First, the development of theory to illuminate social conditions is not generally keyed to specific directions of policy development; there is no automatic match between the knowledge-generating and knowledge-using worlds. Second, confronted with a range of competing theories (and theoreticians), a government R&D organization must usually strike a balance between wide diversity in its investment choice (making it difficult to provide a well-integrated program having cumulative effects) and intensive concentration on a few promising areas of study (running the risk that significant advances in understanding lie along other lines of inquiry). Finally, even the most sensitive evaluation of theories and their future potential offers an incomplete picture of the empirical study that will be needed to both test and utilize theoretical perspectives in the policy and environment. As Marshall's paper intimates, the variety of labor markets may itself be so extensive—as theoretical constructs and as economic and social mechanisms—that a systematic or uniform approach to data gathering and analysis is inconceivable.

Introduction

To clarify the effects of employment programs, it is necessary to understand labor markets and how they work. Such an understanding should be provided by theories of labor markets. Indeed, *all labor market policies are based on explicit or implicit theories of cause and effect relationships*. Implicit theories are often very weak and cannot stand careful scrutiny. For example, we cannot explain the effects of incomes policies on the general level of wages and prices without a theory of inflation. Incomes policies assume cost-push inflation; they will have little effect if inflation is caused by excess demand. Similarly, neoclassical macroeconomic theory assumes homogeneous labor markets and the marginal productivity theory of wages. That theory will be less effective as a guide to policy if labor markets are segmented and the marginal productivity assumption is invalid.

As another example, and indeed the focus of analysis later in this review, we cannot understand the effects of various policies on racial employment patterns without a theory of discrimination. Under neoclassical theory blacks can improve their economic conditions by accepting lower wages than whites for similar work, by becoming more productive than whites for the same wages, or as a byproduct of rigorous enforcement of antitrust laws on the assumption that competitive firms are less discriminatory than firms operating under less than perfectly competitive conditions. By contrast, programs to train the disadvantaged and get them into better jobs assume some queue theory of the labor market in which workers are lined up on the basis of their productivity. If markets are segmented and the queue does not exist, employment programs will not lead to upgrading. If radical economists are correct, the problems employment programs are designed to solve are inextricably bound up with the capitalist system and cannot be solved without revolutionary changes in that system.

Labor market theory thus has important implications for employment policy. But, since employment policy must be considered within the context of overall economic policy, it will be useful to review that context before looking more specifically at particular labor market theories.

Employment and Macroeconomic Concerns

One of the most important economic problems confronting the United States and other industrialized democratic nations is how to simultaneously maintain full employment, stable prices, economic growth, and a reasonably free society with collective bargaining. The difficulty, of course, is that some of these objectives appear to be incompatible. There is, for example, considerable doubt that full employment and stable prices can be maintained together because low levels of unemployment appear to be associated with inflationary pressures.

The generally accepted explanation among economists for inflation-unemployment trade-offs involves the so-called Phillips curve, depicting an inverse relationship between unemployment and inflation. The evidence seems to support the conclusion that there might be a long-run trade-off between unemployment and the rate of wage inflation, though the relationship clearly does not hold, or at least is not always observable, in the short run (Gordon, 1973; Hiestand, 1970: 253; Holt, 1971). If there is a short-run Phillips curve, it seems to shift frequently because factors other than unemployment affect wages, and because there are lags in the impact of unemployment, wages, and other variables on each other. In the early 1970s, for example, inflationary pressure originated with forces—such as the energy crisis and food shortages—largely outside the labor market. The Phillips curve analysis also ignores the inflationary pressures (suboptimal plant capacity, limited investment, and restrictionist attitudes) generated by recessions.

Monetary-fiscal policies, thus, have limited ability to reduce unemployment because they tend to put unacceptable pressures on prices before unemployment reaches acceptable levels. Such policies are limited in other ways as well: (1) by the inability to accurately predict economic conditions so that policy changes can be timed in such a way as to have the desired effect on prices and employment; (2) by the lead time required to get measures through the political process; (3) by lags in the effects of policy changes; and (4) by the fact that monetary policies have effects in markets that are not always desirable from a public policy viewpoint.

Governments in western countries have, therefore, attempted various procedures to supplement monetary-fiscal policies to overcome the so-called Phillips curve dilemma. One of these approaches is to have "incomes" or wage-price policies. Incomes policies, however, have been limited by a number of factors. It is most difficult to devise a formula to fix wages and prices which is equitable and prevents maladjustments in either product or factor markets. For example, there is general agreement that restricting wage changes to changes in productivity is not inflationary, but it is difficult to design a formula relating wage and price changes to specific firms, industries, or workers which would not create problems or to implement such a policy even if the formula could be devised.

Wage-price controls must counteract powerful forces in labor and products markets. When policy-makers create conditions to maintain full employment, they also increase unions' power to raise wages and employers' power to raise prices. An effective incomes policy often requires union leaders not to raise wages when they have the power to do so. Since union leaders are elected by members, there will ordinarily be political ramifications for them if they decline to do all they can to increase wages.[1]

Incomes policies are also limited by technical difficulties involved in controlling wage payments, as contrasted with wage rates. The rates tend to be controlled, but wage payments are influenced by factors like promotion, overtime, and methods of wage payment which are very difficuly to control. "Wages drifts" are particularly likely where there is little pressure on employers to resist wage increases. In Europe local wage drifts have embarrassed union leaders because actual wage payments by employers in tight labor markets have often been higher than negotiated wage increases for which the union leaders could not claim credit (Meidner and Anderson, 1973; Ulman, 1972: 399-405).

Although some controversy continues, the evidence indicates that incomes or wage-price policies have only marginal effects on limiting wage and price increases. There is some agreement that wage-price *freezes* can moderate inflationary psychologies, but that controls are difficult to enforce and become less effective the longer they remain in force. Thus, controls cannot solve the wage-price problem but can be a useful supplement to other policies. Moreover, in order to be even moderately successful, incomes policies must have union support, and unions must have strong incentives to make the policies work. Another requirement appears to be sufficiently restrictive monetary policies that give employers a strong will to resist wage increases. Finally, for success, incomes policies appear to require broad public support, which ordinarily means they must be easily understood, based on equitable formulas, and fairly administered.

Because of the limitations of monetary, fiscal, and incomes policies, employment policies have certain theoretical advantages in overcoming the unemployment-inflation dilemma. Employment policies are designed to provide a better match between workers and jobs, now and in the future. They are therefore "targeted" on specific labor markets in the sense that they are designed to address particular problems in particular labor markets rather than following the general approach of other policies. By providing better labor market information, training, public employment, preemployment preparation, and measures to overcome labor market imperfections, it is *theoretically* possible to shift the Phillips curve to the left, permitting lower levels of unemployment with less inflation.

Employment programs have objectives other than supplementing general economic policies. They attempt to improve conditions for particular groups of workers, to facilitate the development of lagging regions, or ghettos or help people move out of these places, and to provide jobs for people who are not likely to find private employment without unacceptable levels of inflation.

The remainder of this paper defines various labor market concepts, presents brief overviews and critiques of several theories of labor markets and illustrates the applicability of these labor market theories as they relate to the special problem of racial discrimination. In each case the employment implications of these theories are underscored.

Survey of Employment and Labor Market Theories

The term "market" is used in somewhat different contexts. In some cases it means a specific place where buyers and sellers physically come together to arrange exchanges. There are also markets "located" in no particular place or where buyers and sellers are not necessarily brought together physically. Examples include the "secondary labor market" referred to by dual labor market theorists and the market for college graduates. Workers from many different and widely separated places might compete for the same jobs or workers in the same local labor supply might compete for jobs widely separated from each other. Clearly, in this latter sense the labor market concept is an *abstraction* and refers merely to the area within which exchanges frequently take place. Moreover, labor markets might be worldwide for certain highly specialized workers like deep-sea divers, or purely local, as for construction electricians.

The relevant labor market concept depends primarily on two factors. One is the propensity of workers to respond to opportunities at various distances from home. The other is knowledge of market opportunities.

The main functions of labor markets are to fix wages and other terms of employment and to allocate labor among occupations, jobs, and employers.

The Neoclassical Theory

The most generally accepted theory of the labor market is the "neoclassical" or "orthodox" theory. Even though there are many different interpretations, neoclassical theorists emphasize certain common concepts. They attempt to focus on the most significant determinants of wages and employment and on the basis of a few abstract and simplified concepts reach conclusions about a variety of matters, including income distribution, wealth, wages, the allocation of labor, and discrimination. With modifications, neoclassical economists use the same simple mechanism to bridge the gap between consumer behavior, the firm, general equilibrium for the entire economy, and international trade.

ASSUMPTIONS

The usual neoclassical formulation assumes perfect competition, although it can also be used to examine less-than-perfect competition. In a perfectly competitive labor market, the following conditions exist on the supply side: workers have perfect knowledge of the market, including information on wage rates and available opportunities; workers are rational and respond to differences in rates of return, including wages and noncash benefits; workers are perfectly mobile; workers are not organized and make their own decisions on accepting jobs and wages offered.

On the demand side, perfect competition requires that employers have full and perfect knowledge of the market; that employers are rational and attempts to maximize profits; that no employer represents a large enough part of the total demand for labor to affect wages; and that employers act individually, and not in concert, in fixing wages.

The competitive assumption is important to the neoclassical model. Competition is assumed to be a major force, causing relations to spread among sectors. In the labor market, competition expresses itself in the form of actual and potential labor mobility.

The neoclassical model also assumes decisions made on an individual basis rather than in light of group or class interests. Moreover, institutional arrangements are assumed to be constant while the system is moving toward equilibrium.

THE MODEL

The basic neoclassical model assumes wages and employment to be determined by demand and supply. According to the model, demand is determined by the marginal productivity of homogeneous units of labor. Marginal productivity is determined by the contribution of an added unit of labor to an entrepreneur's total revenue from selling the product. As successive units of labor are added, the demand declines because of diminishing returns. Even under less than perfectly competitive conditions, demand declines with additional units of labor because it is assumed that the price must be lowered if these units of production are to be sold, whereas under competitive conditions it is assumed that the entire output can be sold at existing market prices. Under competitive conditions, the supply of labor to the employer is regarded as stabler, meaning that the entrepreneur hires all of the labor he wants at the existing wage. Equilibrium is described as the point where the revenue-related demand for labor intersects with the needed supply of labor. At this point the firm's profits are maximized; at any lower level of labor utilization, additional workers would contribute more to revenue than to cost so it would pay a firm to expand. At a level of labor utilization larger than this point, costs increase more than revenue, and profits must be falling. At the point of intersection, employment and wages of the firm are therefore determined.

LABOR SUPPLY

Because it is based on the concept of marginal productivity, neoclassical labor demand theory is more developed than supply theory. On the supply side there are several intractable difficulties, most of which are associated with workers' inability to "separate" their labor from themselves. Workers have conflicting desires for more income or more leisure as income rises with higher wages. On one hand, workers may want to work longer hours at higher wages because they desire to substitute the things the higher wages can buy for leisure (substitution effect). On the other hand, the worker may indicate a willingness to sell less labor at higher wages, buying more leisure while maintaining a stable income (income effect). As a result of these considerations, a worker's "utility function"—which is determined by a combination of consumption goods purchased at home (paid for by sacrificed leisure or the amount that leisure could be sold for) and leisure—cannot be determined. There is no a priori way of telling whether the income or substitution effect predominates.

Similarly, the aggregate supply curve for the whole economy cannot be determined, although economists commonly assume it to incorporate a positive ratio between wages and labor at lower wages and a negative relationship between labor supplies and income at higher wages.

The aggregate labor supply curve is determined by labor force participation rates (LFPR). LFPRs reflect the tendency for workers to enter the work force at various wage rates and labor market conditions. Unfortunately, however, there are countermovements in labor force participation rates that complicate any analysis. For instance, when unemployment rises, the involuntary loss of jobs by some family members causes others to enter the labor force. This is the so-called additional worker hypothesis. If there are many additional workers in the work force, the official unemployment rate overstates the number of jobs needed to reach full employment because the "additional workers" will withdraw from the work force. On the other hand, some workers become discouraged and withdraw from the work force as unemployment rises. The presence of these discouraged workers causes the official unemployment rate to understate the number of jobs needed to restore full employment because presumably many of these discouraged workers would enter the work force in response to better job opportunities. The evidence suggests that in mild recessions, discouraged workers outnumber additional workers.

IMPLICATIONS OF THE NEOCLASSICAL THEORY

One implication of the theory is that *workers are poor because of their low productivity*. The obvious policy lesson, if this is true, would be to increase workers' productivity through increasing their "human capital."

Second, there is an assumption that income distribution tends to reflect differences in productivity, so *the theory tends to justify income distribution*.

The marginal productivity theory may also support a queue theory of the labor market, according to which employers rank workers and potential workers along a single ordinal vector on the basis of their respective productivity. Many of the employment programs of the 1960s were based on the assumption that disadvantaged workers would be moved up in the employment queue through employment training. In order for the queue theory to be valid, it must assume fairly universal rankings throughout the economy. If different employees have different rankings, analytic relationships are upset.

Human Capital Theory

The concept of human capital was adapted from physical capital investment theory by Becker and Schultz during the late

1950s and early 1960s (Becker, 1964; Samuelson, 1960; Schultz, 1961). Human capital analysis was stimulated by concern for poverty, economic development, income distribution, and unemployment. However, the *human capital concept depends heavily on the assumption that labor force is, in fact, paid its marginal product*. If labor is not paid its marginal product, human capital will not be a good measure of factor inputs.

The human capital concept has considerable appeal for those concerned with human resource development, especially those who desire quantification as a basis for decision-making. It would be good to know, for example, whether a particular employment program would yield a higher return relative to cost than some other program. The calculation of rates of return, or benefit-cost ratios, seems to provide this information.

The human capital concept also appears to provide a more general guide to public policies. Accepting its reasoning, we might try to measure the human capital deficiencies of blacks or the poor, determine the extent to which low incomes are due to inadequate human capital formation, and develop policies to alter this relationship. Moreover, a belief that human capital formation is an important factor in economic growth sparked further interest in the theory and calculation of these values. Denison, for example, estimated that *38 percent of the increase in output in the American economy between 1929 and 1957 could be accounted for by improvements in the quality of labor*, while only 15 percent was due to increases in the quantity and quality of land and physical capital, and 16 percent to increases in the quantity of labor (Denison, 1962).

DIFFICULTIES

Despite its appeal, the human capital concept has many defects that limit its application to labor market problems. First, there is ideological and political resistance to the concept. It implies that differences in the distribution of income and wealth are caused by *individuals* themselves rather than by *social institutions*. Those who want to alter social institutions are less inclined to give weight to the human capital concept, which emphasizes *marketable* benefits, because it is very difficult to put a price on the value of social change. How much is it worth, for example, to eliminate or reduce racial discrimination or imperfections in labor markets? The concept that earned incomes are due to differences in human capital also implies that the poor simply were not interested enough in investing in themselves to improve their earning power, that they made bad choices relative to people who are better off, or that they simply have inferior physical and intellectual abilities. On this basis, it is equally easy to argue politically that since earnings reflect productivity, taxes should not be progressive.

There are, in addition, a number of conceptual problems with the human capital concept. Many of these problems derive from difficulties in applying physical investment theory to people. *Human capital, unlike physical, cannot be separated from its owner and sold.* Physical capital only produces goods and services whereas humans both produce and consume. Hence, it is difficult or impossible to calculate accurate rates of return. For example, in calculating the returns to education or training, nonmonetary benefits like the attractiveness of posttraining jobs should be included but cannot be calculated in monetary terms; actual returns to training are thus underestimated. Similarly, training, education, and health increase a worker's satisfaction but contribute nothing in themselves to measurable national output.

Since labor cannot be separated from its owner, it cannot be sold or "mortgaged." It is therefore more difficult than in the case of physical capital for an individual to borrow funds to make sufficient human investment to equalize his or her costs and returns. Limited resources thus become important constraints on the ability of poor people to make human resource investments.

The owners of physical capital maximize monetary returns from that capital. However, human capital theorists cannot determine what those who make investments in themselves maximize. This is because investors are assumed to maximize a "utility function," incorporating nonmarket factors like prestige, consumption benefits (both from the investment itself and from the nonmarket value of goods and services produced as a result of the investment), and earnings. Once we move from the assumption that all of these things (rather than only earnings) are maximized, it is impossible to tell whether or not an investor made a "rational" choice. If costs are not at least recaptured by earnings, they could be recaptured by these other terms. Moreover, the benefits to be derived from the investment are *expected* utilities and cannot be predetermined, partly because the process of investment itself (education) changes one's utility function. Neoclassical economic analysis requires stable or known preferences. If preferences are unstable or unknown, there is no way to maximize a utility function.

There are also serious conceptual problems in determining costs. People must make expenditures for such things as food, clothing, housing, and medical care, which are maintenance costs of the human investment. But since these things also must be done in order for the worker to live, how much should we attribute to maintenance of human capital and how much to consumption?

Finally, the nature of "human capital" makes it very difficult to specify whose utility function is being maximized. This is always a problem with public investments of all kinds, because there is no uniquely determined welfare function for the whole society. Rather, we must first specify whether the maximizing agent is the federal government, individuals, states, cities or some other entity. But with individuals, and with institutions, decisions are often made on the basis of expected returns to other individuals or institutions, as when parents invest in their children's education.

Measuring future returns from human resource investments presents other very difficult problems. To infer the future by the past is a very hazardous procedure in a dynamic society. One of the most difficult problems for human capital theory is the assumption that there is a direct relationship between a given investment (education) and productivity. There probably is a subrelationship, but it has not been satisfactorily demonstrated. Incomes and education are directly correlated, but we cannot tell which is cause and which is effect. The technique of calculating returns to education through regression equations which account mathematically for the influence on earnings of everything other than training or education is hazardous if there are important facts such as *differences in natural ability which are not taken into account*.

There is no question that employers demand workers with education or training. But this is not the same as demanding workers with certain productive capacities. Education might be used by employers to screen workers even though there is no necessary connection between education and job performance. Human capital theory is unable to specify precisely what it is that employers demand and what it is that workers supply, making the traditional demand and supply analysis much looser than many of its advocates imply.

RELEVANCE TO POLICY

On the basis of calculated rates of return, taken alone, governments might decide to do nothing about the health of older people or training of any other than the brightest or youngest of their citizens. Even if we overcome the formidable obstacles to accurate calculation of human capital, this concept would be an imperfect guide to policy. Whose satisfaction should be maximized? Only value judgments could answer this question.

Human capital theorists meet such objections by inserting new terms in their equations. These changes help clarify some of the theoretical relationships involved in investment decisions, but it usually remains impossible to quantify all of the variables involved. As a result, the human capital approach is an unsatisfactory theoretical and practical way to make manpower or other human resource decisions. It does help in establishing costs and benefits, but these are sufficiently crude for one to argue against placing a great deal of reliance on them for decision-making purposes.

Orthodox Theory of Employment

Orthodox employment theory[2] combines neoclassical microeconomic theory with some aggregative general or macroeconomic concepts. Orthodox theory starts with the competitive assumptions noted earlier. In this system, aggregate labor markets are cleared and *full employment* exists when aggregate demand equals aggregate supply at going real wages (money wages divided by a price index). It must be remembered, however, that this definition of full employment assumes flexible wages, homogeneous workers, and other aspects of perfect competition. All people not working at full employment are voluntarily unemployed in the sense that they will not accept jobs at prevailing real wages.

Orthodox theory also assumes some "frictional" or temporary unemployment at full employment.[3] This is true because some time is required for workers and employers to find each other. The orthodox theory of job search assumes that a frictionally unemployed worker will maximize a utility function that accounts for expected duration of unemployment so that the discounted value of his or her expected net future stream of real and psychic income is maximized. Presumably, frictionally unemployed workers will be willing to endure longer periods of unemployment in order to obtain higher real wages. Under these assumptions, orthodox macroeconomic analysis concludes that frictional unemployment can be reduced only if policy-makers are willing to endure an increased rate of inflation.[4] This is because a one-time change in wages would reduce unemployment only temporarily; it would return to its previous level when wages and prices stabilized. To maintain unemployment at a lower level, policy-makers must take measures to generate wage inflation on a sustained basis. But once workers learn that an inflated wage has less purchasing power, it is assumed they will demand higher money wages, worsening unemployment-inflation trade-offs (shifting the Phillips curve upward and to the right).[5] The Phillips curve is thus assumed to be perpendicular, indicating that extended efforts to reduce unemployment below the frictional level will be dissipated in inflation.

There are several ways aggregate demand might be increased to the full employment level. Classical economists assumed that equilibrium would always be at full employment, and theoretically they were right, but their wage flexibility requirements were not very realistic. In other words, if workers were willing to accept sufficiently low wages and all other prices were flexible, jobs could always be found. But workers are not willing to do this.

Barring wage and price flexibility, the orthodox view is that full employment can be achieved through monetary and fiscal policies to increase aggregate demand to the desired levels. But the homogeneous labor market assumptions underlying this argument make it unlikely that full employment could be achieved through monetary and fiscal policies alone without intolerable levels of inflation. Put another way, monetary-fiscal policy could reduce deficient demand unemployment, but not frictional or structural unemployment.

POLICY IMPLICATIONS AND DEBATES

Frictional Versus Structural Unemployment

Frictional unemployment occurs because people are between jobs for short periods of time. The relationship between aggregate demand and supply can be approximated by comparing unemployment with job vacancies. Under the assumption of homogeneous labor markets, where all workers are qualified for all jobs, the level at which job vacancies equal unemployment depends on what is loosely called frictional unemployment. At full employment, frictional unemployment depends on the frequency of unemployment and the average length of search time required to find a new job.

By contrast, structural unemployment assumes persistent unemployment at different levels in different labor markets. Labor market segmentation and disperson of vacancy-unemployment rates among the different markets will cause greater upward pressure on wages at any given level of aggregate unemployment than would be true in the absence of segmentation (Holt, 1970) because it is more difficult to match people with jobs. Segmentation also increases frictional unemployment because the search time required to find an acceptable new job is assumed to be lower in a large, nonsegmented labor market, where there are economies of size in job search.

Structural unemployment exists when persistent disparities in vacancy-unemployment ratios are found among different labor markets. The concept has always caused economists trouble, especially in debates over structural and deficient demand unemployment that arose during the 1960s (Gordon, 1973). Part of the controversy centered on the distinction between frictional and structural unemployment. What was previously regarded as "structural"—for example, unemployment among teenagers and blacks—was due to high turnover rates rather than prolonged periods of unemployment. This is more appropriately regarded as differentially high frictional unemployment rates rather than structural unemployment.[6]

The distinction between different kinds of unemployment is important because each type calls for different remedies.[7] The remedy for frictional unemployment is to increase labor mobility.

Employment programs could reduce job turnover and search time, especially in those sectors with above-average frictional unemployment. Measures to reduce the seasonality of employment in some industries also would reduce frictional unemployment. Reducing structural unemployment requires remedies to overcome factors like racial or sex discrimination which cause labor markets to be segmented. Employment programs could theoretically shift the Phillips curve to the left by reducing unemployment in areas with above-average unemployment *or* by increasing labor supplies in those sectors with below-average unemployment rates. Mobility projects to move people from labor surplus to labor shortage areas and broadening job opportunities available to people within various sectors with high unemployment rates would also achieve this objective as could measures to eliminate discrimination because of race or sex.

Competitive Markets

Economists who emphasize the efficacy of the competitive labor market in allocating labor and reducing unemployment usually prescribe removal of labor market imperfections to make these markets operate more effectively. These economists are likely to contend, as did the classical economists of the 19th century, that unemployment is more likely to be voluntary and temporary than involuntary and chronic. A modern version of this position has been advanced by Feldstein (1973). Feldstein argues that the degree of labor market imbalance is exaggerated by the official unemployment rates. Many young people, according to Feldstein, prefer casual work patterns and hold jobs only briefly. The availability of unemployment insurance aggravates the problem by allowing workers to remain unemployed for longer periods of time than they otherwise could manage. In Feldstein's view, much of the unemployment in recent years is due not to structural imbalances or inadequate aggregate demand, but to high turnover in low-wage jobs. This analysis leads him to deemphasize public employment as a means of combating unemployment in favor of changes in minimum wages and in the unemployment insurance system. Public employment is rejected as a response because of difficulties in determining the appropriate size of the program and because public jobs are presumed to be "unproductive." Feldstein would modify the minimum wage as it applies to youth because the present system prevents young workers from "purchasing" training from employers by underbidding older workers. He would modify the unemployment insurance system because it encourages workers to "over-invest" in job search time and reduces employers' incentives to reduce seasonal and cyclical job fluctuations.

There are a number of factual and theoretical difficulties with Feldstein's argument. Factually, there is no evidence that workers refuse jobs because they are eligible for unemployment insurance. Very few workers exhaust their unemployment insurance except in times of prolonged recession when there clearly is inadequate aggregate demand. Moreover, there is no evidence at all that young workers or any others *prefer* low status, high turnover, low-paying jobs if more stable ones can be found. Virtually all young workers eventually settle down to permanent jobs mainly *when stable jobs become available to them*. The evidence suggests that the *employer's* attitude has much more to do with restricting teenagers to high turnover jobs than the attitudes of teenagers.

Feldstein's assumption that lowering minimum wages would reduce unemployment is also questionable, even within the neoclassical framework. Lower wages for teenagers might merely cause employers to substitute young workers for older minorities or women, who tend to be concentrated along with teenagers in "secondary" labor markets. Similarly, it is questionable that employers require lower wages before they will train younger workers. Indeed, management has a natural preference for younger workers in training programs which require considerable investment by the employer in the workers.

Feldstein's conclusion on public employment is equally questionable. As to appropriate size, a public employment program might simply be designed to absorb part, say a fourth, of all unemployment above 3 percent. Similarly, it would be relatively easy to assure that public employment programs engage participants in useful work.

Finally, although I cannot prove the proposition, at any given time unemployment has a variety of causes—cyclical, frictional, and structural—all of which require different remedies. I doubt very seriously that lowering minimum wages or weakening the unemployment insurance system would do much to reduce any of these kinds of unemployment. It makes more sense to maintain these systems and strengthen their management while dealing directly with the problem of unemployment not absorbed by the regular economy.

Demand-Pull or Cost-Push Inflation

There has been some controversy among economists over the extent to which inflation is caused by inadequate aggregate demand or by cost-push. As with so many other controversies in economics, semantic confusion, ideological differences, and inadequacies of empirical analysis keep the issues from being laid to rest.

The demand-pull school has argued that inflation is caused by increases in the money supply, usually generated by monetary-fiscal authorities rather than by increases in costs (Friedman, 1966: 17-39). In this view, inflation will not usually result from increasing costs because rising costs will cause prices to rise, sales to fall, and unemployment to increase. Cost-push therefore becomes self-limiting unless the monetary-fiscal authorities take action to sanction wage and price increases by increasing money supplies to prevent unemployment from rising. Because this is partly a "chicken and egg" problem, where cause and effect are difficult to measure empirically, it is a rather futile argument.[8] The problem with the demand-pull thesis is that it is based on restrictive assumptions about the perfection of labor markets and their homogeneity.

Cost-push and demand shift theorists emphasize labor market imperfections and labor market segmentation. An important assumption, supported by considerable evidence, underlying cost-push arguments is that wages rise more rapidly as a result of excess demand than they fall as a result of excess supply. In a dynamic system with segmented markets it is possible to have overall full employment without having full employment in each submarket. Schultz has offered a novel and provocative hypothesis based on apparent cost-push considerations, viewing inflation as the result of differential sectoral shifts in demand during a period when overall demand was more or less steady.[9]

Schultze's hypothesis is supported by Bowen and Masters, who found that when prices were stable during the late 1950s and early 1960s, intersectoral demand (albeit imperfectly measured) was much more uniform than in the period Schultze studied with comparable overall demand (Bowen and Masters, 1964: 975-984). More direct support for Schultze's hypothesis comes from studies which show that the main influence of unions has been to prevent wages from falling when labor markets were slack as much as they did in preunion periods (France, 1962: 171-209; McCattree, 1963: 60-74).[10] If these findings are correct, the nonlinearity of wage responses biases the economy toward rising wages, and aggregate wages will rise at full employment. Wage stability therefore requires some demand deficiency (Tobin, 1972: 1-18).

Effect of Employment Programs on the Phillips Curve

Despite its theoretical potential, employment policy apparently has done very little to shift the Phillips curve to the left. Indeed, during the 1960s, the inflation-unemployment relationship worsened (the long-run Phillips curve shifted to the right), mainly because of a worsening of female and teenage unemployment rates relative to the national average. Employment policy also apparently did very little to counteract the effects of a decline in the relative supply of prime-age males. However, employment programs undoubtedly prevented the Phillips curve from shifting farther to the right.

Employment programs have had a limited impact on the inflation-unemployment trade-off because they were not designed either by function or in scale for that purpose. They are intended mainly to provide labor market information, train and upgrade workers, improve labor market operations, supply preemployment training, and provide public service employment for those who cannot find jobs in the private sector. Our short experience with these programs must be viewed as experimental. They have been reasonably successful in improving conditions for the individual participants, but they were not directed toward macroeconomic goals. *They cannot substitute for monetary-fiscal policies to overcome deficient demand unemployment, but they can do something to reduce frictional and structural unemployment.*

Public service employment is a particularly effective and relatively inexpensive way to reduce structural unemployment. Employment programs can also be coordinated with antidiscrimination measures to reduce labor market segmentation. An adequate income maintenance program would make it possible for employment programs to concentrate more on skill upgrading and be used less as a substitute for welfare. An improved education system might obviate the necessity for employment programs to compensate for educational deficiencies.

On the other side of the ledger, there are also a number of inherent obstacles to the use of employment programs as countercyclical tools. There is a problem of timing: it takes some time to train people in order to overcome skill shortages. Similarly, it is difficult to forecast labor requirements accurately given present data and techniques.

Moreover, while employment programs can improve the inflation-unemployment trade-off, they can also make that trade-off worse. Training can increase unemployment by increasing the supply of labor. Employment programs can also contribute to inflationary pressures because they cost money. Therefore, programs should be emphasized which do as much as possible to improve the operation of labor markets at relatively low cost. Long-term and more expensive training should be undertaken during recessions when the cost of training is lower and inflationary pressures are not as serious. Similarly, types of training such as apprenticeship programs that increase the adaptability of workers would improve the inflation-unemployment trade-off.

In other respects, employment programs can have little effect. Many forces encouraging inflation, such as the energy crisis and shortages of goods and services, originate outside the labor market and are not readily influenced by employment programs. Indeed, these and other developments also make it difficult to use any mode of economic analysis which fails to account for limits on factors of production as a guide to policy.

In short, employment programs have not been specifically designed to have much effect on the inflation-unemployment trade-off. If they had, we would have a very different kind of employment system. Moreover, even if we concentrated more resources on shifting the Phillips curve to the left, the success of employment programs would depend partly on the extent to which they were coordinated with monetary-fiscal policy, economic development programs for lagging regions and other "depressed" areas, education, antidiscrimination, and health, welfare, and income maintenance activities. An expanded, goal-oriented employment program could do much on its own to improve the operation of labor markets, but it could not substitute for these other components of a comprehensive human resource development strategy. We should also emphasize that employment revenue sharing under CETA reduces the ability of manpower policy to be coordinated with aggregate economic policies because the decentralized system will respond more to local than to national needs.

Internal Labor Market Analysis

Although economic theorists usually assume homogeneous labor markets throughout the economy, there has long been a recognition that workers are divided into noncompeting groups. In 1874 Cairnes wrote that there was some mobility between labor markets, but

> the average workman, from whatever rank he be taken, finds his power of competition limited for practical purposes to a certain range of occupations, so that however high the rates of remuneration in those which lie beyond may rise, he is excluded from sharing them. We are thus compelled to recognize the existence of noncompeting industrial groups as a pattern of our economy (Cairnes, 1874: 67-68).

In 1952, Clark Kerr analyzed the significance of internal labor markets for labor market theory (Kerr, 1954). Kerr noted that there were certain "institutional" markets whose dimensions were set by formal and informal rules rather than individual preferences. These rules added structure to labor markets. Although these rules do not require formal labor organization, unions sharpen the boundaries between internal and external labor markets and define more sharply the precise ports of entry into internal markets. External markets are the ones ordinarily considered by neoclassical economic analysis where demand and supply determine wages. Kerr emphasizes the role of the internal market in influencing mobility and potential mobility, which are the ultimate forces tending to relate wage-determining processes throughout the economy. By reducing mobility, the forces at work in the internal labor market lessen external competitive pressures.

Doeringer and Piore have developed the concept of the internal labor market more completely and have related it more specifically to federal employment policy (Doeringer and Piore, 1971). Like Kerr, their concern is primarily with the formal and informal processes governing employment relationships and the forces influencing those processes. Key factors affecting internal employment decisions include labor supplies in external labor markets, the type of technology in the firm or industry, the value of the internal labor market to the firm's present work force, product market conditions, and customs.

A very important theme developed by Doeringer and Piore is

> that differences between the skills and abilities of the labor force are reconciled through a series of instruments which are controlled within the internal labor market. These instruments—recruitment procedures, training, compensation and the like—exist because a number of functions conventionally identified with the competitive labor market have been internalized to the enterprise. These instruments, individually and collectively, constitute a series of labor market adjustment processes by which the internal labor market adapts to changes in both production techniques and labor market conditions (Doeringer and Piore, 1971: 198-190).

Because of such adjustment procedures, Doeringer and Piore tend to discount the argument that structural unemployment reflected rising unemployment rates during the 1960s. This, however, does not necessarily follow. Each firm can adapt labor forces of different skill levels to its own requirements and still avoid hiring large numbers of workers—such as teenagers, women, and minorities—whose supplies have increased. Unless flexible wages or other benefits to entrepreneurs are assumed, there is no reason employers should change their hiring practices to avoid hiring the workers they most prefer.

The internal labor market is generated by the specificity of skills to each firm, the prevalence of on-the-job training, and custom or unwritten rules based largely on past practices or precedent. Doeringer and Piore challenge the neoclassical assumption that the internal labor market, which insulates workers from competitive markets, generates inefficiency. They argue that some of the factors around which internal labor markets are organized—the value of security and advancement to workers and savings to the employer in costs from recruitment, screening, training, and the reduction of turnover—cause efficiencies in labor utilization. There might also be some inefficiencies from attempts by workers to protect job security and insure equitable treatment in internal labor markets. It has not been determined whether the efficiencies outweigh the inefficiencies, but there is a strong presumption that the internal labor market is, on balance, more efficient.

Internal labor market analysis challenges neoclassical assumptions that there are no fixed employment costs and that the employment relationship is temporary. Becker and Oi have worked out the implications of fixed recruitment, screening and training costs within the framework of neoclassical theory (Becker, 1964; Oi, 1962). It can be shown that these fixed costs create incentives for employers to establish more permanent relationships, but that profit maximization no longer requires wages to be equal to marginal products at any given time; workers can be paid more than their marginal products plus training costs at first and less than their marginal products plus training costs later.

However, according to Doeringer and Piore, Becker and Oi failed to emphasize

> the startling implications for neoclassical wage theory of the permanent employment relationship . . . neither employers nor workers necessarily concern themselves with the connection between wages and marginal productivity at any point in time. . . . The disruption of neoclassical equivalencies between the wage and marginal product in each pay period . . . involves the disruption of these equivalencies for a given job as well. The worker, therefore, may *never* produce enough in a particular job classification to cover his wages during the period in which he is employed in that classification (Doeringer and Piore, 1971:p 76).

This means that wages are attached to *jobs* not to workers as the neoclassical theory has assumed. In a competitive society, the wage rate for the job would reflect the marginal productivities of workers holding those jobs, but not in the internal labor market, which tends to be insulated from competitive forces. Moreover, the wage, even at ports of entry, is more likely to reflect the expected productivities of *groups* of workers than it is the productivities of *individuals*. Some workers are therefore paid more than their productivity while others are paid less. "In sum, the forces which in neoclassical theory yield a determinate wage establish, in the internal market, only a series of constraints" (Doeringer and Piore, 1971: 77).

Employment Implications of Internal Labor Markets

One major employment implication of internal labor market analysis is that training should not be provided independently by firms unless there are economies of scale. Most firms can do their own skill training, but are not very well suited for general training in computational, verbal, or reading skills. Moreover, groups of firms, unions, individual workers, or governments must provide training that is not enterprise-specific because particular employers are not likely to choose to incur the costs of training if they derive only partial benefits from it.

Second, the government should provide recruitment and training procedures to accomplish social objectives, like promoting greater employment opportunities for workers likely to be screened out by firms' recruitment and screening procedures. Firms will normally attempt to use the least expensive devices if they can to recruit and screen their work forces. Employers will give heavy weight, for example, to procedures that will, with a given cost, maximize the probability of acquiring the kinds of workers they desire. If public policy-makers want to get blacks, disadvantaged, or indigent populations employed, they might adopt preemployment screening procedures to equalize the probability that employers will be able to obtain qualified workers from among these excluded groups. Indeed, to some extent Manpower Development and Training Act programs accomplished this objective for employers by recruiting and screening workers who were reliable and trainable.

Internal labor market analysis suggests considerable flexibility in the processes whereby employers adjust workers and jobs. However, much of this information is specific to each enterprise, even though it might be useful to other employers and to public policy-makers. Therefore, the need exists for a mechanism to collect information on the operation of internal labor markets, analyze this information, and disseminate it to labor market participants who can profit from it.

Multiple Labor Market Analysis

The basic idea underlying dual labor market theory is that workers are separated into primary and secondary labor markets. The good jobs, characterized by better wages, security, permanence of employment, upward mobility, and the like, are in the primary market, while the least desirable jobs—characterized by limited upward mobility, low wages, little job security, and high turnover—are in the secondary sector. The primary markets have more extensive internal labor markets than secondary markets.

Since workers and employers tend to adapt to jobs, the forces restricting workers to the secondary market can be self-perpetuating. Workers are restricted to this market by residence, inadequate skills, poor and limited education, poor work histories, and discrimination. Employers adjust to these conditions by means of weak employee discipline, piece rates, overstaffing, limited investment in workers' training, and shifting costs of labor force maintenance to the public through welfare and other devices.

There is no doubt that the dual labor market concept focuses on the very important reality of labor market segmentation. There is, however, considerable doubt that labor markets are divided into only primary and secondary segments, even at the macrolevel. The dual labor market classification system does not, for example, fit the facts of professional or construction labor markets.[11] Moreover, the dual labor market perspective is, at this stage, more a description of extreme labor markets than it is a complete theory of major labor market segments.

The manpower implications of segmented labor markets are nevertheless fairly clear. Measures can be taken, such as reducing discrimination, providing training for workers in skilled jobs, and improving labor market information, to reduce barriers between markets. Alternatively, manpower programs can be used to improve the jobs within marginal and submarginal markets for those who either are not likely to move into other labor markets or who do not wish to do so. As noted earlier, however, these kinds of programs will not only improve the conditions of the workers involved but could serve as an adjunct to general economic policy by improving the operation of labor markets and reducing structural unemployment.

Economics of Discrimination[12]

Discrimination has been an important cause of labor market segmentation and low incomes. A major objective of employment policy has been to improve the conditions of minorities. It is, therefore, very important to develop adequate theory to help understand the causes and effects of discrimination.

An analysis of the economics of discrimination also makes it possible to examine the usefulness of labor market theories—especially the neoclassical theory. This section also explores the ideas of dual labor market economists with respect to the problem of discrimination.

The Neoclassical View

While the first statement of the neoclassical theory of discrimination was apparently offered by Edgeworth in 1922 (Edgeworth, 1921: 431-457), most of the major work in this country follows Becker's *The Economics of Discrimination* (Becker, 1971).[13] It should be emphasized, however, that theorists who follow the neoclassical tradition differ among themselves. They agree only on the form of the theory, not on details or even major conclusions.

According to Becker, "If an individual has a 'taste for discrimination,' he must act as if he were willing to pay something, either directly or in the form of reduced income, to be associated with some persons instead of others" (Becker, 1971: 14). Becker defines a coefficient of discrimination to measure this "taste for discrimination" in money terms for different factors of production, for employers and for consumers, where it is assumed that the factors of production are equally productive. The obvious implication is that the employer is willing to pay favored workers more than those workers who are discriminated against.[14] The Becker-type model has a number of limitations for those interested in using the theory of discrimination to explain reality. For example, the long-run implication of the model is that employers with no discrimination coefficients would hire blacks, because of their lower wage rate, forcing their competitors to do the same. Thus a long-run equilibrium would be established where wages of minorities equaled the wages of whites in either integrated or completely segregated situations.[15] This suggests that employers would change their work forces in response to changes in wage rates. The analysis leads to the conclusion that economic discrimination is mainly a reflection of "market imperfections" and monopoly power; otherwise discrimination should tend to disappear in the long run.

Discrimination in the Dual Labor Market Analysis

An approach that has specifically challenged the neoclassical model of discrimination is the "dual labor market" hypothesis. Economists have long known that the labor market was "Balkanized" or divided into noncompeting groups, but the dual labor market idea became more popular with scholars who were studying ghetto employment during the 1960s and early 1970s. These analysts studied ghetto labor markets in detail and began reformulating some of the ideas about segmented markets developed by Kerr, Fisher, Killingsworth, and others (Kerr, 1954; Doeringer and Piore, 1953; Killingsworth, 1968).

The dual labor market approach deals with discrimination mainly as a factor in labor market segmentation, with no special theory of discrimination. Because of discrimination, blacks have a high probability of being restricted to secondary labor markets. Once they get into these markets, the adaptive forces at work in that sector make it difficult for them to move into primary markets.

Piore (1970) explains the separation of markets by a number of specific arguments. Secondary markets are distinguished from primary markets by the behavior patterns, especially unstable employment, which they impose on the workers in those markets. Employers and workers adapt to unstable conditions, and labor market institutions contribute to the perpetuation of these conditions. Welfare, for example, contributes to segmentation by providing such limited support that workers are forced into the secondary market. Unions operate mainly in the primary market and therefore contribute to the perpetuation of better wages, hours, and job protection in that sector. Unions have more difficulty in the secondary sector because the workers have insufficient power to win strikes. Workers tend to be barred from primary jobs not because of their lack of job skills but because they work intermittently and are not reliable.

In this view, discrimination perpetuates segmentation by restricting certain workers to secondary markets—not because of their education and skills but because they have outward characteristics resembling most workers in the secondary markets. Doeringer and Piore emphasize that many workers in the secondary market have stable employment even though their jobs encourage instability (Doeringer and Piore, 1971).

While technology influences the allocation of jobs between the primary and secondary sectors, many kinds of work can be performed in either sector and are where they are because of historical decisions to locate them there.

The behavior patterns of workers in the various labor markets are reinforced by class associations. Jobs in the various sectors tend to be filled by people from particular classes. Piore (1970) defines "mobility chains" through which people pass. Workers enter these chains from a limited and distinct number of points which have economic and social significance. "Thus people in a given job will tend to be drawn from a limited range of schools, neighborhoods, and types of family backgrounds. And conversely, people leaving the same school or neighborhood will move into a limited set of employment stations."

Finally, institutions and historical forces strengthen labor market segmentation. The importance of on-the-job training as a means of acquiring skills has increased the employer's incentive to hold some workers in more stable jobs, whereas other institutions have perpetuated instability. Migration of disadvantaged workers into urban areas has helped maintain the supply of workers in secondary markets. The lower-class subculture is mainly a function of "the rate of in-migration of ethnic and racial groups, and the size of the stock of second and third generation members of these groups relative to the in-flow of new members."

The dual labor market analysis is still in its formative stage and therefore scarcely qualifies as a "theory." So far it is a classification system more than a theory. Moreover, the analysis and description apply to only parts of the economy and are therefore not a complete system. Many labor markets, like those for craftsmen and independent professional and technical workers, do not fit neatly into that system. Moreover, the origin and causes of labor market segmentation are not satisfactorily formulated.

Critique of the Neoclassical Theory of Discrimination

There is no commonly accepted standard for evaluating a theory of discrimination. For example, if we accept Arrow's objectives of making the neoclassical analysis of discrimination compatible with the competitive equilibrium mode and of explaining racial wage differentials, we might conclude that he has succeeded on both counts but could still argue that he has failed to provide a satisfactory theory of discrimination. Such a theory would explain the basic causal forces at work in the real world and would serve as a dependable guide to policy. Conversely, a particular theory of discrimination designed to support policy and provide a better fit with reality might be less congruent with competitive equilibrium theory.

Because of a preoccupation with theoretical compatibility, neoclassical economists fail to present a convincing definition of discrimination. Indeed, they treat discrimination as exogenous and therefore not to be directly analyzed. Mechanical results follow from the way the model is specified; therefore little is added to our understanding of discrimination. Neoclassicists tend to exclude important variables that influence economic discrimination, concentrating instead on phenomena considered to be central to economic discrimination (racial wage differentials for homogeneous units of labor) that are not proved and probably do not play the role stipulated by the neoclassical model. This produces misleading policy suggestions.

CONCEPTION OF DISCRIMINATION

To adhere to the wage theory mold, neoclassical economists define discrimination as a taste "to be associated with some persons rather than others" for which an economic agent is willing to pay. This definition creates a number of conceptual problems. First, to the extent it assumes discrimination to be a "physical" phenomenon—for example, a desire by whites not to associate with blacks—it scarcely conforms with reality, where whites have been in close physical association with blacks in the workplace. Clearly, discrimination is more a status or caste phenomenon, a concept forcing the neoclassical approach into a more general posture. Discriminators object to discriminatees *partly* because the latter are generally regarded to be "inferior" people who would lower the status of the discriminators.

MOTIVES OF THE ECONOMIC AGENTS

An economic theory of discrimination should show how discrimination interacts with the motives of certain economic actors. The neoclassical model does this, in part, by assuming that actors with "discrimination coefficients" modify the usual motives specified in neoclassical utility functions. The model assumes, I think correctly, that employers are motivated mainly by profits but that this motive is modified by a "taste for discrimination" or a "perception of reality." Yet, "physical association" is a problem; it is difficult to see why employers, especially in large firms, would discriminate against blue-collar workers with whom top management would not be associating.

Krueger attempts to overcome this difficulty by assuming that employees are motivated by the desire to maximize incomes among white workers, an unrealistic assertion at best. However, it is possible that the discrimination coefficients of employees could be transmitted to the employer, as Arrow specifies, causing the employer to behave *as if* it had a discrimination coefficient. If the employer has a status motive for discrimination, there would be no objection to hiring discriminatees for "inferior" jobs, but employers would object to hiring them for higher status jobs. Bergmann's analysis implies this tendency, but Arrow ignores it.

I cannot prove status motives are more realistic than benevolence toward white workers or envy-malice toward blacks, but the empirical evidence seems to support this conclusion. Whites clearly have been more strongly motivated to bar blacks from such status jobs as mechanical craftworkers in the construction industry, railroad conductors and engineers, and managers and supervisors of integrated work forces than they have from such jobs as carriers (not a low wage job), foundry work (also not low wage), cement masons, service workers, and laborers, all of which are considered to have lower status. Empirical analysis is complicated by the fact that occupants of higher status jobs also usually have more power to bar blacks, making it difficult to distinguish motive from power.

The neoclassical model also makes unrealistic assumptions about the motives of white workers, who probably are more responsible than employers for discrimination in *blue-collar* jobs. The neoclassicists assume white workers with discrimination coefficients to be mainly motivated by wage rates. This assumption leads to some curious results. First, white workers are presumed to demand higher wages to work with blacks who are perfect substitutes. This is curious in view of the usual neoclassical assumption that people act rationally. Surely, white workers could see that such demands would be self-defeating; blacks would displace whites, as the neoclassical model stipulates. White workers are more likely to demand that blacks be excluded entirely from "status" jobs than to demand racial wage differentials. As noted below, however, whether white workers succeed in barring blacks depends on the power relations between the parties. If employers are firm in hiring blacks, and if adequate supplies of black workers are available, whites are not likely to quit good jobs because blacks are hired. White workers' basic motivation is likely to be *job control* rather than wage rates. The wage rate is an important part of the job, but the job's status, working conditions, stability, opportunity for advancement, and the extent to which workers participate in the formulation of job rules also are important considerations. Discriminators are likely to want to monopolize the better jobs for themselves and will use race, sex, or any other argument as a means for doing so.

POWER RELATIONS AMONG THE AGENTS

A theory of discrimination should be able to say something about what gives discriminators the power to exclude discriminatees. The neoclassical model fails to do this because it does not deal with bargaining between groups, assumes wages to be workers' sole objective, and posits wage differentials and wage changes to be basic causal forces. The neoclassical model is also silent with respect to the motives of black workers and the determinants of their power to overcome discrimination by white workers and employers.

INSTITUTIONAL DISCRIMINATION

The neoclassical model also fails to distinguish between specific overt acts of discrimination (where, for example, a worker is not hired or promoted because of race) and the discrimination which pervades social and economic institutions. When discrimination becomes institutionalized, as it has become for blacks, overt discrimination becomes a relatively less important cause of disadvantage among discriminatees. Inadequate education, segregated labor market institutions, and other forces which deny equal access to jobs, training, or information greatly reduce the probability that those discriminated against will aspire to, prepare for, or seek to enter the status occupations. In neoclassical language, institutional discrimination makes it less likely that black and white workers will be homogeneous substitutes.

I do not wish to imply, however, that overt and institutional discrimination are completely dichotomous. While the distinction is important, discriminators can practice overt discrimination while appearing to be objective, as, for example, when they use recruiting sources or screening devices strongly infused with the results of institutional discrimination.

Neoclassical theory does not deal with institutional discrimination because it assumes, I think mistakenly, that institutions are unchanging and therefore do not interact with basic variables. However, since the discrimination coefficient is itself considered exogenous to the system, the neoclassicists can hardly claim to have a *theory of discrimination*. A theory of discrimination would help explain the causes of discrimination and show how economic variables relate to the central phenomenon to be explained. Because of the way they specify the model, neoclassicists must rely on competition, operating through wage differentials, to produce equilibrium. Thus, discriminators must either disappear in the long run or change their "tastes." There is, however, no indication of the relationship between competitive market forces and discrimination itself. We do not know, for example, whether the "taste for discrimination" persists among those who have it even though they are eliminated from the market in the long run, or whether economic pressures cause discriminators to cease discriminating, therefore causing discrimination itself to be reduced or eliminated. These alternatives, while perhaps producing the same ultimate results, are substantively quite different.

A realistic specification of the process of change would indicate the pressures (from government, the black community, or market forces) that provide employers or employees some motive to change black employment patterns with no necessary change in racial attitudes. Once actors are required to cease discriminating, in an overt sense, that part of their action based on inaccurate "perceptions of reality" changes immediately. But negative racial attitudes may persist. These are probably eroded by a tendency for people to rationalize actions governed by economic or other "imposed" motives. Gradually, as discrimination declines, those discriminated against cease being regarded as "inferior" people, and status considerations for excluding them are reduced. Thus, the line of causation probably is: overt discrimination is changed, attitudes change, and institutions change.

WAGES AND COMPETITION

To make the neoclassical model compatible with competitive equilibrium theory, it is necessary to assume that wage differentials and wage and price competition are basic causal forces. But these assumptions also cause some problems for the theory, as does the assumption that racial wage differentials are important facts to be explained. If job control and status are primary objectives among workers, and if profits and status are the main objectives of employers, then discriminatory wage differentials for homogeneous labor in the same firms are not likely to be very significant forces in the real world. Indeed, there is no evidence that such differentials exist for workers who are perfect substitutes. Because of the importance of job specificity and on-the-job training, it would almost be necessary to show that blacks and whites in the same firms and occupations were paid different wages, a highly unlikely occurrence.

There is, however, considerable evidence of job segregation and of concentration of blacks in certain kinds of jobs. The larger supplies of blacks in these "traditional" jobs undoubtedly tend to cause wages in these jobs to be lower than otherwise. But there is at least a partial compensation on the demand side because the "dependable" supply of blacks may cause employers to prefer blacks for these jobs. The neoclassical model does not ordinarily deal with this problem because of its questionable assumption that demand is independent of supply. There are, to be sure, racial *income* differentials. But this is not the same as showing racial *wage* differentials for ***homogeneous units of labor***, as specified in the neoclassical model, even though neoclassical analysts sometimes use incomes and wages as if they were interchangeable concepts. Incomes are influenced by such factors as nonwage income, occupation, hours worked, and method of wage payment, as well as by wage rates.

The neoclassical formulation therefore becomes nearly a theory of wages with an extra term, the discrimination coefficient, where the specification of the model predetermines the outcome. This certainly is more so than a theory explaining the basic forces behind discrimination. The results of this formulation are predefined —blacks must accept lower wages than whites in order to get jobs.

The neoclassical competitive assumptions also ignore the importance of bargaining and group activity, which seem to be very important in changing racial employment patterns. The usual neoclassical assumption is that decisions are made on the basis of *individual* motivations and that these in the long run will erode any *group rules* incompatible with individual marginal productivities and wage- and profit-maximizing motives. However, there may be no way for an employer to determine the productivity of an individual worker, especially when adding a black worker to a group of whites. The employer must calculate the costs to him of reactions of the whites as well as the gain from hiring a qualified black. This will often become a bargaining problem between groups of blacks and their supporters, white workers and their organizations, and employers. Power relations among the parties will determine whether or not blacks get hired. Within a broad institutional framework (including laws and prevailing race relations in the larger society), the capacity of blacks to gain access to jobs ordinarily will be determined by their ability to inflict losses on or to convey profits to employers and by their control of supplies of labor qualified to satisfy the employers' demands if whites boycott or strike in protest against the hiring of blacks. Employers are motivated by net profits resulting from the racial employment bargain. Black or white workers' power will therefore not flow from the *marginal* productivities of *individual* workers, but from the productivities of *groups* of workers. Moreover, the effect of change on the *net* productivity of *work groups* will determine the extent to which employers are likely to make new racial rules.

Employers will not only be influenced by the net effect of the employment decision but also by the impact of such external pressures as government, general employment conditions, and the nature of product markets. Product markets are important in bargaining situations because they influence the employer's vulnerability to consumer pressures. Generally, consumer-oriented companies are more vulnerable to prevailing racial attitudes, negative or positive, than those whose main output is producers' goods.

No model of employment discrimination would be complete that ignored the influence of unions, but these are generally ignored by the neoclassical model. A union's racial practices are determined mainly by the influence of race on the union's control mechanisms (Marshall, 1965, 1967). These mechanisms are the procedures used by the labor organization to protect and promote its basic objectives, which vary with the type of organization. On balance, a labor organization is not a basic force creating discrimination; it is a force to be used by its members to carry out their objectives whether they be discrimination by whites or the eradication of discrimination. Ashenfelter, for instance, shows that, on balance, craft unions have caused black wages to be lower than they would have been, while industrial unions have caused them to be higher (Ashenfelter, 1974).

This suggests another major problem with the neoclassical model. It assumes that competition necessarily erodes both discrimination and divergent group interests. A showing that competition does not play this role would cause considerable difficulty for the model. Where the primary motivation for discrimination at the blue-collar level comes from white workers —which I think is a more realistic assumption than that it comes from employers—oligopolistic firms might hire black workers faster than competitive firms in order, for example, to weaken the bargaining power of white-controlled unions. There is considerable historical evidence that blacks broke into oligopolies like the steel and auto industries as strikebreakers long before they were ever hired in more competitive industries like textiles, which has avoided black areas in the South and has been known as a "white man's industry."

It is true that black workers are concentrated more in industries with low product-market concentration ratios. But this does not prove that competitive industries are less discriminatory or that competition tends to erode discrimination. Blacks tend to be concentrated in "competitive" industries because these are low wage areas that hire mainly unskilled and semiskilled workers, where there are greater supplies of black labor. Industries with higher product-market concentration ratios tend to have fewer blacks, at least partly because they also have higher skill requirements than competitive firms, and blacks generally have lower skill levels than whites.

The neoclassical emphasis on competition also ignores the possible effects or bargaining on the racial employment practices of the large employer. Because of low skills, white or black workers in small competitive firms have very limited bargaining power. By the same token, the competitive employer has less "slack" to respond to black demands for better jobs. These employers are more likely to be consumer oriented and concerned that unpopular racial policies will reduce their sales and profits. Consumer boycotts can be more effective against these firms than against intermediate goods-producing oligopolists, who are less vulnerable to consumer boycotts but might be more responsive to threats of lawsuits or the loss of government contracts.

Some economists who follow the neoclassical tradition think that the civil rights laws have caused great improvements in black incomes. But they fail to show within their theoretical formulation a convincing statement of the process through which these laws reduce discrimination.[16] To say that employers and white workers have discrimination coefficients is to *assume* that the law worked directly to counteract these "tastes." An alternative assumption, that employers have no discrimination coefficient for blue-collar workers, leads to a prediction that the laws would help the employer by making it possible for employers who discriminated because of fear of white worker or customer reaction to use the law as an excuse to make profitable black personnel changes. The neoclassical model seems to require whites to demand higher wages in this case or to quit; but there is no evidence that either has occurred.

There is an important distinction between arguing, as neoclassical economists do, that competitive market forces tend to reduce discrimination and that *industrialization* and the efficiency requirements of enterprises do so, as argued, for example, by Kerr, Dunlop, Harbison, and Myers (Killingsworth, 1960). These scholars rely on evidence from international studies to conclude that the logic of industrialism helps erode discrimination. Industrial societies, in their view, are more often open societies "inconsistent with the assignment of managers or workers to occupations or to jobs by traditional caste, racial groups, by sex or by family status" (Killingsworth, 1960). This formulation emphasizes the interactions of employers' decisions with major institutions in the larger society, so that industrialization, rather than the neoclassical competitive market, affects discrimination. Industrial societies not only tend to be open, but they also tend to produce urbanization and to be pluralistic, both of which increase the political and economic power of blacks to combat discrimination. Industrial societies are also characterized by more intensive government involvement in markets and by more consistent use of political processes to achieve economic ends.

Conclusions

This section outlined theoretical conceptions of racial discrimination advanced by neoclassical and dual labor market economists. It emphasized lack of agreement among the various proponents of the various systems and the formative nature of dual labor market and radical approaches. These theories also differ in their purposes. In general, discrimination does not occupy a central place in any of these formulations, but is only one part of a broader conceptual framework. The neoclassical theory has been developed more systematically than the others. But except in terms of compatibility with competitive neoclassical general equilibrium theory, it seems to me to be inadequate in its definition and conception of discrimination. It treats discrimination as "given" and not to be explained by the model, fails to take into consideration the influence of groups and bargaining, uses deductive (rather than empirically derived) concepts which are difficult to validate, produces mechanical results which add little information about the forces increasing or reducing discrimination, omits significant factors impinging on discrimination, and generally leads to inadequate policy recommendations.

To understand racial discrimination in employment and to produce strategies, tactics, and policies for changing discrimination, a broader bargaining model is needed. Such a model would distinguish between overt and institutional discrimination, facilitate analysis of the motives of various factors impinging on the employment decision, emphasize examination of power relations between market actors, and would stress the need to assess the broader social and economic context within which these actors establish formal, informal, and institutionalized rules governing racial employment problems. While there are clear overlaps between the neoclassical, dual labor market, and bargaining conceptions, the last provides a better framework for both understanding the dynamics of racial phenomena in the labor market and formulating policies to improve minority opportunities.

NOTES

1. On the other hand, incomes policies are not always incompatible with collective bargaining. During the early 1970s, for example, wage and price controls were relatively effective in the construction industry because inflation had created a different set of challenges for union leaders; wage inflation meant that each succeeding wage settlement tended to be higher than the last one, causing those responsible for the earlier settlements to be compared unfavorably by their members with those who made later (higher) settlements. A system of controls permitting leaders to help formulate the ground rules for confronting such problems in a collective bargaining context, getting credit from their members for equitable settlements, leads to greater political stability for union leaders.

2. I use the term "orthodox" to refer to generally accepted theory. Orthodox employment theory combines the neoclassical microeconomic analysis and the macroeconomic theories of John Maynard Keynes. However, some theorists rejected Keynesian analysis and attempted to construct a macroeconomic analysis largely of neoclassical principles alone.

3. Employment is assumed to be frictional and voluntary if: (1) it results from unemployment due to a search for a preferred option; (2) the unemployed worker

could always find a less favorable option; (3) employment does not result in the displacement of existing workers; and (4) the frictionally unemployed worker eventually arrives at an acceptance wage that results in a positive change in income.

4. In the orthodox formulation, unemployment may also result from *demand deficiency*, meaning that there are not enough jobs for those who wish to work at prevailing real wages. This kind of unemployment can arise because the amount of goods and services producers try to produce is greater than the amount all buyers are willing to buy at existing prices.

5. For a discussion of the "deception theory," see Alchia, 1970: 42).

6. Gordon makes a realistic appraisal of structural and frictional unemployment. He makes immobility the key to defining structural unemployment, which "may exist in a sector with persistently above-average unemployment, even if vacancies equal unemployment, provided that workers cannot freely move out of that sector to others with lower unemployment rates when and if they wish to do so" (Gordon, 1973: 20). However, "If the relatively high unemployment rates resulting from such above-average job turnover or time spent in search are offset by high wages or other attractions so that workers do not move to other labor submarkets, even though they are free to do so, then . . . these high rates are due to differentially high frictional unemployment" (Gordon, 1973: 2).

7. Gordon offers the following classifications: "the position of the Phillips curve depends on (1) 'normal' frictional unemployment, however defined; (2) differentially high frictional unemployment in some markets which is offset by relatively high wages or other attractions of the job, but with workers choosing not to move to other submarkets, although they are able to do so; and (3) two types of 'structural' unemployment—(a) differentially high frictional unemployment (with vacancies equal to, or greater than, unemployment) which is not offset by higher wages or other attractions of the job, but where workers are not able to move to other submarkets, and (b) relatively high unemployment resulting from vacancies being less than unemployment in a particular sector of the labor market even though vacancies equal or exceed unemployment in the entire economy, again with no offsetting attractions such as higher wages and with workers unable to move to sectors with lower unemployment rates" (Gordon, 1973: 21).

8. See Samuelson and Solow, 1960: 149-177. Samuelson and Solow note that, as compared with the British experience, the American Phillips curve has been less stable and lies to the right. That is, wage and price stability in the United States, despite a higher productivity growth rate, can be attained only at higher unemployment rates than in England.

9. Wages and prices tended to rise in sectors of increasing demand, but the overall rise in prices appeared when sectors losing demand failed to experience wage and price declines. This wage-price behavior in declining sectors was an expression of cost-price pressure, since demand considerations alone called for declines to offset increases occurring in the expanding sectors (Schultze, 1959).

10. Collective bargaining is a mechanism that can cause cost-push inflation. Unions' power to raise wages will increase when unemployment declines because workers become more willing to strike for higher wages; and employers, whose profits probably are rising, will offer less resistance to wage increases that can be

passed on to consumers as higher prices. Wage increases are spread throughout the economy through pattern bargaining and the tendency for comparisons with pattern setters to powerfully influence wage changes in nonunion as well as union sectors (See Ross, 1958).

11. For a framework which might be more appropriate for this purpose, see Levitan et al., 1972: Ch. 12.

12. I will deal mainly with the economic theories of *racial* discrimination, although some aspects of the discussion probably are applicable to sex and other forms of discrimination. For a review of empirical research, see Hiestand, 1970.

13. The most complete statement of this neoclassical view is by Kenneth Arrow (1972, 1974).

14. If an employer faces a money wage rate of W for workers, then $W(1+d_i)$ defines a *net wage* rate, where d_i is the *discrimination* coefficient for labor. The employer is willing to pay the favored workers $(W+d_i)$ and the ones discriminated against $(W-d_i)$, so that if W_w is the wage of white workers and W_B is the wage of black workers and the employer prefers W's to B's, $W_w < W_B$.

15. If $W_W - W_B < d_i$ (where d_i is the money value of the discrimination coefficient), employers would hire B's; if $W_W - W_B B > d_i$, employers would hire only W's; and if $W_W - W_B = d_i$, work forces would be integrated.

16. Freeman (1973), for example, argues that enforcement of the Civil Rights Act of 1964 must have been responsible for the significant improvements he found in black relative income positions during the 1960s. However, careful studies of the direct enforcement of laws conclude that direct enforcement activities failed to exert much influence (Adams, 1972).

REFERENCES

ADAMS, A. V. (1972) *Toward Fair Employment and the EEOC: A Study of Compliance Procedures Under Title VII of the Civil Rights Act of 1962.* Columbus, OH. Center for Human Resource Research, Ohio State University.

ALCHIA, A. (1970) "Information costs, pricing and resource unemployment." In Edmund S. Phelps et al., *Microeconomic Foundations of Employment and Inflation Theory.* New York: W. W. Norton.

ARROW, K.J. (1972) "Models of job discrimination" and "Some models of race in the labor market." In A. H. Pascal (ed.), *Racial Discrimination in Economic Life.* Lexington, MA. D.C. Heath.

______(1974) "The theory of discrimination." In Orley Ashenfelter and Albert Rees (eds.), *Discrimination in Labor Markets.* Princeton, NJ: Princeton University Press.

ASHENFELTER, O. (1974) "Discrimination and Trade Unions." In Ashenfelter and Rees (eds.), *Discrimination in Labor Markets.* Princeton, NJ: Princeton University Press.

BECKER, G. S. (1964) *Human Capital.* New York: National Bureau of Economic Research.

_____(1971) *The Economics of Discrimination*. Chicago: University of Chicago Press.

BERGMANN, B. R. (1970) *Occupation Segregation, Wages, and Profits When Employers Discriminate by Race and Sex*. College Park, MD: Project on the Economics of Discrimination (mimeograph).

_____(1971) "The effect on white incomes of discrimination in employment." *Journal of Political Economy* 79, 2 (March/April).

BOWEN, W. G. and MASTERS, S. H. (1964) "Shifts in the composition of demand and the inflation problem." *American Economic Review* (December).

CAIRNES, J. E. (1874) *Political Economy*. New York: Harper.

DENISON, E. F. (1962) *The Sources of Economic Growth in the United States and the Alternative Before Us*. New York: Committee for Economic Development.

DOERINGER, P. and PIORE, M. (1971) *Internal Labor Markets and Manpower Analysis*. Lexington, MA: D. C. Heath.

DUNLOP, J. (1958) *Industrial Relations Systems*. New York: Henry Holt.

EDGEWORTH, F. Y. (1921) "Equal pay to men and women for equal work." *Economic Journal* 31.

FELDSTEIN, M. (1973) "The economics of the new unemployment." *Public Interest* (Fall).

FISHER, L. (1953) *The Harvest Labor Market in California*. Cambridge, MA: Harvard University Press.

FRANCE, R. R. (1962) "Wages, unemployment, and prices in the United States, 1890-1932, 1947-1957." *Industrial and Labor Relations Review* (January).

FRANKLIN, R. J. and RESNIK, S. (1974) *The Political Economy of Racism*. New York: Holt, Rinehart and Winston.

FREEMAN, R. B. (1973) "Changes in the labor market for black Americans." In A. K. Odun and G. L. Perry (eds.), *Brookings Papers on Economic Activity*. Washington, D.C.: Brookings Institution.

FRIEDMAN, M. (1966) "What price guideposts?" In George Schultz and Robert Aliber, *Guideposts, Informal Controls and the Market Place.* Chicago: University of Chicago Press.

GORDON, D. (1972) *Theories of Poverty and Unemployment*. Lexington, MA: D.C. Heath.

GORDON, R. A. (1973) "Some macroeconomic aspects of manpower policy." In Lloyd Ulman (ed.), *Manpower Programs in the Policy Mix*. Baltimore: Johns Hopkins University Press.

HIESTAND, D. (1970) *Discrimination in Employment: An Appraisal of the Research*. Ann Arbor: Institute of Labor and Industrial Relations, University of Michigan and National Manpower Policy Task Force.

HOLT, C. C. (1970) "How can the Phillips curve be moved to reduce both inflation and unemployment?" In Edmund S. Phelps et al., *Microeconomic Foundations of Employment and Inflation Theory*. New York: W. W. Norton.

_____(1971) *The Unemployment-Inflation Dilemma: A Manpower Solution*. Washington, DC: Urban Institute.

KERR, C. (1954) "The Balkanization of labor markets." In E. Wright Bakke, et al., *Labor Mobility and Economic Opportunity*. Cambridge, MA: Technology Press.

_____, DUNLOP J., HARBISON, F., and MYERS, C. (1960) *Industrialism and Industrial Man*. Cambridge, MA: Harvard University Press.

KILLINGSWORTH, C. (1968) *Jobs and Incomes for Negroes*. Ann Arbor: Institute of Labor and Industrial Relations, University of Michigan.

KRUEGER, A. O. (1963) "The economics of discrimination." *Journal of Political Economy* 71, 5 (October).

LEVITAN, S (1973) "Manpower programs for a healthier economy." In Lloyd Ulman (ed.), *Manpower Programs in the Policy Mix*. Baltimore: Johns Hopkins University Press.

_____, MANGUM, G., and MARSHALL, R. (1972) *Human Resources and Labor Markets*. New York: Harper and Row.

MARSHALL, R. (1965) *The Negro and Organized Labor*. New York: John Wiley.

_____(1967) *The Negro Worker*. New York: Random House.

_____and CHRISTIAN, V. [eds.] (1978) *Black Employment in the South*. Austin: University of Texas Press.

McCAFFREE, K. M. (1963) "A further consideration of wages, unemployment and prices in the United States, 1945-1958." *Industrial and Labor Relations Review* (October).

McCALL, J. J. (1971) *Racial Discrimination in the Job Market: The Role of Information and Search*. Santa Monica, CA: Rand Corporation.

MEIDNER, R. and ANDERSSON, R. (1973) "The overall impact of an active labor market policy in Sweden." In Lloyd Ulman (ed.), *Manpower Programs in the Policy Mix*. Baltimore: Johns Hopkins University Press.

OI, W. Y. (1962) "Labor as a quasi-fixed factor." *Journal of Political Economy* (December).

PHELPS, E. S. (1972) "The statistical theory of racism and sexism." *American Economic Review* 62, 4 (September).

PIORE, M. J. (1970) "Manpower policy." In S. Beer and R. Barringer (eds.), *The State and the Poor*. Cambridge, MA: Winthrop.

_____(1972) "Notes for a theory of labor market stratification." *Working Paper No. 95*. Cambridge, MA: MIT.

ROSS, A. M. (1958) *Trade Union Wage Policy*. Berkeley: University of California Press.

SAMUELSON, P. A. and SOLOW, R. M. (1960) "Analytical aspects of anti-inflation policy." *American Economic Review* (May).

SCHULTZ, T. W. (1960) "Capital formation by education." *Journal of Political Economy* (December).

_____(1961) "Investment in human capital." *American Economic Review* (March).

SCHULTZE, C. L. (1959) *Recent Inflation in the United States*. Washington, DC: Joint Economic Committee.

THUROW, L (1969) *Economics of Poverty and Discrimination*. Washington, DC: Brookings Institution.

_____(1970) *Investment in Human Capital*. Belmont, CA: Wadsworth.

TOBIN, J. (1972) "Inflation and unemployment." *American Economic Review* (March).

ULMAN, L (1972) "Wage-price policies: Some lessons from abroad." In Ray Marshall and Richard Perlman (eds.), *An Anthology of Labor Economics*. New York: John Wiley.

WALKER, J. L. (1973) *Economic Development, Black Employment, and Black Migration in the Nonmetropolitan Deep South*. Austin: Center for the Study of Human Resources, University of Texas (mimeograph).

WELCH, F. (1967) "Labor market discrimination: An interpretation of income differences in the rural South." *Journal of Political Economy* 75, 3 (June).

Chapter 2

The U.S. Labor Force in a Changing Economy: Implications for Manpower Policy and Research

Denis F. Johnston
Center for Demographic Studies
Bureau of the Census

Denis Johnston uses systematic forecasts of population and labor force changes as a platform for considering possible new needs for and directions in manpower research and development. Such an approach to thinking about inquiry may be far less limited than others considered in this volume. Many of the future conditions, states, and events discussed in the Johnston paper already exist in the sense that tomorrow's population is here today. Thus, barring catastrophic occurrences, we are safe in associating a relatively high order of certainty with major features of the nation's population and labor force over the coming 10 to 20 years. We can even make plausible assertions about likely changes in these features without worrying excessively about related developments, such as the rate of economic growth or the pace of technological innovation, or about continuity in patterns of social behavior, as for example with respect to labor force participation.

At the same time, however, quantitative representations of the future tend to create illusions of certainty that are problematic in several ways. First, the corespondence between anticipated and actual experience may turn out to be satisfying in broad terms but insufficient in critical specific dimensions, as where a forecast on female labor force participation is accurate on the whole yet

AUTHOR'S NOTE: *The views and interpretations expressed in this paper are the author's, and do not necessarily reflect the positions or policies of the agencies with which he is or has been affiliated.*

mistaken as to rates by age group, marital status, race, and education level. Second, we can only speculate as to how states, conditions, and events that have been satisfactorily anticipated will be perceived and addressed when they actually occur. Finally, when forecasts are regarded as accurate predictions of the future, they may serve as self-fulfilling or self-defeating prophecies. Johnston's assessment takes frank account of these limitations.

Assumptions

The supply of workers is a product of many factors, the most important of which in the long run is the number of people of working age from whom that supply must be drawn. But the timing, intensity, and duration of labor force participation by persons of working age (conventionally defined as persons 16 years and over) reflect the complex interaction of a host of additional factors, including individual and family work-leisure trade-off decisions, the felt need for formal education or training, the incidence of disability, provisions for retirement, familial obligations, and, of course, the demand for labor.

The first of these determinants, the population of working age, is itself a function of the interaction of the fundamental elements in population change—mortality, fertility, and migration. The national population projections developed by the Bureau of the Census have usually assumed a slow but steady decline in mortality and a constant volume of net immigration to the United States (currently assumed to equal 400,000 persons per year). While both assumptions are open to question, there is far greater uncertainty associated with the path of fertility. Instead of attempting to "predict" fertility, the Census Bureau has resorted to the development of alternative sets of projections which assume a common trend of mortality and a constant volume of net immigration, combined with different levels of fertility.[1]

The mortality assumptions adopted in the most recent set of population projections were taken from the Social Security Administration's Actuarial Study No. 76.[2] On this basis, the projected average length of life at birth for males increases from 68.6 years (1974-1976 average) to 69.6 years by the year 2000. Among females, the corresponding increase is from 76.3 years to 77.8 years. Recent increases in average life expectancy demonstrate the volatility of these estimates. The latest actuarial study, issued in June 1978, projects a male life expectancy of 70.3 years and a female life expectancy of 78.0 years in 2000.[3] When we compare these latest projections with past trends, it is apparent that alternative assumptions could readily be defended as equally plausible. For example, the average annual change in life expectancy at birth over the past decade (1965-1967 to 1975-1977) has amounted to 0.22 years for males and 0.29 years for females—changes that are considerably different from those projected till the end of the century.

Table 2.1: Estimates and Projections of Life Expectancy at Birth, by Sex, 1924-1926, 1949-1951, 1975-1977, 2000, and 2050

	1924-1926	1949-1951	1975-1977	2000	2050
Males	57.1	65.5	69.0	70.3	71.6
Females	60.0	71.1	76.8	78.0	80.4
Average annual change:					
Males	0.34	0.13	0.05	0.03	
Females	0.44	0.22	0.05	0.05	

Immigration

Observed fluctuations in the volume of net immigration to the United States during the past three decades, together with the cumulative impact of illegal immigration whose magnitude defies reliable estimation, suggest that the assumption of a constant volume of 400,000 per year might also be supplemented by a range of alternative assumptions.[4] The total population of the United States is now projected to increase by about 42 million (from 218 to 260 million) between 1978 and the year 2000. About 12 million of this projected gain is accounted for by the cumulative effects of a net immigration of 400,000 persons per year, plus their eventual offspring. Thus, a 50 percent increase in net immigration over this period would add another 6 million to the population by the end of the century, while a 50 percent reduction would reduce our total population growth by about 14 percent (from 42 to 36 million increase).[5]

Fertility

Wide swings in the fertility rates of American women during the past half-century are the basic source of the considerable variation in the age distribution of the population of working age we have experienced during the postwar period, and they are the root cause of the similar changes in age distribution which are in prospect over the next two decades. In 1920, the general fertility rate was 117.9—a rate which declined quite steadily to an all-time low of 75.8 in the depression year of 1936. A gradual climb which accelerated during the postwar "baby boom" caused it to reach a peak of 122.7 in 1957. Thereafter, it again declined steadily, falling to a new all-time low of 65.8 in 1976.[6] Thus the general fertility rate dropped by 36 percent from 1920 to the trough of 1936; it then rose by 62 percent between 1936 and the peak year of 1957, and subsequently declined again by 45 percent over the 1957-1977 period.

During the 1960 decade, the most dramatic changes in the age distribution of the population of working ages (16 and over) occurred in the 16 to 24 age group (up from 18 to 23 percent of the total population 16 and over) and in the 35 to 44 age group (down from 20 to 16 percent of that total). These changes reflect the effects of the postwar "baby boom" and the reduced births of the depression years, respectively. During the 1970 decade, the aging of these same cohort groups accounts for the major observed changes: a rise in the proportion aged 25 to 34 and a decline in the proportion aged 45 to 54.

Prospects for the 1980 decade reveal corresponding changes in the 35 to 44 age-group (up from 15 to 20 percent) and in the 55 to 64 age-group (down from 13 to 11 percent). However, the most significant change in prospect for the 1980s is the sharp drop in the proportion of young adults in the population of working ages; persons aged 16 to 24 will decline from 22 percent of the total in 1980 to 17 percent of the total in 1990.

An important consequence of the declining fertility of the past 20 years and the corresponding rise in the economic activity of women is the change in the nonworker/worker ratio (i.e., the number of persons not in the labor force per 100 persons in the labor force; see Table 2.2).[7]

Table 2.2: Nonworker/Worker Ratios, United States, 1950-1990

	1950	1960	1970	1978	1990
Total population (all ages)	152,271	180,671	204,878	218,548	243,513
Total labor force (16 and over)	63,858	72,142	85,903	102,537	121,456
Ratio	138.4	150.4	138.5	113.1	100.5

The prospective decline in the nonworker/worker ratio from a high of 150 in 1960 to 100 by 1990 signals major changes in domestic consumption patterns, dependency needs, and the nature of the work-leisure trade-off. Noteworthy in this regard is the drop in the proportion of nonworkers aged 16 to 64 (mostly homekeepers and students) from 40 percent in 1950 to 30 percent in 1990, and the rise in the proportion of nonworkers aged 65 and over (from 11 percent in 1950 to 22 percent in 1990). These changes imply continuing demand for home-care and child-care services and for goods and services designed to meet the needs of elderly dependents.

The most recent set of population projections issued by the Bureau of the Census provides three series (I, II, and III) that differ only in the assumed trend in completed fertility.[8] Evidence from recent surveys of birth expectations confirms the downward shift in average family size from the three-child norm of the 1950s to the two-child norm at present (see Table 2.3).[9]

Table 2.3: Lifetime Births Expected, 1967, 1972, and 1978

		Percentage distribution				
	Year	Total	0 or 1	2	3	4 or More
All wives aged 18 to 34 years	1967	100.0	8.2	30.7	29.7	31.4
	1972	100.0	12.3	47.0	24.0	16.7
	1978	100.0	17.4	49.2	22.5	10.9
Black wives aged 18 to 34 years	1967	100.0	11.7	25.0	25.1	38.2
	1972	100.0	15.1	34.0	20.7	30.2
	1978	100.0	17.6	36.2	25.5	20.7

These data indicate that two-thirds of these young married women now expect to have two children or less. Meanwhile, the total fertility rate has been well below the bare replacement level since 1972, although it has been fluctuating around 1.8 children per woman since 1976.[10]

The conjectural leap from these data to projections of future fertility is notoriously hazardous but inescapable. The series II projections assume a gradual rise in completed fertility to the bare replacement level of 2.1 children per woman, on average. Series III, on the other hand, assumes a continuing gradual decline to an ultimate completed fertility of 1.7 children per women, on average. On balance, the adoption of the series II population projection as representing the most likely growth path seems defensible, but series III is equally plausible.

The Changing Structure and Characteristics of the U.S. Labor Force

Patterns of Growth and Participation

Between 1950 and 1960, the total labor force increased by 828,000 per year, on average; women workers comprised nearly 60 percent of this net gain, while nearly all of it was concentrated among workers (of both sexes) aged 35 years and over. The 1960 decade witnessed a major change in this pattern of growth, with an average annual net gain of 1,376,000, of which 60 percent was again comprised of women workers. But with the inflow (from the mid-1960s onward) of the postwar "baby-boom" cohorts who entered the working ages, about 70 percent of this next gain occurred among workers 16 to 34 years old. During the current decade (1970-1978) the pace of labor force growth has been accelerated, averaging 2,079,000 per year. Women workers have amounted to 62 percent of this increase, while workers aged 16 to 34 (of both sexes) have comprised 87 percent of this net growth.

According to the most recent projections of labor force, the prospective growth, 1978-1990, shall be at a slower pace, amounting to 1,576,000 per year, on average, with 65 percent of the increase comprising women workers and the same proportion comprising workers (of both sexes) aged 35 and over. The average annual rates of change in these labor force components provide impressive evidence of these historically unprecedented fluctuations (see Table 2.4).

Table 2.4: Average Annual Rates of Change (in percentages) in Total Labor Force, 1950-1990

	1950-1960	1960-1970	1970-1978	1978-1990
Total labor force, both sexes	1.2	1.7	2.2	1.4
Males	0.7	1.1	1.4	0.8
Females	2.3	3.0	3.6	2.2
Both sexes, 16 to 34 years old	0.2	3.0	3.6	2.2
Both sexes, 35 years old and over	2.0	0.9	0.5	1.8

Long-term trends and projections of the labor force participation rates of men and women over the 40-year span, 1950 to 1990, display a major change in the composition of the labor force. In the aggregate, rising proportions of the population in the prime working ages, combined with large increases in the rates of economic activity among women, more than offset the gradual declines in the participation rates of men. Thus, the proportion of the population 16 and over in the labor force rose from 58.5 percent in 1950 to 62.7 percent in 1978 and is projected at 65.6 percent in 1990. Among men of working age, the corresponding proportions declined steadily from 84.3 percent in 1950 to 77.2 percent in 1978 and are projected at 75.7 percent in 1990. But among women, the proportion in the labor force rose from 33.3 percent in 1950 to 49.3 percent in 1978 and is projected at 56.4 percent in 1990. In short, the proportion of the labor force comprising women workers rose from 29 percent in 1950 to 41 percent in 1978 and is projected at 45 percent by 1990.

Impact on the Demand for Labor

Annual changes in the volume of births are reflected, with an average time-lag of about 18 years, in the volume of new young workers who enter the labor force in search of entry-level jobs. To that number must be added the substantial numbers of mostly women workers who reenter the labor force each year. Beginning in the mid-1960s, when the first of the "baby-boom" cohorts began to enter the labor force in significant numbers, the annual volume of new job seekers has increased steadily and is expected to reach a peak by 1979 or 1980, when the birth cohorts of 1961 move into the labor force. A large proportion of the demand for entry-level jobs depends upon net growth in employment within given occupations or the development of new occupations, but the bulk of job openings are attributable to replacement needs occasioned by death or retirement. In general, about two-thirds of the more than 4 million job openings each year, 1960 to1976, resulted from replacement needs, while the remaining third was attributable to net growth in total employment. During this period, the proportion of total job openings created by net growth ranged from a low of about 25 percent in managerial and administrative occupations to a high of about 50 percent in professional and technical occupations.

According to the latest BLS projections of employment, the outlook for the period 1976-1985 is for continued rapid expansion in the volume of job openings, averaging 5.1 million per year. Of that total, fully 36 percent are assumed to stem from net growth in employment. That proportion ranges from a low of 31 percent for nonfarm labor to a high of 45 percent for clerical workers.[11] Both white-collar and blue-collar occupations are expected to share equally in this projected growth, with about 40 percent of the total job openings in both sectors attributable to net growth. A similar proportion of the anticipated job openings in service occupations (other than private household workers) is also due to net growth. Only two major occupation groups are expected to continue their long-term decline in number: private household workers and farm workers. The former group declined from 2.0 to1.1 million and the latter from 4.2 to 2.8 million between 1960 and 1976. They are projected at 900,000 and 1.9 million, respectively, in 1985.

When the above employment projections are compared with the most recent projections of total labor force (under the moderate growth assumption), it is evident that even the above pace of employment growth may not suffice to bring about significant reductions in unemployment. With a projected civilian labor force in 1985 of 113 million, the projected employment total of 104.3 million implies an unemployment rate of 7.7 percent.

Educational Attainment of Workers

THE HIGHLY EDUCATED

Further insight into the employment needs of the nation's workforce may be gained by considering long-term trends in the educational attainment of adult workers (persons 25 and over in the civilian labor force). As recently as the late 1950s, only 46 percent of these adult workers had graduated from high school and only 10 percent were college graduates. By March 1977, the proportion of the adult workers with four years of high school or more had risen to 74 percent, and the proportion completing four years or more of college had reached 20 percent of the total adult workforce. Noteworthy in this regard is the fact that over 40 percent of these college graduates had completed at least one year of graduate school. According to projections prepared by the author in 1973, the proportion of high school and college graduates in the civilian labor force 25 years and over would reach 81 and 24 percent, respectively, by 1990.[12]

The magnitude of these increases in educational attainment cannot be conveyed by percentage figures alone. In the late 1950s, there were 5.7 million adult workers with four years or more of college. By the late 1960s, their number had risen to about 8.7 million, of whom 3.6 million had completed at least one year of graduate schooling. By March 1977, there were 14.5 million college graduates in the adult labor force, of whom 6.3 million had completed one year or more of graduate schooling.

It is becoming evident that a growing proportion of these highly educated workers are finding employment in occupations that did not formerly attract significant numbers of college graduates. Between March 1968 and March 1978, for example, the number of college graduates (25 and over) employed in professional, technical, managerial, or administrative occupations rose from 7.7 to 12.3 million—a 60 percent increase. Over the same period, however, the number employed in all other occupations rose from 1.5 to 4.0 million—an increase of 167 percent.[13] Earlier BLS studies of the components of growth in demand for the better educated workers called attention to the phenomenon of educational upgrading—i.e., the imposition of higher educational qualifications on particular jobs without corresponding change in job content. Although continuing technological advances and the creation of new technical occupations account for much of the demand for highly educated workers, a large proportion of that demand may reflect only the educational upgrading that accompanies the rising educational attainment of job-seekers.

It is evident that any excess supply of college graduates in the labor force will not be reflected in unemployment rates; the unemployment rate among all college graduates in March 1978 was 2.5 percent, as compared with 6.6 percent for the civilian labor force as a whole. What is indicated, however, is the movement of growing numbers of highly educated workers into occupations that may not fully utilize their educational qualifications and training. In short, the problem of underemployment, in the form of college graduates who are overqualified for their jobs, shows signs of growing in severity during the coming decade.

The differential growth rates of the labor force as a whole and of the highly educated segments of the labor force provide further indication that the problem of accommodating an ever-growing proportion of highly educated workers remains serious (see Table 2.5).

Table 2.5: Average Annual Rates of Change (in percentages) in Labor Force, 1958-1968, 1968-1978, and 1978-1990

	1958 to 1968	1968 to 1978	1978 to 1990
Total Labor Force, 16 and Over:			
Both sexes	1.6	2.2	1.4
Males	1.0	1.3	0.8
Females	2.8	3.6	2.2
Civilian Labor Force with 4 Years or More of College:			
Both sexes	4.3	5.8	3.6
Males	3.9	5.3	2.8
Females	5.4	6.9	4.9

Job prospects for women college graduates are especially problematic. The number of these women employed in clerical, sales, blue-collar, service, or farm occupations nearly quadrupled between 1968 and 1978—up from 424,000 to 1.5 million. Noteworthy in this regard is the relatively slow rise in the number of these college graduates who are employed as primary and secondary school teachers—traditionally a major source of their employment. In 1968, half of all college graduate women in the labor force were so employed; by 1978, that proportion had fallen to one-third. Of course, the opening of many male-dominated occupations to these highly educated women has had salutary effects. Between 1968 and 1978, the number of these women employed in professional, technical, managerial, and administrative jobs (other than in primary and secondary school teaching) rose 900,000 to 2.2 million. But these gains have been accompanied by a parallel rise in the number of male college graduates employed in clerical, sales, blue-collar, service, or farm occupations —up from 1.1 million in 1968 to 2.5 million in 1978.

During the coming decade, the anticipated growth in the number of college graduates in the labor force and the more moderate growth expected in the number of professional and managerial jobs they have traditionally filled, point to severe competition among both men and women college graduates for such positions.

THE POORLY EDUCATED

The supply-demand outlook for workers at the lower end of the educational ladder poses a different problem. The number of workers with less than eight years of formal education declined from 9.9 million in the late 1950s to 7.1 million in 1968 and to 4.7 million in 1978. By 1990, their number is expected to have declined to about 2.7 million. Although these workers are less concentrated in particular occupations than college graduates, their prospective employment opportunities can be gauged by considering job requirements in service occupations, operative occupations and nonfarm labor. In March 1977, for example, 65 percent of the 4.3 million employed workers with less than eight years of formal education were employed in these three occupation groups.

The prospective increase in the number of jobs in these three groups, averaging close to 600,000 per year during the next decade, suggests that the steadily diminishing number of less educated workers will find ample opportunities for employment, provided that educational upgrading in these occupations is not excessive. However, the changing educational composition of workers in all blue-collar, service and farm occupations between 1967 and 1977 suggests that substantial educational upgrading is taking place among these occupation groups. The proportion of workers in these occupations who have completed four years of high school or more rose from 41 to 58 percent during this period, and the proportion completing 4 or more years of college rose from 1.4 to 3.2 percent (up from 500,000 to 1.4 million).

In short, the continued upgrading in the educational attainment of workers which is in prospect gives rise to considerable pressure for educational upgrading within occupation groups, quite apart from the upgrading which would occur in tandem with technological advances. These pressures are most evident when we examine the trends and projections which relate to the employment of workers at opposite extremes of the educational ladder. What these projections imply is a significant surplus of college graduate workers after 1980, together with a growing shortage of workers who would normally find employment in occupations requiring minimal amounts of formal education. In both cases, the process of matching supply and demand entails a considerable upgrading in educational terms, and this, in turn, suggests the possible emergence of a labor supply which is overqualified for the actual requirements of available jobs. The current outlook suggests the possible emergence of a job-worker matching problem—the reverse of the problem of "structural unemployment," which was of primary concern at the beginning of large-scale government involvement in manpower training in the early 1960s. To be sure, the problem of qualifying the hard core unemployed and otherwise handicapped workers for available employment will remain, albeit in smaller magnitude. But in addition, there looms the possibility of serious adjustment problems with a potential oversupply of workers with formal educational qualifications far in excess of the actual requirements of the jobs which are available to them. If, as is indicated by the current outlook, the number of jobs for which the highly educated are formally qualified fails to increase rapidly enough to absorb these workers, there might be an accelerating movement of increasing number of highly educated workers into occupations which have traditionally been the preserve of the less educated majority. Such movement, in turn, is likely to generate considerable strain stemming from both frustrated ambitions and expectations among the more highly educated and increased competition for advancement among the less educated.[14]

The Changing Structure of the U.S. Economy

Occupational Distribution

In 1978, for the first time, over half of the employed civilian workers were employed in white-collar jobs, a rise from 43 percent in 1960. Over the same 18-year period, farm employment declined from 7.9 to 3.0 of total employment. The rates of change in the distribution of the employed in the major occupational sectors have been quite varied during the past two decades and that disparity is expected to continue into the 1980 decade (see Table 2.6).

Table 2.6: Average Annual Rates of Change (in percentages) in Major Occupational Sectors, 1960-1985

	1960-1972	1972-1978	1978-1985
All occupations	1.8	2.4	1.9
Total white-collar occupations	2.6	3.1	2.2
Total blue-collar occupations	1.4	1.6	1.5
Total service occupations	2.6	2.6	2.4
Total farm occupations	−1.5	−1.5	−1.0

According to these projections, the number of persons employed in the civilian economy would increase by 1.9 million per year, on average, from 1978 to 1985 and would total 107.6 million by 1985.[15] This represents a modest reduction in the pace of employment growth in the recent past, which averaged 2.1 million jobs per year from 1972 to 1978. The distribution of this projected growth in employment is quite different from that of the past few years. Comparing the average annual increase in jobs during the 1972-1978 period and the 1978-1985 period, employment in the higher white-collar occupations (professional, technical, managerial, and administrative jobs) will fall from an 800,000 to a 500,000 rate. Sales and clerical jobs will increase slightly more rapidly in the projected period, from a 540,000 to a 600,000 yearly increment. The average annual growth in blue-collar occupations remains constant at 490,000 during both periods. Service occupations will expand at a slightly faster pace, from 310,000 to 335,000 jobs per year. Farm occupations, which declined by 45,000 per year, 1972-1978, are projected to decline by 28,000 jobs per year, 1978-1985. In summary, the only major slowdown that is anticipated in the growth of employment in the 1978-1985 period is concentrated in the professional and managerial groups. This finding lends further support to the argument that growing numbers of college-educated workers are likely to be forced into occupations that have not traditionally attracted them to a significant extent.

Industrial Distribution

During the period 1959 to 1968, the most rapid growth in employment by far was in the government sector, which expanded at an average annual rate of 4.2 percent at a time when the overall rate of job growth averaged 1.8 percent per year. Only two other sectors of the economy grew more than 2 percent per year during this period: finance, insurance, and real estate (2.7 percent per year) and all services (2.9 percent per year). The slowest growth occurred in transportation, communication and public utilities (0.7 percent per year) and contract construction (0.8 percent per year). Agriculture and mining registered losses in jobs, at rates of −4.5 and −2.1 percent per year, on average, during this period.[16]

These patterns of change were quite different during the following nine-year span, 1968 to 1977. Total employment again grew by 1.8 percent per year, on average, but the rate of growth was now led by mining (3.5 percent per year) and finance, insurance, and real estate (3.2 percent per year). The government sector continued to grow, but at the substantially lower rate of 2.8 percent per year during this period; that growth rate was matched by wholesale and retail trade and by all services. Transportation, communication, and public utilities continued to expand slowly (0.8 percent per year) while contract construction grew at a faster pace than before (1.9 percent per year). Only agriculture (−2.5 percent per year) and total manufacturing (−0.1 percent per year) registered declines.

The outlook for the period 1977-1985, according to these projections, is for an accelerated rate of growth in total civilian employment, averaging 2.2 percent per year. Three sectors of the economy are projected to grow considerably faster than this average rate: all services (3.0 percent), finance, insurance, and real estate (2.8 percent), and wholesale and retail trade (2.7 percent). The slowest projected annual growth rates are in total manufacturing (1.8 percent), transportation, communications, and public utilities (1.6 percent), and the government sector (1.3 percent). Mining and contract construction are expected to grow at an annual rate of 2.4 and 2.2 percent, respectively, while agricultural employment is expected to remain constant during this period.

Expressed on an average annual basis, the number of jobs in the civilian economy increased by 1.4 million, 1959-1968; by 1.5 million, 1968-1977; and is projected to increase by 2.3 million, 1977-1985. The bulk of this accelerated growth to 1985 is concentrated in durable and nondurable goods manufacturing, where an average annual decline of 22,000 jobs, 1968-1977, is converted to an average annual increase of 396,000 jobs, 1977-1985. The anticipated growth in the trade and services sectors of the economy is also substantial, from 1.0 million jobs a year, 1968-1977, to 1.3 million jobs a year, 1977-1985. Only the government sector is expected to grow at a substantially slower pace than during the past decade, from 370,000 jobs a year, 1968-1977, to 210,000 jobs per year, 1977-1985. Three major sectors—manufacturing, trade, and services—are expected to account for three-fourths of the total growth in jobs during the 1977-1985 period, as compared with only 63 percent of the total during the 1968-1977 period.

It must be stressed that the above projections reflect the assumption that long-term trends in labor supply will be more closely matched by demand for labor than they have been in the recent past. Both the projections of civilian employment by major occupation group (based on the number of persons employed) and the projection of civilian employment by major industrial sector (based on the number of jobs available) assume a gradual reduction in the aggregate unemployment rate to about 4.5 percent by 1985. Given that assumption, these projections, and the average annual rates and amounts of change derived therefrom, provide plausible estimates of the pace of economic growth that must be sustained if that underlying assumption is to be realized. In addition, the projections portend continuing shifts in both the occupational and industrial distribution of the labor force, with the locus of most rapid growth moving from the white-collar occupations to the blue-collar and service occupations.

Output per Worker and GNP

The projection of private gross national product (GNP) per hour of work is derived from projections of labor force and employment, combined with assumptions concerning long-term trends in average annual hours worked per worker and in average productivity. Average annual hours worked per worker are expected to continue their long-term gradual decline, from 2,001 in 1968 to 1,918 in 1977 and 1,867 in 1985. However, this reduction in hours is overshadowed by the continuing growth in the number of employed workers in the private sector, which, expressed in terms of jobs held, has increased from 69.3 million in 1968 to 80.0 million in 1977 and is projected at 96.9 million in 1985. Combining these figures, we obtain an increase in private hours of work per year from 139 billion in 1968 to 154 billion in 1977 and 181 billion in 1985.

Productivity, as measured by the value (in 1972 dollars) of output per hour of work in the private sector, rose from $6.63 to 1968 to $7.72 in 1977 and is projected at $9.07 in 1985. Combining these estimates with the number of hours of work per year in the private sector, we obtain an estimate of private gross national product (GNP) of $920 billion in 1968, $1,186 billion in 1977, and $1,641 billion in 1985, again in 1972 dollars. The GNP component associated with general government is estimated at $132 billion in 1968, $147 billion in 1977, and $163 billion in 1985, so that total GNP (in 1972 dollars) comes to $1,052, $1,333, and $1,803 billion in 1968, 1977, and 1985.

Here also, the average annual rates of growth in these components over the two periods 1968-1977 and 1977-1985 reveal a number of significant changes (see Table 2.7).[17]

These projections indicate that long-term trends in improved material levels of living are expected to continue into the 1980

Table 2.7: Average Annual Rates of Change (in percentages) in Components of GNP, 1968-1977 and 1977-1985

	1968-1977	1977-1985
Average annual hours per job (private)	−0.47	−0.34
Total employment (private sector jobs)	1.59	2.39
Total hours worked (private sector)	1.12	2.05
Private GNP per hour (1972 dollars)	1.69	2.01
Total private sector GNP (1972 dollars)	2.82	4.06
Government GNP (1972 dollars)	1.23	1.27
Total GNP (1972 dollars)	2.63	3.78
Total disposable personal income (1972 dollars)	2.93	3.92
Per capita disposable personal income	2.07	3.03

decade, despite the impact of inflation and the energy shortage. However, the critical factor in sustaining this improvement is productivity (output per hour of work). During the 1960-1968 period, output per hour increased at an average annual rate of 3.8 percent, but during the 1968-1977 period, that rate of increase dropped sharply to 1.7 percent per year, on average, and is projected at 2.0 percent per year from 1977 to 1985. The effect of this slower rate of increase on disposable personal income is diminished somewhat by the growing proportion of the population that is economically active, but the rate of increase in disposable personal income still reflects the slowdown in productivity increases. Between 1960 and 1968, disposable personal income increased (in 1972 dollars) by 5.2 percent per year, on average. From 1968 to 1977, that increase dropped to 2.93 percent per year and is projected at 3.92 percent per year, 1977 to 1985. On a per capita basis, the average annual rate of increase during these three periods amounts to 3.84 percent, 2.07 percent, and 3.03 percent, respectively. In summary, the outlook to 1985 is for some improvement in the rate of increase in productivity and disposable personal income, with the latter (expressed in 1972 dollars) moving from a per capita level of $2,610 in 1960, $3,549 in 1968, $4,275 in 1977, and $5,449 in 1985.

Implications for Manpower Policy

In principle, it is possible to distinguish between two broad types of manpower policy: policy that seeks to influence the supply of labor, and policy that seeks to affect labor demand.[18] The manpower policies and related programs that have emerged during the 1960 and 1970 decades have been almost exclusively of the first type. They have viewed the demand for labor as essentially exogenous and have sought to adjust the supply of labor to given or anticipated labor demand by improving the skills of job-seekers, encouraging provision of on-the-job training for workers, encouraging migration to localities of high labor demand, and a variety of other methods. Policies of the second type have emerged mostly in response to local emergencies, such as factory closings.[19]

One of the basic issues to emerge from continuing concern with the effectiveness of existing manpower policies is the extent to which their focus should shift from efforts to improve the skills and qualifications of job-seekers toward efforts to match the existing supply of labor by generating a corresponding labor demand.[20] The original focus of manpower development programs initiated in the 1960s placed them clearly in the first type; they were designed largely to improve the employability of the hard-core unemployed. These programs were criticized for their failure to address other salient problems affecting the match between labor supply and demand. In particular, they did not directly address problems of discrimination, the need for improved job-market information, the need to facilitate access to available jobs, or, most importantly, the need to introduce measures to create and sustain high levels of aggregate demand for labor. It was also pointed out that primary emphasis on the disadvantaged tended to create a secondary labor market in which these workers would remain isolated from the mainstream of economic activity.[21] Concentration on efforts to improve the qualifications of the less advantaged workers and job-seekers was further criticized on the ground that such upgrading, unless accompanied by adequate levels of aggregate labor demand, merely give rise to a corresponding upgrading of job requirements, regardless of the actual demand related to adequate job performance.[22] Finally, it has been argued that greater effort focused on job training for the more highly skilled jobs where real shortages exist would have a desirable multiplier effect. It would permit the beneficiaries of such training to move into more rewarding occupations and it would, in addition, open opportunities for advancement among workers at lower skill levels. By removing bottlenecks in the supply of highly skilled labor, such training would also reduce the inflationary impact of such bottlenecks during periods of rapid economic growth.[23]

It is hardly surprising that critical evaluations of the several manpower programs of the past two decades have tended to stress the limitations stemming from their basic goal, which was to improve the competitive position of the most disadvantaged workers in the existing labor market. The underlying manpower policy which inspired these programs sought, first and foremost, to provide immediate assistance to those target groups where the perceived need was the greatest. Given this priority, the limited resources available, and the lack of information as to the secondary and tertiary effects of these programs, the programs which emerged were both imaginative and highly relevant. Unfortunately, the real world seldom provides clean-cut tests of the effectiveness of any large-scale social program. To the critics who argue that the alleged beneficiaries of MDTA and CETA programs would have achieved equivalent gains on their own in the course of time, there can be no conclusive rejoinder. By the same token, it is impossible to demonstrate how much worse off these individuals, or the society as a whole, might have been in the absence of the programs that were implemented.

Manpower Policies in the 1980s

The manpower outlook for the 1980 decade is dominated by several developments. First, the large inflow of new young workers that has been observed during the past 15 years is not expected to continue at the same pace. The teenage entrants to the labor force in 1975 were drawn from the large birth cohorts of 1956 to 1959; those in 1980 are from the birth cohorts of 1961 to 1964; the latter group is about 300,000 smaller than the former. The peak number of new young entrants are to be found in 1978 or 1979 and may be expected to diminish gradually each year thereafter. Thus, while there remains a need for programs designed to ease the transition from school to work, that need should become more manageable, other things equal, in the course of the next decade.

Second, the large increase that can be foreseen in the number of younger adult workers (25 to 44 years old) strongly suggests the need for closer monitoring of their work experience, occupational mobility, and job satisfaction. The emerging needs of this burgeoning group may also call for the development of special programs designed to facilitate necessary adjustments to changing labor demands, upgrading of skills, and the like. Between 1978 and 1990, the population in this broad age group will increase by over 19 million, and the corresponding number in the labor force is expected to increase by over 20 million—increases of 33 and 45 percent, respectively. This group is the greatest potential source of demand for new housing, consumer durables, and a host of goods and services associated with family formation and child rearing. It also offers the greatest potential for further improvements in the nation's productivity, for innovative approaches toward the solution of persistent social, economic, and ecological problems, and for the development of flexible and adaptive life styles in response to the growing challenge of natural resource constraints and environmental problems. But if the educational attainment and skills of this group of workers have reached unprecedented heights, its levels of aspiration and its expectations are correspondingly high. Most of these workers have trained for and aspire to jobs with career potential, work that is both challenging and meaningful, and a work setting that encourages and is responsive to creative innovations.

Within this broad population group, two segments can readily be identified as the locus of the greatest potential strain during the coming decade: the educationally disadvantaged and career-oriented college graduate women. Despite the continuing improvement in the educational attainment of the work force, the number of young adult workers (20 to 34 years old) with less than four years of high school education is expected to decline only moderately during the 1980s, from 5.6 million in 1977 to about 4.9 million by 1990. Thus the demand for remedial education, vocational training, and other services aimed at providing basic education and job-related skills to this group will continue. It should be added, in this connection, that growing numbers of high school graduates may also find themselves in need of such remedial education and training, inasmuch as they have not acquired the proficiencies formerly associated with high school graduation.

It is more difficult to anticipate the kinds of manpower policies and programs that may be called for in order to make optimal use of the skills and potentials of the highly educated women who are expected to continue the pursuit of career objectives. As has been noted, a large proportion of these women have traditionally found employment as teachers in primary and secondary schools—where the anticipated growth in job opportunities is not expected to match the potential supply of qualified workers. Under these circumstances, and with the added encouragement of antidiscrimination legislation, we can anticipate a continuing movement of these women workers into occupations which have been largely the preserve of working men in the past. Such movement, in turn, may generate increasing competition for the available jobs. In addition, the growing labor force participation of young adult women may give rise to increased demands for greater flexibility in the conditions of work (in regard to hours worked, day care arrangements, etc.). In short, the manpower policies that are called for over the next few years should be aimed at removing the remaining barriers to the employment of women in any and all occupations for which they may be qualified, and at ensuring their compensation and promotion in accordance with demonstrated qualifications and performance.[24]

Third, there are significant features of the socioeconomic status of minority populations which must be taken into account in the formulation of manpower policies in the immediate future. The relative "youth" of the black and other population means that the inflow of new young workers is considerably greater in this group than in the population as a whole. The lower aggregate labor force participation rates of black and other men (relative to white men) suggest the relatively greater impact of disability, discouragement, and irregular labor force participation. The persistent 2 to 1 ratio of black and other to white unemployment rates points to a condition which, if extended to the work force as a whole, would be regarded as a severe depression.

With respect to the family status, it is apparent that black and other families are about four times as likely as white families to be in the low income category, and that this differential is attributable, in part, to the larger proportion of dependents and the higher incidence of female-headed families among the black and other group. In view of the substantial disparities which remain between white and minority populations, the need for manpower policies which continue to focus on the latter group is evident.

A fourth problem area requiring the attention of manpower policy planners relates to the elusive and somewhat controversial question of worker "alienation." Attitudinal data are notoriously difficult to interpret, and the high proportion of employed workers who continue to report that they are "satisfied" with their employment is frequently cited as evidence that the problem of worker dissatisfaction is of marginal significance. In his careful review of the statistical evidence relating to job performance, productivity, worker absenteeism, strikes, grievances, and the like, Peter Henle evaluated the situation as follows:[25]

> In summary, Americans may be more unhappy at work, but there is very little evidence to show that this has affected their economic performance. An individual's job may be the most important aspect of his life, but his contribution to the economy may not diminish simply because he has problems with his supervisor, is disgusted with his working conditions, or feels that his job is too rigidly defined. On the other hand, the absence of any clear-cut economic data pointing to disaffection with work raises the possibility that people may be more satisfied with their jobs than many writers have suspected. If so, the force of two underlying developments may have been overlooked:
>
> 1. A number of industrial and economic changes over the past two decades have had the effect of making many jobs more satisfying.
> 2. With respect to the less satisfying elements, some progress has been made and avenues to improve these aspects of the job remain open.

Nevertheless, the unenviable but essential task of manpower policy planning is to try to anticipate possible strains before they assume crisis proportions, and there is considerable evidence to suggest that a closer monitoring of trends in the general area of worker satisfaction is called for. For example, it is instructive that the proportion of a cross section of white-collar workers who would choose similar work again was 43 percent, and the corresponding proportion of a cross-section of blue-collar workers was only 24 percent.[26] Even if the incidence of acute dissatisfaction with one's job is rare, and its effect on productivity is minimal, the possibility remains that the continued heavy inflow of highly educated young adult workers could lead to a heightened degree of job dissatisfaction in the future, stemming both from increased competition for the more prestigious jobs and the greater movement of these workers into occupations where the better educated come into direct competition with less educated workers. It is also possible that greater attention to the several dimensions of job satisfaction could yield useful policy guidelines whereby significant improvements in worker satisfaction could be achieved—an objective which might have important pay-offs in improved worker productivity.[27]

Finally, the manpower policies evolving over the next few years will have to deal with the worsening terms of the trade-off between inflation and unemployment. Several strategies have been proposed here. First, the development of improved mechanisms for anticipating skill shortages and overcoming them by means of flexible training programs would benefit both the recipients of such training and those who could then replace the better-trained workers as they moved into shortage occupations. Such programs would also reduce the inflationary pressures generated by skill shortages and reduce the impact of labor-supply bottlenecks on production. By the same token, improved employment, training, and promotion opportunities for minority and women workers would increase the supply of qualified workers in areas of potential shortage, and thus reduce the potential oversupply of workers in occupations where many of these workers have traditionally been concentrated.[28] Second, the decentralization of manpower planning which is called for under the provisions of the Comprehensive Employment and Training Act of 1973 (CETA) entails the maintenance of active manpower policy planning units in a large number of local areas. This act greatly enhances the possibilities for the gradual development, testing, and revision of a flexible mix of manpower programs designed to meet the unique conditions of the particular area in which they are formulated.[29] As experience with state and local-area manpower planning accumulates, it should be possible to determine the kinds of national manpower policies which can best complement those which are evolved at the state and local area levels.[30]

One of the major lessons of the decade of experience with the Manpower Development and Training Act has a direct implication for the formulation of manpower policy in the future: such policies must be viewed as complementary to, rather than in conflict with, or independent of the variety of social and economic, policies which are developed in such diverse areas as health, education, welfare, and within the private sector. As Solomon Barkin has pointed out, all advanced industrialized societies have witnessed an increased blending of conventional economic objectives with a variety of social objectives.[31] An obvious corollary of this recognized interdependence of economic, social and political goals is that no major economic policy can be adequately evaluated solely in economic terms, any more than a social goal, no matter how intrinsically desirable, can be evaluated without regard for its economic costs and implications.

If the two-child fertility norm continues to prevail, the 1980 decade may witness some further decline in average family size and a corresponding increase in the ratio of earners to "dependents." The smaller size and higher per capita income of families also suggest possible increases in savings rates, and/or possible increases in "discretionary" income and in the desire for leisure pursuits. If slower population growth is accompanied by a continued growth in material affluence, a greater range of options in regard to work versus leisure may be opened, a gradual blending of work, leisure, and continuing education may emerge. A more highly educated labor force, enjoying a high level of material affluence and correspondingly advanced tastes and expectations regarding the ingredients of a "good" life, may be expected to explore a variety of options in regard to the place of work in the life of the individual, the conditions under which it is performed, and the kinds of rewards which are sought via work activities.[32]

But this outlook is essentially "surprise-free" in that it reflects a fairly smooth continuation of current trends in rates of economic activity and in labor productivity.[33] Two major "surprises" could drastically alter this picture. First, the continuing extension of automated techniques in both primary production and service sectors suggests the possible reemergence of the fundamental issue raised (albeit prematurely) at the start of the 1960s: the extent to which automation should be permitted to "displace" jobs in the interests of greater productivity. Our experience to date in regard to this issue is certainly reassuring. Increased automation has not led to increased output with fewer jobs. Instead, it has permitted widespread upgrading of jobs by reducing or eliminating work that is especially onerous, dangerous, or unpleasant while creating increased demand for a host of service and maintenance occupations. But the necessary displacement of workers which this process entails is not without social costs, and the accelerating pace of automation merits watching, particularly when, as in the 1980s, the net growth in job opportunities will be substantially smaller than at present.[34]

Second, the potential impact of natural resource constraints on employment is now a problem of undeniable significance. There is an extensive list of raw materials which could fall in short supply over the next ten to fifteen years (whether the shortages are artificially induced or real) and the employment implications of such shortages are quite severe, even when the shortages in question are of short duration.[35] Our recent experience with oil shortages and current uncertainties concerning energy supplies and costs suggest the need for the development of a variety of contingency manpower policies which would be designed to minimize the employment impact of possible future shortages and to provide general guidelines for the allocation of skilled human resources under alternative combinations of natural resource constraints. In the long run, manpower policies will have to be integrated not only with social and economic policies within the nation, but with policies relating to international trade and the socioeconomic goals of other nations as well.

Ultimately, the continuation of long-term trends in labor force growth and in productivity yield aggregate levels of output and consumption which raise staggering problems of congestion, pollution, and waste disposal, and which at the same time impose tremendous demands on natural resources. A labor force which continued to supply hours of work at an increase of 1 percent a year, enjoying an average annual increase in productivity of 3 percent a year, would yield (ceteris paribus) a doubling of the nation's total output every 17 years. The fact that a similar rate of increase has been characteristic of most industrialized nations over the course of this century does not warrant complacency. As one of the host of recent critics of "growthmanship" has put it:[36]

> Obviously, there are two conflicting trends at work: either the present system will lead to overabundance and technological unemployment, or environmental destruction will enforce the end of further economic growth and technological innovation. In either case the reorientation of values we have described will have to take place. Overabundance will require a redirection of our life-style into the economic and nontechnical directions; and so will the ecological limits placed on further growth.

Whether or not continued technological innovation proves equal to the challenge of resource limitations and ecological problems, the magnitude of the adjustments which are likely to be called for may be expected to induce major changes in the allocation of human skills and energies in the future. If the "surprise-free" outlook suggests the appearance of a wider range of options in regard to the relation between work and leisure, the possibility of encountering a progressively severe series of shocks in the form of material shortages, pollution problems, etc., raises a different set of possible options, involving more painful trade-offs. In either event, the kinds of manpower policies which are called for will necessarily reflect changing conceptions of the meaning and purpose of work in our society.

Implications for Manpower Research and Development

Any program of manpower research and development reflects a complex series of compromises involving a host of short-term demands and long-term objectives. Such a program is expected to preserve some capacity for flexible response to immediate demands for information and guidance, as the need arises. It must maintain some facility for the systematic accumulation and regular dissemination of research findings. Such a facility must also be strongly oriented toward the expression of these research findings in terms of their practical implications, and in a language useful to the manpower planners and analysts. Finally, such a program must recognize the need to establish criteria for the evaluation of existing and proposed manpower research, and for assessing progress toward the attainment of specified manpower development objectives.[37]

Research

The most pressing need for concentrated manpower research in the immediate future arises directly from the increased data requirements imposed by the provisions of CETA. With the decentralization of responsibility for manpower plans and progress called for under this act, there has been a corresponding increase in the need for current information relating to the local labor market areas for which these plans and programs are to be developed. Furthermore, the kinds of information that are required cover a wide range of subjects—demographic and socioeconomic characteristics of the population, the economic characteristics of the area in question, measures of economic growth trends, economic development plans, migratory flows, relations with outside areas, and unique natural and cultural resources and features within a given area.

As the state and local-area manpower planners accumulate practical experience in the development and revision of manpower plans and programs, an essential function of a centralized manpower R&D program is to monitor this experience, disseminate of information relating to successful (and unsuccessful) examples, and provide extensive training, general guidelines, and other instructional material so as to ensure adherence to minimum standards in the manpower planning and related technical estimates and projections of each of the jurisdictions.

A second area for manpower research activity is population migration and distribution. Estimates and projections of the flow and distribution of the population are of critical importance in the development of manpower plans at the local-area level. In particular, the inability of central-city minority populations to relocate themselves in areas of growing employment opportunity poses serious economic and social problems in these cities. The persistence of "pockets of poverty" in a number of rural areas also points to the need for integrated manpower and economic planning at the local level.[38]

A third area for manpower research is job mobility. As was pointed out above, the proportion of job openings attributable to replacement needs is expected to increase, particularly after 1980, when net growth in employment is expected to slow down. This trend calls for additional information relating to the transferability of skills and work experience from one occupation to another, so that the social and economic costs of such transfers can be minimized. Such information would, in addition, facilitate the development of training programs for specified clusters of occupations among which job mobility could occur with minimal costs.

Fourth, the improvement of our understanding of the factors which aid or impede the adaptation of workers to the changing skill needs of the economy requires more adequate measures of the skills, knowledge, and experience of workers, together with some assessment of their potential for acquiring further education and training.[39] The need for such an assessment is indicated by the accumulation of evidence that "years of school completed," "major field of study," and other conveniently obtainable indicators of acquired knowledge, even when supplemented with work experience information, do not provide an adequate picture of an individual's capabilities or potential for further training. Improved guidance and counseling, both in school and on the job, also requires better tools for measuring capabilities.

A fifth research area which has profound implications for our understanding of short-term labor force dynamics is the sensitivity or responsiveness of labor supply to change in labor demand.[40] According to the results of an earlier BLS study, the responsiveness of labor supply to a growth in labor demand was such that three jobs would be required in order to put two unemployed persons to work.[41] This 3 to 2 ratio resulted from the finding that favorable demand conditions tended to attract, on average, one new worker from outside the labor force directly into employment for every two unemployed workers who found employment. But the attempts to further specify the nature and magnitude of this relationship have yielded a wide variety of estimates. More recent research within BLS tends to confirm the principal research conclusion of Bowen and Finegan with respect to the research problem:[42]

> we have found no convincing evidence in the postwar record that short-period changes in the overall rate of unemployment have had a large impact on the labor force participation rate of any population group other than teenagers and possibly males 65+.

Nevertheless, the large year-to-year fluctuations which have been observed in net labor force growth can hardly be dismissed as a function of sampling variability, and the usefulness of improved estimates of the locus, magnitude, and determinants of these fluctuations in labor supply for purposes of manpower policy and planning is obvious.[43]

Finally, growing concern with the issue of the "quality of work" gives rise to a wide variety of research problems, ranging from specific studies of trends in the incidence of job turnover, absenteeism, and similar indicators of job dissatisfaction to general inquiries relating to changing conceptions of the meaning of work and its place in the life of the individual. The former kinds of studies can readily be carried out on the basis of information which is conventionally obtainable and familiar to labor economists. The latter kinds, however, require considerable involvement with the vagaries of attitudinal data and the metaphysical imponderables of the meaning and purpose of life itself. Between these extremes, there remains a large area of research relating to the several dimensions of job satisfaction, such as material rewards, financial security, the challenge and intrinsic significance of the work, job comfort or discomfort, the social relations on the job, and the adequacy of available resources (including the amount of autonomy enjoyed). Information on the relative importance of these factors to persons classified by age, sex, race, educational attainment, etc., combined with corresponding rankings of different occupations along these dimensions, would be of considerable value in job counseling and might, in addition, furnish important clues as to the directions of needed improvement in particular occupations.[44]

Development

The remaining areas of concern for manpower research and development activities over the next decade are shaded toward the "development" side of the "research and development" continuum. Three major problem areas can be distinguished: (1) the assessment of the manpower impact of the federal budget; (2) the assessment of the manpower impact of social legislation; and (3) the integration of manpower planning and policy with economic policy and broader social goals and priorities.

With respect to the manpower impact of the federal budget, the Comprehensive Employment and Training Act called for the establishment of a National Commission for Manpower Policy, "charged with the long-term responsibility of identifying manpower goals and needs and assessing the impact on the present and potential labor force of various governmental programs and activities."[45] In discharging its responsibilities, this commission would establish some methodology for expressing established and proposed federal, state, and local budget expenditures in terms of their manpower requirements and manpower effects. On the requirements side, the pioneering work of Leonard A. Lecht and his associates at the National Planning Association should prove highly useful.[46] In extending these estimates and projections of manpower requirements to state and local areas, the work of the Bureau of Labor Statistics offers a wealth of technical experience.[47] The Bureau has also carried out a number of studies relating to the manpower impact associated with state and local government spending.[48]

Equally significant is the need for estimates of the manpower impact (and manpower requirements) of existing and proposed social legislation, and the incorporation of these estimates in calculations of their benefit-cost ratios. Eli Ginzberg cites the substantial manpower impact of past legislation relating to farm policy, defense expenditures, aerospace programs, and the like. For example, he points out that defense-related employed rose from about 4 million in 1964 to about 6 million in 1968 (with the Vietnam build-up), and subsequently declined to about 4 million by 1972.[49] An even greater potential impact can be envisioned (if not precisely estimated), with the possible passage of legislation relating to health and disability, or to income maintenance.[50]

Many other areas can be mentioned where the passage of new legislation might be expected to have a significant impact on labor supply and/or labor requirements, such as extensive provision of day care facilities, the widespread adoption of work-study arrangements for upgrading the skills of older workers, new forms of sheltered workshops for the severely disabled, graduated work-retirement schemes, and the like. The need to anticipate, rather than merely respond to budgetary or legislative enactments which are bound to have significant effects on manpower supply and requirements is of paramount importance in any viable program of manpower research and development. As Henry David pointed out over a decade ago:[51]

> There is no end to the number of critical assumptions which must be made and of difficult questions which must be answered when the task of discerning a future wrapped in uncertainty is undertaken. Yet, there is no escaping this difficult and hazardous task, once there is a commitment to a fuller realization of human potentialities. This objective can be attained only if alternative future strategies for manpower development and utilization are carefully weighed in developing long-range policies.

Finally, the integration of manpower plans and policies with socioeconomic policies and broader social goals entails the development of a common frame of reference and language of discourse. This is an extremely ambitious undertaking, implying as it does the establishment of conventional agreement in regard to a common measure of value applicable to the entire spectrum of objectives under consideration. In particular, the advocates of such an interpretation must deal with the accusations of "Philistinism" which have been raised against attempts to apply a singular valuational calculus to diverse issues of public welfare.[52] In addition, there is the more general question of the extent to which the currently popular "systems" metaphors are appropriate to the consideration of policy issues involving a plurality of interacting systems. Paul Diesing, for example, has stressed the need to retain an awareness of the different "criteria of rationality" which pertain to such major social institutions as the polity, the economy, the system of education, and the religious sector. He argues that each of these major societal "systems" functions in accordance with a unique set of means in pursuit of unique ends or values. Of course, the performance of such systems can be evaluated in terms which are extrinsic to their basic orientation; it is legitimate and fruitful, for example, to consider the economics of religious organizations. But in turning to considerations of public policy, it is essential to consider each of these individual systems in terms of criteria which are derived from the norms which govern its particular operation. At this level of concern, the plurality of normative systems must be recognized.[53]

The point of these considerations in the present context is to serve as a reminder that the ultimate norms which govern the development and evaluation of manpower policies are not identical to, and cannot legitimately be subsumed under those pertaining to economic conduct.[54] But to argue that manpower policy should be formulated in accordance with its own goals and evaluative criteria is not to deny the existence of the substantial area of common concern with economic and social policies. If the idea of an all-encompassing social accounting system is premature and possibly chimerical, the more modest aim of assessing the social and economic consequences of alternative manpower policies and the reverse effects of particular economic and social policies on manpower is both vital and attainable. Short of a complete integration, there exists the possibility of dialogue and of achieving a measure of common understanding and mutual agreement among the proponents of manpower goals and those whose primary concern rests with political, economic, or social objectives. Optimism that such agreements can be reached arises from our growing awareness of the interdependence of these objectives, and the potential complementarity of the means offered by these several policy instruments.

NOTES

1. In 1953, the Bureau of the Census began to issue multiple series of population projections, designed to reflect different assumptions in regard to future fertility combined with a single assumption in regard to future mortality and net immigration (see *Current Population Reports*, Series P-25, No. 78). That practice has been followed in the several subsequent revisions to be issued by the Bureau. By July 1977, when the most recent set of national population projections was released, three sets of projections were provided: Series I, reflecting an ultimate level of completed fertility of 2.7 births per woman, on average; Series II, 2.1 births per woman; and Series III, 1.7 births per woman (see *Current Population Reports*, Series P-25, No. 704).

2. Social Security Administration, Office of the Actuary, *United States Population Projections of OASDHI Cost Estimates* (Actuarial Study No. 76, June 1977).

3. U.S. Department of Health, Education, and Welfare, National Center for Health Statistics, *Vital Statistics of the United States, 1976*, Volume II, Section 5, Life Tables, table 5-5; and Social Security Administration, Office of the Actuary, *United States Population Projections for OASDHI Cost Estimates* (Actuarial Study No. 77, June 1978), table 7B.

4. The total volume of officially reported net immigration to the United States rose from 1.0 million (1941-1950) to 2.5 million (1951-1960) and 3.3 million (1961-1970). See the Commission on Population Growth and the American Future, Research Reports, Vol. 1, *Demographic and Social Aspects of Population Growth* (Washington, DC: U.S. Government Printing Office, 1972), Part 2, table 2, p. 170. The recorded level of net (legal) immigration has averaged close to 400,000 per year in the 1970s, but estimates of the true volume of net immigration are highly uncertain due to both the poorly estimated volume of emigration and the unknown proportion of undocumented aliens who may remain in the country permanently or for long periods of time.

5. Bureau of the Census, *Current Population Reports*, Series P-25, No. 704, tables 8 and D-1.

6. The general fertility rate is the number of births occurring during a specified calendar year per 1,000 women 15 to 44 years old. It is a more sensitive indicator of fertility levels than the more commonly reported crude birth rate, which is the number of births in a year per 1,000 population. Preliminary estimates of the general fertility rate in 1977 indicate a small increase to 67.8.

7. Population: Bureau of the Census, *Current Population Reports*, Series P-25, No. 311 (for 1950); No. 519 (for 1960); No. 721 (for 1970); No. 800 (for 1978); and No. 704 (for 1990, Series II projection). Total labor force: *1979 Employment and Training Report of the President*, tables A-1 and A-2; and Paul O. Flaim and Howard N. Fullerton, Jr., "Labor force projections to 1990: three possible paths," *Monthly Labor Review* 101 (December 1978): 25-35, to be reprinted with additional tables as a BLS Special Labor Force Report. In table 2.2 and subsequent tables, Series II population projections and the moderate growth series of labor force projections are used exclusively.

8. See note 1.

9. Bureau of the Census, *Current Population Reports*, Series P-20, Nos. 211, 248 and unpublished data for 1978.

10. Bureau of the Census, *Current Population Reports,* Series P-20, No. 336, table 3.

11. Bureau of Labor Statistics, *Occupational Projections and Training Data* (Bulletin 2020, 1979), tables 1 and 2.

12. Harvey R. Hamel, "Educational attainment of workers, March 1967," BLS Special Labor Force Report No. 92, reprinted with additional tables from *Monthly Labor Review* 91 (February 1968); Denis F. Johnston, "Education of workers: projections to 1990," BLS Special Labor Force Report No. 160, reprinted from *Monthly Labor Review* 96 (November 1973). These estimates exclude a substantial number of college graduates in the labor force who are under

25 years old and a small number who are in the armed forces and who may enter the civilian labor force at a later date. In March 1977, for example, there were about 1.7 million workers under 25 years of age with four years or more of college. Additional workers in this age group, especially those with one to three years of college education, may eventually complete their college education.

13. Elizabeth Waldman, "Educational attainment of workers, March 1968," BLS Special Labor Force Report No. 103, reprinted with additional tables from *Monthly Labor Review* 92 (February 1969); Scott Campbell Brown, "Educational attainment of workers, 1975 to 1978," *Monthly Labor Review* 102 (February 1979): 54-58.

14. For more detailed discussion of these and related issues, see Max. L. Carey, "Revised occupational projections to 1985," *Monthly Labor Review* 99 (November 1976): 10-22; and BLS Bulletin No. 2020 (op. cit.). With respect to the college-educated, also see A. J. Jaffe and Joseph Froomkin, "Occupational opportunities for college-educated workers, 1950-75," *Monthly Labor Review* 101 (June 1978): 15-21. With respect to the educationally limited workers, see T. Aldrich Finegan, "Improving our information on discouraged workers," *Monthly Labor Review* 101 (September 1978): 15-25.

15. *1978 Employment and Training Report of the President*, table A-15; Philip L. Rones and Carol Leon, " Employment and unemployment during 1978: an analysis," BLS Special Labor Force Report No. 218, reprinted with additional tables from*Monthly Labor Review* 102 (February 1979); and BLS Bulletin 2020 (op. cit.), table 2. The projected occupational distribution of the employed labor force in 1985 as shown in the latter report was adjusted by the author to correspond with the latest BLS projections of the civilian labor force and an assumed unemployment rate in 1985 of 4.7 percent. That adjustment increases the total employed civilian labor force in 1985 from 104.3 to 107.6 million.

16. Valeria A. Personick, "Industry output and employment: BLS projections to 1990," *Monthly Labor Review* 102 (April 1979): 2-14, table 5. Also see Arthur Andreassen, "Changing patterns of demand: BLS projections to 1990," *Monthly Labor Review* 101 (December 1978): 47-55.

17. Norman C. Saunders, "The U.S. economy to 1990: two projections for growth," *Monthly Labor Review* 101 (December 1978): 36-46. In regard to recent productivity declines, see Ronald E. Kutscher, Jerome A. Mark, and John R. Norsworthy, "The productivity slowdown and the outlook to 1985," *Monthly Labor Review* 100 (May 1977): 3-8.

18. The same distinction has been made with respect to population policy. See the statement by Roger Revelle, pp. 28-31 in The Commission on Population Growth and the American Future, *Statements at Public Hearings of the Commission on Population Growth and the American Future*, Vol. 7 (Washington, DC: U.S. Government Printing Office, 1972).

19. Manpower policies that regard labor demand as an "independent" variable have of course been supplementary to monetary and fiscal policies aimed at generating and sustaining appropriate levels of aggregate labor demand. But direct employment creation, particularly in the public sector, is by no means a new development. Furthermore, policies that assume a need to manipulate labor supply in the interests of productivity, price stability, or other economic objectives

are subject, in principle, to the same kinds of criticism that are provoked by equivalent policy proposals in the area of population. See, for example, Goran Ohlin, "Is 'labor force' a policy variable?" A paper presented at the annual meeting of the Population Association of America, April 18-20, 1974.

20. As Willard Wirtz and others have pointed out repeatedly, the Employment Act of 1946 implies a commitment to the provision of suitable and adequate employment to all who wish to work and are able to do so. See, for example, Willard W. Wirtz, "Earning and learning to live," pp. 14-26 in Seymour L. Wolfbein (ed.) *Manpower Policy: Perspectives and Prospects* (Philadelphia: Temple University School of Business Administration, 1973).

21. On the dual labor market theory, see Michael J. Piore, "The dual labor market: theory and implications," in David Gordon (ed.) *Problems in Political Economy: An Urban Perspective* (Lexington, MA: Lexington Books, 1971).

22. For a brief discussion of this issue, see Andre Daniere, "The economics of higher education," *The Annals* 404 (November 1972): 58-70. Also pertinent is Ivor Berg, *Education and Jobs: The Great Training Robbery* (Boston, MA: Beacon, 1971). For a fuller treatment, see Margaret S. Gordon (ed.) *Higher Education and the Labor Market* (New York: McGraw-Hill, 1974).

23. On this point, see Gösta Rehn, "Manpower policy as an instrument of national economic policy" and Lloyd Ulman, "Imperfect labor markets and manpower policy," pp. 171-192 and 193-207 in Wolfbein (ed.) op. cit. Also see E. Wight Bakke, *The Mission of Manpower Policy* (Kalamazoo, MI: W. E. Upjohn Institute for Employment Research, April 1969). For a wide-ranging treatment, see Sar A. Levitan, Garth L. Mangum, and Ray Marshall, *Human Resources and Labor Markets* (New York: Harper & Row, 1972), especially Chapter 29, "Issues for the 1970's."

24. On this issue, see Isabel V. Sawhill, "The economics of discrimination against women: some new findings," *Journal of Human Resources* 8 (Summer 1973): 383-396; and "Women and the workplace: special section," *Monthly Labor Review* 97 (May 1974). A related policy issue is that of volunteer work whose contribution to social well-being is enormous but whose participants are typically ineligible for social insurance or formal credit for experience and training they acquire in the course of their volunteer activities. For information on the scope and significance of volunteer work, see the U. S. Department of Labor, Manpower Administration (now Employment and Training Administration), Manpower Research Monograph No. 10 (April 1969). Also see ACTION, *American Volunteer—1974* (February 1975).

25. Peter Henle, "Economic effects: reviewing the evidence," pp. 119-148 in The American Assembly, Columbia University, *The Worker and the Job: Coping With Change* (Englewood Cliffs. NJ: Prentice-Hall, 1974). Compare the findings of Robert P. Quinn et al., *Job Satisfaction: Is There a Trend?"* U.S. Department of Labor, Manpower Administration, Manpower Research Monograph No. 30 (Washington, DC: U.S. Government Printing Office, 1974). The original quality of employment survey, taken in 1969-1970, was repeated in 1972-1973 and again in 1977. The trends revealed in these three surveys afford small grounds for complacency in regard to job satisfaction. See Robert P. Quinn and Graham L. Staines, *The 1977 Quality of Employment Survey* (Ann Arbor, MI: Survey Research Center, Institute for Social Research, University of Michigan, 1979).

26. Report of a Special Task Force to the Secretary of Health, Education, and Welfare, *Work in America* (Cambridge, MA: M.I.T. Press, 1973), "Introduction." Compare G. Staines and R. Quinn, "American workers evaluate the quality of their jobs," *Monthly Labor Review* 102 (January 1979): 3-12.

27. A detailed listing of policy recommendations in this area is provided by Sam Zagoria, "Policy implications and future agenda," pp. 177-201 in The American Assembly, Columbia University, op. cit.

28. On the "Phillips curve" problem in relation to manpower policy, see Charles C. Holt, C. Duncan MacRae, Stuart O. Schweitzer, and Ralph E. Smith, *The Unemployment-Inflation Dilemma: A Manpower Solution* (Washington, DC: The Urban Institute, 1971); and the critical discussion by Robert E. Hall, "Prospects for shifting the Phillips curve through manpower policy," *Brookings Papers on Economic Activity* 3 (1971): 664f. Also see Chapter 26, pp. 509-527 in Sar A. Levitan et al., op. cit.

29. For a summary of the provisions of this act, see "Manpower programs: moving toward decentralization," pp. 37-66 in the *Manpower Report of the President,* April 1962.

30. On the need for a "flexible manpower service capacity," see the remarks of Stanley H. Ruttenberg, "Recent developments in manpower administration," pp. 141-153 in Wolfbein (ed.) op. cit.

31. Solomon Barkin, *Manpower Policy: Economic Policy Instrument and Independent Policy System* (U.S. Department of Labor, Manpower Administration, December 1973), especially Part I, pp. 3-32.

32. For further speculations in this vein, see the writer's "Illustrative projections of the labor force of the United States to 2040," pp. 163-187 in Commission on Population Growth and the American Future, Research Reports, Vol. 2, *Economic Aspects of Population Change* (Washington, DC: U.S. Government Printing Office, 1972). Also see his "The future of work: three possible alternatives," *Monthly Labor Review* 95 (May 1972): 3-11; and Fred Best (ed.) *The Future of Work* (Englewood Cliffs, NJ: Prentice-Hall, 1973). For more recent insights, see Brigitte Berger, "People work: the youth culture and the labor market," *Public Interest* 35 (Spring 1974): 55-66; and Fred Best and Barry Stern, "Education, work, and leisure: must they come in that order?" *Monthly Labor Review* 100 (July 1977): 3-10.

33. All projections and forecasts are "surprise-free" in the sense that they must assume some continuity of observed trends and structural relationships. To introduce shocks or disturbances (surprises) into such projections is merely to subsume them under the same set of assumed determinants. On this point, see William Ascher, *Forecasting: An Appraisal for Policy-Makers and Planners* (Baltimore: Johns Hopkins University Press, 1978), especially pp. 199-214. Compare the trenchant remarks of Robert A. Nisbet, "The year 2000 and all that" and "Postscript: June, 1971," pp. 257-278 in Albert Somit (ed.) *Political Science and the Study of the Future* (Hinsdale, IL: Dryden, 1974).

34. According to a study conducted by Harold Wool in the early 1970s, employment in professional, technical and kindred occupations was expected to increase by about 39 percent between 1970 and 1980, while the prospective labor supply in these occupations was expected to rise by 45 percent. At the opposite

end of the spectrum, the increase in employment in laboring and semiskilled service occupations was projected ro rise by about 10 percent, while the prospective supply of labor for these occupations would rise by only about 4 percent. See table 3 in "Changing patterns of occupational opportunity," pp. 103-127 in *Manpower Report of the President*, April 1974. The complete study is Harold Wool, *The Labor Study for Lower Level Occupations* (Washington, DC: National Planning Association, 1973). Actual trends in employment during the 1970-1978 period suggest that employment in professional, technical, and kindred occupations will rise by about 35 percent during the 1970 decade, while employment in nonfarm labor and all services combined will rise by about 39 percent. Although the latter estimates are imprecise, they suggest that the imbalance cited by Wool may be more serious than he envisaged.

35. For example, see Ronald E. Kutscher and Charles T. Bowman, "Industrial use of petroleum: effect on employment," *Monthly Labor Review* 97 (March 1974): 3-8.

36. Walter A. Weisskopf, *Alienation and Economics* (New York: E. P. Dutton, 1971), p. 179. On this general issue, see Herman E. Daly (ed.) *Toward A Steady-State Economy* (San Francisco: W. H. Freeman, 1973), especially the editor's chapter, "Electrical power, employment, and economic growth: a case study in growthmania," pp. 252-277; and John H. Cumberland and James R Hibbs, "Alternative future environments: some economic aspects," pp. 115-128 in Walter A. Hahn and Kenneth F. Gordon (eds.) *Assessing the Future and Policy Planning* (New York: Gordon and Breach, 1973). A more recent study in this vein is Fred Hirsch, *Social Limits to Growth* (Cambridge, MA: Harvard University Press, 1976), especially pp. 161-190.

37. For a schematic summary of alternative strategies for the utilization of manpower research findings in manpower development, see Ronald G. Havelock and David A. Lingwood, *R&D Utilization Stategies and Functions: An Analytical Comparison of Four Systems* (Ann Arbor: Institute for Social Research, University of Michigan, 1973).

38. For a recent assessment of migration, see "The new geography of employment: migration and the American worker," pp. 69-99 in *Manpower Report of the President*, April 1974.

39. This recommendation is included as one of the principal needs for a future manpower research agenda. See Ray Marshall, "Research and development: innovations in manpower policy," pp. 65-86 in Wolfbein (ed.) op cit. Also see Dixie Sommers and Alan Eck, "Occupational mobility in the American labor force," *Monthly Labor Review* 100 (January 1977): 3-19; and Fred Best, "Preference on worklife scheduling and work-leisure trade-offs," *Monthly Labor Review* 101 (June 1978): 31-37.

40. Major studies in the area include Peter S. Barth, "Unemployment and labor force participation," *Southern Economic Journal* 34 (January 1968): 375-382; William G. Bowen and T. Aldrich Finegan, *The Economics of Labor Force Participation* (Princeton, NJ: Princeton University Press, 1969); Arthur D. Butler and George D. Demopoulos, "Labor force behavior in a full employment economy," *Industrial and Labor Relations Review* 24 (April 1971): 375-388; Kenneth Strand and Thomas Dernberg, "Cyclical variation in civilian labor force

participation," *Review of Economics and Statistics* (November 1964): 378-391, and "Hidden unemployment, 1953-62: a quantitative analysis by age and sex," *American Economic Review* 56 (March 1966): 71-95; and Alfred Tella, "Labor force sensitivity to employment by age, sex," *Industrial Relations* 4 (February 1965): 69-83. Critical reviews of this research include Jacob Mincer, "Labor force participation and unemployment: a review of recent experience," pp. 73-112 in Robert A. Gordon and Margaret S. Gordon (eds.) *Prosperity and Unemployment* (New York: John Wiley, 1966); and William G. Bowen and T. Aldrich Finegan, op. cit., pp. 503-537.

41. Sophia Copper and Denis F. Johnston, "Labor force projections for 1970-80," *Monthly Labor Review* 88 (February 1965): 129-140, reprinted as BLS Special Labor Force Report No. 49.

42. Bowen and Finegan, op. cit., p. 515.

43. Concern for the issue of labor force sensitivity stems in part from the observed decline in the ratio of so-called "primary workers" (males 25 to 54 years old in the labor force) to "secondary workers" (comprising all other members of the labor force). That ratio has declined from .84 in 1950 to .57 in 1978; the latest projections of labor force yield a corresponding ratio of .62 by 1990. In theory, "primary" workers would be insensitive to changes in the demand for labor, whereas the "secondary" workers would not; hence a decline in the ratio of primary to secondary workers would imply, ceteris paribus, a greater responsiveness of labor supply to demand conditions. It has since become evident to most observers that this simple dichotomy of the labor force does not accord with the realities. Many workers in the secondary worker category are fully committed to labor force participation by reason of economic necessity and are therefore as insensitive to demand conditions as males in the 25 to 54 year-old age group.

44. Research in this area, as well as in areas of job mobility and labor force sensitivity, would be greatly facilitated by continuation (and expansion) of the kinds of longitudinal surveys that have been conducted by Herbert S. Parnes and associates. Exclusive reliance on cross-sectional or "in-time" survey data severely limits the usefulness and reliability of the results obtained. On this point, see James L. Peterson, "Work and life cycles: agenda for longitudinal research," *Monthly Labor Review* 102 (February 1979): 23-27; and Edward Kalachek, "Longitudinal job market surveys: asking 'how come,' and not 'how many'," *Monthly Labor Review* 101 (September 1978): 8-14.

45. Manpower Report of the President, April 1974, op. cit., p. 66. This provision corresponds closely to the recommendations of Eli Ginzberg, among others, as summarized in Wolfbein (ed.) op. cit., pp. 216f.

46. Leonard A. Lecht, *Manpower Needs for National Goals in the 1970's* (New York: Frederick A. Praeger, 1969).

47. U. S. Department of Labor, Bureau of Labor Statistics, *Tomorrow's Manpower Needs* (Washington, DC: U. S. Government Printing Office, 1969-1972).

48. See, for example, Thomas F. Fleming, Jr., "Manpower impact of state, local government purchases," *Monthly Labor Review* 96 (June 1973): 33-39.

49. Eli Ginzberg, pp. 209-217 in Wolfbein (ed.) op. cit.

50. On the estimated impact of health and disability on labor force participation, see Monroe Berkowitz and William G. Johnson, "Health and labor force participation," *Journal of Human Resources* 9 (Winter 1974): 117-128. In regard to the labor-supply effects of the New Jersey-Pennsylvania Graduated Work Incentive Experiment (commonly known as the "Negative Income Tax Experiment"), see the entire issue of the *Journal of Human Resources* 9 (Spring 1974).

51. Henry David, *Manpower Policies for a Democratic Society*—the final statement of the National Manpower Council (New York: Columbia University Press, 1965), p. 110.

52. On this issue, see Eleanor Bernert Sheldon and Howard E. Freeman, "Notes on social indicators: promises and potential," *Policy Sciences* 1 (Spring 1970): 97-111; and Bertram M. Gross, "The state of the nation: social systems accounting," pp. 154-271 in Raymond A. Bauer (ed.) *Social Indicators* (Cambridge, MA: M.I.T. Press, 1966).

53. Paul Diesing, *Reason in Society* (Urbana: University of Illinois Press, 1962). In this study, Diesing distinguishes among five major types of rationality: technical, economic, social, legal, and political. Also pertinent are his earlier articles, "The nature and limitations of economic rationality," *Ethics* 61 (October 1950): 12-26, and "Non-economic decision-making," *Ethics* 66 (October 1955): 18-35.

54. The "transeconomic" nature of manpower policy is stressed by Henry David, op. cit., p. 95 and by Sar A. Levitan, "Manpower programs for a healthier economy," in Lloyd Ulman (ed.) *Manpower Programs in the Policy Mix* (Baltimore, MD: Johns Hopkins University Press, 1973), p. 115.

Chapter 3

Conceptualization of Labor Market Reality

Michael J. Piore
MIT

Michael Piore offers a very different view of the labor market and labor market theory. He traces the emergence of the predominant manpower "paradigms" of the 1960s. These are examined not just as analytic frameworks, but, more important, as reflections of prevailing values within society and among academic researchers during that decade. The usefulness of such paradigms for examining the nation's recent manpower experience is contrasted with perspectives and policy perscriptions provided by the dual labor market hypothesis.

As a proponent of the dual market concept, and as a perceptive commentator on its intellectual, social, and political origins, Piore adds new dimensions to themes developed in the two preceding papers. The importance of diversity of thought for both policy and scientific study is emphasized, particularly with respect to the backgrounds and beliefs of the more influential members of the manpower community as these characteristics sometimes encouraged and other times inhibited that diversity. Again, substantial tension between broad theoretical propositions and localized observation is seen to mark the evolution of thinking about unemployment, poverty, and other manpower problems. The task of accommodating models of reality in any manpower strategy is complicated further by the fact that some of the models may themselves require careful specification of a dual (or even more highly differentiated) market structure before they come to represent a sound basis for policy analysis. In his concluding discussion, Piore attempts a critical bit of interpretation by relating such points as these to the organization, orientation, and prospects of the Labor Department's manpower research effort.

Introduction

This paper attempts to review the research program of the Manpower Administration, Department of Labor, in terms of the role of social science theory in the development of public policy. The paper is motivated by a particular view of the relationship between scientific theory and social policy.

This view begins with the theory of scientific inquiry developed by Thomas S. Kuhn in *The Structure of Scientific Revolutions.*[1] Kuhn argues that a scientific theory is basically what he calls a *paradigm*—a set of concepts or intellectual constructs that "explain" an agreed-upon set of "facts." The concepts are perceived by the scientific community as having coherence and are thought to fit together in a tight, internally consistent logic. Kuhn suggests that scientific advancement takes place in two modes. *Normal* science proceeds within the paradigm, working out its detailed logic, extending that logic into areas where its implications are not clearly perceived, collecting data that buttress the empirical base upon which the paradigm is thought to rest, and measuring those things which the paradigm suggests are important in controlling and manipulating the physical world. The second mode of scientific advancement is *revolutionary*, and focuses on overthrowing the old paradigm and developing a new structure of thought. Examples of major scientific revolutions in this sense are the works of Copernicus, Newton, and Einstein. In economics, an area that Kuhn does not discuss, Keynes created such a revolution. The central questions posed by Kuhn's interpretation of the enterprise of science are: (1) what is it that holds a paradigm together and leads scientific inquiry to follow, under most circumstances, the normal mode; and (2) what generates scientific revolutions?

While Kuhn's answer to these questions is not altogether clear or satisfactory, it seems to involve two distinct processes. One of these processes is intellectual. Kuhn appears to argue that a paradigm is a logical construct, but one whose logic is in certain respects flawed and incomplete. As normal scientific inquiry proceeds, it turns up an increasing number of these flaws and an expanding variety of phenomena that cannot be incorporated to the existing logic. Eventually, these cumulate to the point where they suggest an alternative logic; and when that alternative is perceived and articulated, a scientific revolution occurs.

Kuhn also appears to argue that a paradigm is a social rather than a logical construct; that it is the *ideology* of the particular part of the scientific community subscribing to it. Work proceeds within the paradigm because such work wins the approval of the profession. There is no necessary logic to the paradigm; logical coherence simply *seems* to be present because the paradigm is enunciated by a single social group. Further scientific work tends to follow within the paradigm and to support it because only such work is accorded professional (and hence social and financial) recognition. In this context, revolutions are created by outsiders, social deviants who for one reason or another do not fully adhere to professional norms. For this view of the process, it is important that Einstein was educated outside the social milieu in which the science that he revolutionized was then generally practiced, and that Keynes was a homosexual.

The intellectual and the social models of scientific inquiry are readily integrated. While the underlying basis of a paradigm may well be intellectual, the process through which it achieves initial scientific recognition and is later superceded is essentially social. Thus, logical coherence may be critical to the acceptance of a paradigm, and its logical flaws and inconsistencies critical to its overthrow, but social factors may govern the way in which this process is realized. Those social factors may help determine the rate at which flaws and inconsistencies which surround an accepted paradigm are uncovered through normal scientific inquiry, the weight of such evidence that must accumulate before the old paradigm is rejected and a new construction set forth in its place, and the particular individuals who engineer the scientific revolution when it occurs.

Such a view of the process of scientific inquiry underlies the discussion of this paper, *but there is one important addition.* Kuhn is predominantly concerned with the physical sciences. In manpower policy, as in social policy more generally, there is a primary concern with social science. In our society the implications of social science for economic welfare and social position are more readily and immediately perceived than appears to be the case for the physical sciences. This makes social, as opposed to purely intellectual, elements of scientific inquiry far more important for the social sciences; it places social forces in a context much broader than the "profession" around which Kuhn centers his discussion of the social character of scientific revolutions. If one connotes the social dimension of the process of inquiry in the physical sciences by the term professional *ideology*, the social dimension of the social sciences involves ideologies of nonprofessional economic interests, of social classes, and sometimes of whole nations and international cultures.

This implies that research in the social sciences is fundamentally a political process in the sense that it inevitably deals with justifying the position of individual members of the society. Research in the social sciences may be political in a way and to a degree that research in the physical sciences is not. This, of course, raises the question of whether standards of evaluation and methods of organization applicable to governmentally supported research in the physical sciences are relevant in reviewing social science research programs.

The comparison of social and physical sciences also suggests that social pressures emanating from the profession itself need not necessarily coincide with social pressures generated by the interaction of social science theory and political ideologies in society. This has been particularly true for manpower policy and research. The manpower program was originally a response to a set of political pressures; but dominant opinion in the economics profession viewed the conception of that program as misguided. This meant that the program was forced to rely for its intellectual support on a set of professionals detached from the professional mainstream who were "deviants" in terms of the predominant climate of economic thought. From this relationship, the manpower research program has derived what I think is its basic strength. But for the same reason, it has also been vulnerable to attack from the main body of professional economic opinion.

Initial Conceptions of Manpower

Active manpower policy in the United States dates from the Manpower Development and Training Act of 1962. Policy developed under this act was very much a product of the intellectual climate of the late 1950s and early 1960s, especially the changing views of government that marked the shift from the Eisenhower to the Kennedy Administration. There was, it is true, a major reorientation in manpower programs very early in their history from a emphasis on facilitating labor market adjustment to the task of eliminating of poverty. This shift in program goal masks a basic continuity in the underlying intellectual foundation.

The salient feature of this orientation was a conviction that major social problems could be solved through increases in the production of goods and services: it led to a concern with problems of economic growth and efficiency to the virtual exclusion of issues of distribution. The idea that the country might face social problems of such a magnitude that no feasible increase in the rate of growth or in the efficiency of production could overcome them was simply not considered. That social issues might revolve around relative incomes or involve the distribution of such inherently limited "commodities" as status or power was completely foreign to prevailing thought.

While conceived in this general climate, the immediate intellectual foundations for manpower policy are three basic theories. Together these theories form a kind of Kuhnian paradigm—a loosely related series of ideas which combined to suggest a single, more or less coherent view of the world. Whether they had the logical coherence or empirical support of most scientific paradigms is debatable, but whatever their failings as intellectual constructs, the characterization of social reality they provided was sufficiently attractive to gain them widespread acceptance in the academic, political, and private sectors. It should be added, however, that they never achieved wide acceptance among professional economists. The theories were: structural unemployment; automation; and enclave poverty.

Structural Unemployment[2]

The theory of structural unemployment was developed in the late 1950s and early 1960s to explain an apparent secular trend toward higher unemployment rates. The theory attributed these rates to an imbalance or mismatch between the structure of the labor force and the structure of jobs. It was thought that attempts to reduce unemployment through the conventional Keynsian remedy, an expansion in aggregate demand, would be unsuccessful because of this mismatch. New jobs created in an expanding economy would not coincide with the characteristics of the unemployed labor force. Instead of a reduction in unemployment, the result would be wage inflation—firms with new jobs would compete for qualified workers with establishments in which such workers were already employed. Real reduction of unemployment required adjustment in labor force structure, and it was as an instrument for making this adjustment that the proponents of this theory advocated manpower policy. The structural theory conceives of the unemployed as consisting of a pool of people essentially unable to find work and suggests an image of jobs and workers as fitting into neatly defined categories. The labor market attempts to match appropriate categories through processes such as education and training, processes that manpower policy might improve.

Manpower policy in the early 1960s may be seen as a political concession to the power of the trade unions who supported a structural view of unemployment. Academic adherents of the structural theory were a definite minority at that time. The majority of the economics profession, who provided the intellectual foundations for official economic policy, attributed higher unemployment rates to a simple lack of aggregate demand and were convinced that these rates could be reduced to levels which had prevailed in the early and mid-1950s without undue inflation. But this majority did believe that unemployment would eventually fall to a level beyond which further expansion of aggregate demand could not alone reduce it; at that point, the structural diagnosis might be appropriate. Obviously, the profession had not really thought through this problem; when it did so in the late 1960s, a radically different view tended to prevail.

Automation[3]

The second important intellectual current underlying the manpower programs in the 1960s was the "automation crisis." The sense of crisis, especially strong in the trade union movement, derived from observations that the economy was undergoing a major, qualitatively new wave of technological change associated with the integration of computing systems with manufacturing processes. The logic of development—thought to be the elimination of the need for labor—was seldom fully realized. Even the most integrated production procedures seemed to require some monitors. But new technologies did sometimes result in drastic reductions in labor requirements, with most remaining jobs regarded as temporary vestiges of the earlier mode of production.

Extreme fears about the impact of automation were never generally shared by economists. So long as society continued to demand more goods and services and the production of these goods and services required *some* labor, it was theoretically possible to absorb anyone displaced by automation. If existing GNP could be produced by one worker, output could be doubled by employing two workers, tripled by employing three workers, and so on until full employment was reached. Expansion would, of course, be halted if society should become saturated with goods and services, but then it was not clear that people would need or want to work.

Where this logic was weak, and its more optimistic conclusions broke down, was in the implicit assumption that the workers displaced by automation would be able to perform jobs created by an expansion of aggregate demand. Indeed, there was no particular reason to assume that this would be the case. At this juncture the notion of an "automation" crisis became one with the theory of structural unemployment; it was in these terms that it was treated, to the extent that it was treated at all, by professional economists.

It is worth distinguishing between the general statement of the problem that came to achieve intellectual respectability among economists and the specific concerns over automation outside the academic sphere which make the crisis view politically compelling. Theoretical abstraction tended to revolve around the question of unemployment. By contrast, public focus upon displaced workers, although it tended most often to be expressed as a concern about their unemployment, was really broader and encompassed not only unemployment but loss of security, social status, downward economic mobility, and the disappointment of legitimate expectations among the workers directly affected and among those remaining in the industrial sectors and social strata from which these workers came.

The Enclave Theory of Poverty

The third major component of the manpower paradigm was the *enclave* or *insular* theory of poverty. This was a view of poverty associated first with John Kenneth Galbraith[4] and, in its subsequent public policy dimensions, with Michael Harrington.[5]

Galbraith was a major dissenter in the intellectual milieu of the late 1950s and early 1960s from which manpower policy emerged. His dissent, however, centered upon issues that had very little direct relevance to either manpower policy or to matters of unemployment, poverty, and race toward which that policy came to be directed. But paradoxically, the terms in which Galbraith phrased his critique tended to reinforce those tenets of the dominant economic view underlying manpower policy as it emerged.

The heart of Galbraith's argument was that American society had recently emerged from the state of scarcity characteristic of all prior human societies into a state of affluence. In this new state, the central problem was no longer the amount of material production but its quality (or composition). That quality, Galbraith argued, was being systematically distorted by a psychology of scarcity and more seriously and systematically, by advertising campaigns of major corporations, which biased consumption toward the private sector and away from public goods. While this was a major departure from the emphasis placed by other economists upon material growth, it led Galbraith to view poverty a vestige of the age of scarcity. In the affluent society there was only insular poverty hidden from view, and hence forgotten, and isolated from modern society. Insofar as this poverty was in any way fundamental to the functioning of the affluent state, it was because funds necessary to eliminate such enclaves were diverted to private consumption by corporate advertising.

While the continuation of poverty was basically attributable to inaction by society, the actual sources of poverty were to be found in the characteristics of the poor themselves. Of these characteristics, Galbraith himself mentions only the unwillingness of the poor to move geographically (principally, out of Appalachia). But Michael Harrington, who was really concerned with poverty rather than affluence, speaks more broadly of a culture of poverty and develops much more fully the images that have now become familiar: of a welfare culture, of southern rural black poverty, reinforced by a debased education system, and so on.[6]

The theories of structural unemployment, automation, and enclave (or insular) poverty are not the same. In certain respects, in fact, they lead to different policy conclusions and suggest different manpower programs. The structural theory was concerned with unemployment and inflation. In automation, the concern was displacement, whether or not people were unemployed. In insular poverty, the concern was persistent, intergenerational low incomes, not unemployment or automation. That the difference between the theories was real is underscored by the shift in manpower policy in middle sixties from the original programs, directed by a concern for automation, to programs designed to support the war on poverty.

The Manpower "Paradigm"

While different, the three theories nonetheless fit together to suggest a single construct to describe the economic and social phenomena toward which manpower policy was aimed. Indeed, one might very well argue that a sort of manpower paradigm emerged precisely *because* the theories were different; policymakers and their various constituencies sought to preserve a sense of continuity as they moved back and forth across different intellectual orientations. In any case, the story is one in which the essential manpower problem has been regarded as restoring a balance between the structure of jobs and the structure of the labor force. Failure to maintain this balance results in unemployment that is long term, persistent, and unresponsive to treatment through expanding aggregate demand. In this framework, automation becomes a theory about the determinants of the job structure; poverty enclaves a theory about the structure of the labor force. Both tend to be viewed historically in terms of an industrial society evolving over time away from relatively simple, rural antecedents: technology becomes increasingly complex and sophisticated, requiring a corresponding increase in the education and industrial sophistication of the labor force; automation is merely the latest manifestation of this long term trend; certain portions of the labor force are unable to keep pace with advancing technology, largely because they are associated with enclaves connected with an earlier and more primitive technological structure. While some enclaves are associated with technologies recently rendered obsolete by automation, most of them (e.g., rural Appalachia, the black South) are associated with *much* earlier technological systems. Thus, the role of manpower policy is to bridge the large gap between the demands of modern technology and the qualifications of these backward workers. In principle, such a policy might operate on either the demand side of the market to adjust jobs or on the supply side of the market to adjust workers. In fact, however, the story is strongly biased in favor of a solution that seeks to adjust workers to jobs since any other approach works against long-term historical trends.

The other common element in these three theories, again carried into the broader paradigm which they formed, was that each represented a dissenting view within the economics profession. In board terms, these views departed from the mainstream along two axes. First, they were directed at microeconomic, or structural concerns, whereas the profession in the early sixties was preoccupied with much wider, macroeconomic aggregates. Second, all three theories seemed to imply that microeconomic processes were governed by mechanics other than and outside the effective control of the price system. In orthodox economic theory, the pace of technological change is determined by relative prices (or wages), not by autonomous forces such as automation. Likewise, enclaves exhibiting "adverse" labor force characteristics were, however vaguely specified in the manpower policy paradigm, clearly not a predicted outcome of a competitive market system.

Two further points should be made. The relationship between micro- and macro-economic theory, in the early 1960s and increasingly in the decade that followed, was a matter of some dispute and a source of considerable strain for mainstream economic thinking. The Keynesian macrotheory which dominated professional interest at the time when manpower policy was first promulgated was really no more consistent with price theory than were any of the components of the manpower paradigm. In the early sixties, when leading economists had the ear of the president and were on the verge of converting the political establishment to Keynes's economics, capping an intellectual revolution begun when they were graduate students and thus in many ways vindicating their profession and professional careers, there was little incentive to face up to these contradictions.

Furthermore, one strand of orthodox microeconomics attracting significant interest among economists was carried into government along with the "new economics": benefit-cost analysis. It was first introduced in the Defense Department by McNamara, and was later generally prescribed for the evaluation of all government policy including manpower programs. Benefit-cost analysis is normative and prescriptive; it is not a positive theory of the public sector. One might argue that one of its major attractions is that it avoids the necessity of developing such a theory.

Conflicts in the Manpower Experience

Among the characteristics of the ghetto labor market most conspicuously in conflict with established theory in the midsixties were widespread indication of a *labor shortage.* Low-wage employers in ghetto areas were continually complaining about such shortages. In the North, despite political rhetoric to the contrary, community leaders and the workers themselves generally admitted that anybody who really wanted a job could find one. Also indicative of a labor shortage,and in direct contradiction to the structural unemployment theory, employers were actively engaged in recruiting new workers from the American South, Puerto Rico, the Caribbean, Latin America, and elsewhere for low income jobs. Most new recruits came from backward, rural areas, were unfamiliar with modern industry, were illiterate in their own language, and could not speak English. That these people were not only able to perform industrial jobs, but were actively sought for this purpose seems particularly damaging to a view of the world that relates poverty to the increasing sophistication of modern industrial technology. This overall impression was confirmed by data generated in studies of the urban riots during the middle sixties: indicators of social pathology in the ghetto, especially *unemployment*, were not highest among recent migrants as the enclave theories seemed to suggest they should be, but instead among second generation workers who had grown up in urban areas.

The Dual Labor Market Hypotheses

The attempt to understand these apparent paradoxes and to formulate a view of low income markets reflecting the self-perception of those who were involved in them led to the *dual labor market hypothesis*. In essence, the hypothesis asserts that problems of race and poverty must be understood not in terms of a single labor market from which disadvantaged social groups are excluded, but in terms of an active sector of the economy to which those groups are confined. The central idea is that the overall market can be conceived as divided into a primary and a secondary sector. The jobs in the two sectors are distinguished by certain characteristics. In the case of primary jobs, these include relatively high wages, good working conditions, considerable job security, potential for advancement, and a structured relationship between supervisor and workers mediated by a set of written or customary work rules and where dispute resolution involves a kind of due process. By contrast, secondary jobs tend to have lower wages, poorer working conditions, connoting inferior social status, insecurely limited without chances of advancement, and they involve a highly personalized and often arbitrary relationship between supervisor and worker, which lends itself to abuse in the form of favoritism and supervisory tyranny. The essential difference between the two sectors is not, however, the distinguishing features of the jobs within them. There is a *tendency* for the jobs to display these characteristics, but not all jobs possess all of the characteristics, and the attempt to classify jobs as primary and secondary on the basis of these characteristics alone has proved consistently frustrating. Rather, the point is that secondary jobs are *perceived by the people who hold them* as being "secondary"; any list of characteristics is merely an attempt to capture the essence of that perception. Because jobs are viewed as essentially similar and in any case not very attractive, a large portion of the secondary sector labor force is indifferent as to which particular job they hold. When the labor market is tight and such jobs are plentiful, they move back and forth between them and in and out of the labor market, and that movement generates the high unemployment rates associated with low income work.

The dual labor market hypothesis was originally formulated to explain the employment experience of balcks, but a broader formulation now recognizes that the labor force of the secondary sector is not composed of blacks alone. In the United States it tends to include ethnic and racial minorities generally, youth, and women to a certain extent. In Europe, a similar set of jobs is held by recent migrants from rural areas, who, in northern Europe at least, are primarily immigrants.

The dual labor market hypothesis poses two basic analytical challenges: what determines the distribution of employment opportunities between the primary and the secondary sector (or, more broadly, why is there a dual labor market in the first place; and why are secondary jobs allocated to particular socioeconomic groups?

The Orthodox Explanation[8]

In answering these questions, orthodox economic theory has focused upon the education and training. Its response is that primary employment is associated with higher levels of skill. Skill must either be acquired by the individual through an investment in himself or provided through on-the-job training by an employer for whom it is also an investment. The higher wages earned in the primary sector, and presumably better working conditions, higher social status, and more humanitarian relationships between supervisor and workers, are all a return to the past investment made by the worker in himself and an incentive to remain with the firm so that it can recoup its phase of the investment in on-the-job training. Chances for advancement and job security are also connected with the process of on-the-job training, reflecting the employer's desire to hold workers in whose training he has invested. Workers in the secondary sector are presumably there because of an unwillingness or inability to invest in themselves, coupled with their relative unattractiveness as candidates for investment by employers. This, in turn, possibly reflects worker preferences, abilities, or preemployment educational opportunities. Lack of employer investment is also readily explained in orthodox theory by a propensity toward high turnover, which, in the case of youth, can be attributed to a process of gathering information about the labor market and, in the case of women, to a prior overriding commitment to family responsibilities and to periodic interruption of careers for child-bearing.

The orthodox explanation for the distribution of jobs mirrors the explanation of the distribution of workers. Employers decide upon a job structure by weighing the cost of the job relative to its returns. Primary jobs yield higher gross returns but, because of the higher wages and investments in on-the-job training, are more costly to fill. The economy will generate such jobs so long as the returns exceed the cost (until it has exhausted the labor supply in which it is profitable to invest). Thus, the number of such jobs ultimately depends on the "trainability" of the labor force.

This line of explanation originated as a theoretical extension of neoclassical economic theory. It has been developed over the last ten or more years, largely in response to the public concerns about race and poverty, and in that sense is related to the dual labor market hypothesis. But it is not generally presented, as it has been here, in the vocabulary of that hypothesis and has never been popular among those involved in the original work on the dual labor market. The dual market view is not exactly inconsistent with neoclassical theory, but it is essentially alien to the basic tenor of neoclassical thought designed to fit a world in which behavior is basically continuous.

But the more fundamental reason why the neoclassical explanation is not popular among the proponents of the dualistic hypothesis is that the processes of education and training envisaged in that explanation are not consistent with the world which generated the dualistic hypothesis in the first place. The line between the primary and the secondary sector appears to be essentially a social one; the chief barrier to entry of secondary workers into primary jobs appears to be a refusal of the work groups in the latter to accept them. The acquisition of job skills seems to be largely incidental, automatic, and costless if one wins acceptance into the work group and basically impossible if one does not. Educational requirements seem to be used essentially as screening and rationing devices, designed to assure that newly admitted workers are acceptable to the labor force. Employers are largely ignorant of what is taught in the schools whose certification they require of new employees, do not seem to care, and frequently waive educational requirements in favor of other proof of acceptability, such as previous work experience. While it is difficult to believe that education has *no* direct influence upon job performance, exposure to the operating labor market leads one to be very skeptical of explanations which place great weight upon such a relationship.

Proponents of the dual labor market hypothesis have thus tended to emphasize other factors in the market structure. The explanations fall into two groups: explanations of the job structure, and explanations of job distribution among workers.

The Job Structure in Dualistic Theory of the Labor Market

Proponents of the dual labor market hypothesis have tended to place a great deal of weight on factors operating upon the demand side of the labor market to generate a job structure that is in large measure, if not completely, independent of the characteristics of the labor force, a job structure to which workers are forced to adapt. This line of inquiry has led to three distinct views of the job structure. While not necessarily mutually exclusive, they may provide very different policy conclusions.

The most radical explanation emphasizes the inferior social status of secondary jobs, and traces the job structure (in particular the dualistic character of the labor market) to a need in capitalistic societies to maintain hierarchical systems of production.[9] Such systems are presumably necessary to motivate the labor force, to prevent the unification of the working class, and forestall the revolution. The secondary labor force is thus regarded primarily as a Marxian "lumpenproletariat." It enables other workers to value their place in the social system; in the positive sense, their lot may seem "better" than those below them. It also has a negative value of an implicit threat: there is a world to which recalcitrant employees can be relegated should they ever fail to cooperate in the productive process.

As an explanation of the *dual* labor market, this hypothesis suffers from some of the problems of neoclassical theory. It is not clear why the requisite hierarchy should be discontinuous; indeed, a continuous hierarchy would seem to be much more powerful as a motivator than as a divisive force within the working class. And yet if one were to draw up a list of those jobs perceived as secondary in the northern ghetto (or, to take cases where the list is much clearer, "nigger" in the South or "immigrant" in western

Europe), inferior social status would probably prove to be the only unifying characteristic.

A second explanation of the job structure emphasizes insecurity.[10] The distinguishing characteristic of labor as a factor of production is its "variability"; unlike capital, it is something which can be hired and fired freely in response to variations in demand for products. Not all demand, however, is equally variable in this sense, and the secondary sector appears to be dominated by the jobs most sensitive to such variability because of pronounced cyclical or seasonal variations in demand. The industries in which they are located are declining, or it is difficult to inventory the product and thus maintain continuity of production in the face of fluctuating demand. The division between stable and unstable work has probably been aggravated by the success of organized workers in building "shelters" in the labor market through restrictions on lay-off and discharge. Such restrictions generate incentives for employers to compartmentalize demand, reserving the stable portion for the work force to which they have certain permanent employment obligations and using subcontractors or temporary help to handle the rest.

A third explanation returns to classical economic theory and associates the job structure with the process of the division of labor in response to the extent of the market.[11] This is not a hypothesis to be developed convincingly in brief compass. The essential idea is that secondary jobs are associated with small batch production for a limited market. In such production, job tasks are split into a set of very complex operations that require craftmen and very simple functions that virtually anyone can perform. The latter are allocated to the secondary sector. While they are often found in association with more highly skilled work, the gap in skill level is such that it is almost impossible to proceed from one level to the other. By contrast, large scale production involves a much more continuous job structure in which on-the-job learning sequences exist, eliminating the dichotomy present in small scale production and creating opportunities for upward mobility.

The common characteristic of all three of these views, distinguishing them from the enclave and structural unemployment theories that supported the original poverty program and from neoclassical theories that emphasize individual traits, is that each implies that the secondary sector plays a functional role in the operation of an industrial economy. This, in turn, suggests that that secondary sector cannot be eliminated without considerable cost to the rest of the society. Certainly, the hierarchical hypothesis implies in its most extreme version that the price of elimination of the secondary sector is revolution; in less extreme versions, it anticipates a considerable change in the methods of motivating the primary work force. But it is equally true in the other hypotheses. The second hypothesis, for example, implies that the elimination of the secondary sector will create a threat to job security arrangements in the primary sector and, hence, to the gains of the American trade union movement. To the extent that the source of insecurity in secondary jobs is the decline of the industry involved, and that decline results from its movement abroad (as appears to be the case in New England), a reduction in the number of secondary jobs is intimately bound up with our international balance of payments. The third hypothesis, linking secondary jobs to small scale, nonstandardized production, implies, among other things, that elimination poses a threat to current consumption patterns in services and in specialized manufactured goods. This, too, might well be reflected in our balance of payments, to say nothing of the job security of the highly skilled workers to whom secondary labor appears to be a complement in the production process. Thus, all of these interpretations of the job structure suggest that in addition to the narrow interest of the particular employers who utilize secondary workers, there is a much greater social interest in the existence of the secondary sector. The war on poverty, to the extent that it portends the elimination of that sector, is by no means the unmixed blessing it appears to be in the enclave theory where the poor are simply artifacts of some earlier stage of economic development.

The Distribution of Jobs Among Workers

It is thus possible to return to the question of why certain groups of workers appear to predominate in the secondary labor market and whether it is possible to alter the procedure through which these jobs are manned rather than to eliminate the jobs themselves. My own thinking about this matter has come to focus increasingly upon the process of migration from rural agricultural to urban industrial regions. As noted above, continued in-migration in the face of high unemployment is one of the paradoxes of low income labor markets which the dual labor market hypothesis was developed to resolve. The paradox prompted a study of new Puerto Rican migration to Boston, and my own views are largely a product of that study.[12]

The Puerto Rican migration to Boston was apparently percipitated by the changing attitude of black workers in the middle sixties toward secondary job opportunities. There was an increasing intractability of the black work force, to which employers responded by recruiting new workers directly from the backward rural regions of Puerto Rico. Utilization of this new labor force posed certain cultural and linguistic problems, but these were more than compensated for by the readiness of the Puerto Ricans to accept the work and respond to supervision. The transient character of the Puerto Rican commitment to the Boston labor market appears to explain the differing responses of the Puerto Rican and black workers in these same jobs. Most of the Puerto Rican labor force sees itself in Boston temporarily, hoping to accumulate funds to invest in some means of permanent livelihood on the island. Very few actually succeed in this ambition, but the stay in Boston *is* generally temporary. The effect of this transitory commitment is twofold: First, the Puerto Rican migrants are not greatly bothered by the insecurity and lack of advancement opportunity which, for blacks who expect to live their entire lives in Boston, are serious disadvantages of secondary jobs. Second, the Puerto Ricans do not view the work in terms of the social structure of Boston as do the blacks, but instead in terms of the job hierarchy of the island, rooted in traditional agricultural labor, compared to which the manufacturing and service jobs available in Boston carry much higher social status.

The character of the Puerto Rican migration is essentially similar to the migration patterns of blacks from the South in the 1940s and 1950s, and to that of immigrant (foreign) workers today in Europe. Migrants are recruited to take jobs that native workers will not accept. Migration is viewed by the migrants themselves as temporary, and they remain committed to their place of origin and its perspective on the labor market; that commitment gives them a time horizon more commensurate with the insecurity and limited advancement opportunities of secondary work and a point of reference in which the relative social status of their jobs is considerably higher than it is for native workers.

These characteristics suggest that migration from low wage, rural areas may be a general solution to the problem of obtaining labor for secondary jobs. As a solution, however, it poses one basic problem: large numbers of migrants do not, in fact, return quickly to their place of origin. Instead, they remain at the destination long enough to raise their children. The children, growing up in an industrial environment, expect to remain there. They adopt the perspective of the native labor force and become, like other native workers, contemptuous of the jobs which their parents had been recruited to fill. The shift from a first to a second generation labor force appears to be largely responsible for the increasing intransigence of the black workers whom the Puerto Ricans were recruited to replace.

As the Boston case illustrates, the development of a second generation poses two distinct problems: (1) the problem of the upward mobility of the second generation, and (2) the problem of finding a new source of labor to fill secondary jobs. The first problem is complicated by the fact that the desire for upward mobility brings the second generation into competition with those above them in the socioeconomic scale, and gives the latter an incentive to block advancement. Their attempt to do so is facilitated by the social character of training and learning in the lower level primary jobs where such advancement would normally take place. In the case of the second generation, public institutions —particularly the educational system—also act as a barrier to advancement. These institutions are controlled by native workers and ill-adapted to the needs of migrants. Meanwhile, the turnover in the migrant community forestalls the development of sufficient political cohesion to gain control over these institutions and redirect them in light of migrant needs. By the time that cohesion is realized in the second generation, it is already too late for public institutions to serve that generation as a vehicle for social advancement.

The second problem, that of recruiting new sources of labor, is also compounded by certain self-limiting features of the migration process. At the place of destination, the emergence of a migrant community dominated by the second generation seems to affect the job attitudes of the whole racial or ethnic group; after some point, even first generation workers, newly arrived in a social and ethnic community of long standing, tend to reject secondary jobs. Thus, blacks who have just come to Boston from the South are not much more tractable than workers raised in the North. Puerto Ricans from the same rural areas which are contributing to the Boston labor supply migrating to the older areas of resettlement in New York are apparently hesitant to take work that is eminently acceptable in Boston. At the same time, the migratory process and especially the large reverse flow accompanying it, act to change work attitudes at the place of origin as well as the place of destination. Thus, Puerto Rican workers now refuse to do traditional agricultural work on the island very much as second generation blacks are reluctant to perform secondary jobs in Boston, and there is a parallel phenomenon in rural Puerto Rico of high unemployment mixed with severe labor shortages. A very similar pattern has been noted in the rural areas contributing labor to Northern Europe. In the long run, these changes in worker attitudes also force structural changes in the economy of the place of origin that may act to limit its capacity to supply secondary workers and force industrial countries, as the European nations have in fact been forced, to extend their recruitment networks increasingly far afield.

In the American context, these hypotheses about rural-urban migration as a source of labor for secondary jobs lead to a very particular interpretation of the racial crisis of the 1960s which has dominated our manpower policy thinking. They suggest that the roots of that crisis are to be found in the closing off of foreign immigration, first by the World War in 1914 and ultimately by legislation in 1923. Before that time, the needs of the "secondary" sector were filled by foreign labor. The conventional picture of that migration does not correspond to the temporary character of the migratory process as we have described it, but there was in fact a much heavier reverse flow than is generally recognized. By the last decade of open migration, outflows were fully half as large as the inflow. Once the borders were closed, the country was forced to turn toward its domestic labor reserves in the rural South; heavy black migration does indeed date from the First World War. The full impact of the closing of the border was delayed, however, by the Depression. Therefore, massive migrations out of the South were really a phenomenon of the Second World War and the postwar boom. During the 1940s and 1950s black communities in the North were still dominated by first generation migrants. But by the 1960s the black labor force had come to be dominated by a second generation who had grown up in the North. This, although it is undoubtedly not the whole story, becomes a basic factor explaining the social upheavals of the last decade.

It is important to recognize that migration is not, by any means, the only source of secondary labor. Earlier discussion has focused upon women and youth as major alternatives. These groups may share with migrants a foreshortened time perspective. The impact of the social status of the job upon the worker's self-conception may also differ, as it does with migrants, from that of prime age native men. In these respects, youth and female workers are easily incorporated into a single theory of the secondary labor market. The major difference between migrants and native women or youth as sources of secondary labor is that specific locations and hours of work of the latter appear tightly circumscribed by the family units of which they are a part and, for youth, by educational commitments.

There is, however, another major alternative to all three groups: a racial caste system, a group of workers socialized to accept as their permanent station in life, from one generation to the next, low status, insecure jobs. This was the southern solution to the problem of the labor market. And in the 1960s, one can well argue that the North, having closed off foreign immigration in the 1920s, facing the exhaustion of domestic labor reserves and increasing pressure for upward mobility from a labor force which had once seemed largely complementary to white employment, was bound to find the southern solution increasingly attractive. In one sense, then, the conflict between the southern and the northern solutions to the problem of manning the secondary sector may be taken as the central manpower issue of the 1960s. Having resolved that conflict in favor of the northern solution, and having exhausted our domestic labor reserves, the country is turning once again to immigration.[13]

Labor Market Theory, Manpower Programs, and Manpower Research

It remains in this final section to discuss the implications of the preceding theories for an evaluation of the Manpower Administration's research program. That research effort, however, must be placed in the context of the administrative problems of manpower programs generally.

The conventional diagnosis of poverty under which the manpower program began viewed administrative problems as technical in nature. Under theories of structural unemployment the poor were excluded from the on-going economic activity, and, hence, largely idle. Since they were idle, they respresented basically an economic resource from whose employment in productive activity all stood to gain. The fact that poverty nonetheless continued was attributed to the enclaves in which it was concentrated. Once the problem of incorporating the poor into society was recognized, the amelioration of poverty was thought to be a relatively simple task of education and training. The administrative task was to select from an array of possible education and training approaches which would be most successful and to insure that those successful programs were efficiently run. Modern benefit-cost analysis provided a set of techniques for both comparing alternative programs and monitoring the efficiency of any given program over time. Ultimately, the administrator's problem became one of winning acceptance for these techniques within the federal establishment and, because of the cumbersome structure of the U. S. Employment Service, within state bureaucracies as well.

The dual labor market hypothesis suggests a more complicated, political interpretation of the poverty problem and its administrative dimensions. The poor are not an idle, forgotten remnant of some past stage of economic development whose incorporation into the modern economy is a free good, economically and politically. Instead, they participate actively in society, and their participation generates a series of vested interests in the continued existence of the poverty class. These interests are bound to be resistant to any program designed to eliminate that class and to have a strong economic incentive either to "capture" existing programs, directing them in such a manner as would facilitate the secondary sector operators, or to isolate the programs from genuine labor market activity. Even if one accepts the neoclassical interpretation of dualism, attributing market distinctions to differences in the underlying tastes and endowments of the labor force, the administrative task is no longer a purely technical one. The bureaucracy becomes the focus of a political battle over whether or not "poverty" should be eliminated at all, and issues of technical efficiency become clouded by conflicts about fundamental program goals and whether people should be assisted in moving out of the secondary sector or merely directed so as to facilitate circulation within it.

If we begin with the less orthodox view, assuming that the existence of the secondary sector is intertwined completely with the operation of the overall industrial economy, the politics of manpower policy become even more involved. Economic interests to be recognized extend considerably beyond those with an immediate stake in business organizations employing secondary workers; indeed, they include elements of the society far removed from immediate contact with the poor but who depend on secondary workers to provide personal services, absorb fluctuations in the demand for products against which they have managed to construct shelters, to complement highly skilled craft workers in the production of nonstandard items, or to maintain domestic production which would otherwise be forced overseas. The problem of opening primary jobs is no longer so clearly associated with identifiable processes of education and training, but involves processes of socialization in the work place. Political and strategic dimensions of manpower programs are not readily encompassed in terms of narrow technical efficiency. Ultimately, as we have seen, manpower programs may involve a basic contradiction in our national ideology between the melting pot imagery of the North and the racial caste system of the South. Thus, structuralist enclave theories upon which the manpower programs were originally founded appear as an attempt to reconcile the contradictions between the ideology and practice: between a commitment to equality and social mobility and material dependence upon an economic structure that renders such values difficult, if not impossible, to achieve. This last point should be emphasized because it implies that not only the administration, but also the theory upon which it was based and the research program that grew up around it were deeply political in character.

Whether the manpower programs were political in this deep, ideological sense of the term is, I suppose, debatable. That they were political in the more conventional sense cannot be denied. The programs were political in at least two specific respects: First, the manpower policy of the 1962 MDTA was built upon a long-standing complex of government labor market institutions, of which the most important were the school system and the federal-state employment service. *These institutions under the manpower program were nationally funded but locally controlled.* The school system has historically been a local institution and, nominally, the chief effect of the manpower program was to provide it with new funds. The Employment Service has been federally funded but locally controlled. While some students of government considered it to be for this reason a unique and peculiar institution, from the perspective of those active at the local level attempting to influence policy, it did not appear very different from local units of HEW or of the Department of Agriculture. The importance of local control was that national policy was tailored to local circumstances and that local political and ideological interests were respected in the administration of programs.

Manpower programs represented an attempt to impose, largely through the distribution of funds, national in place of local standards. The federal bureaucracy was in the middle of this conflict—its position complicated by the fact that political appointees who administered the manpower programs were not always, especially in the beginning, aware of the nature of the decentralized system they were attempting to manage. Moreover, their views conflicted on this point with those of a number of congressional leaders to whom the career civil service also felt a certain allegience.

The second respect in which the manpower programs were political was that the fight between national and local policy also involved the question of who precisely was going to run local programs, determine program policy and content, and have access to what was, particularly in the eyes of the minority groups who were leading contenders in the battle, lucrative and prestigious employment in the programs themselves.[14]

As far as I know, nobody has attempted to look systematically at the way in which federal officials reacted to this dilemma. It would make a nice study; but perhaps it is too late. The people with whom I had contact reacted in different ways. The most courageous was a county loan officer of the Farmers' Home Loan Administration in Mississippi in the summer of 1964, who responded to local civil rights pressure from below and a White House directive from above by opening his office, as federal regulations had always said it must be open, to black farmers. The white community that summer was up in arms and, in the fall, after three crosses had been burned on his lawn and his wife and children ostracized by their neighbors, he finally moved from the town where he and his father had been raised and out of the state. He was a man without illusions who knew, I am sure, how his own community would react. But he was also a moral man who ultimately acted in accordance with his *own* sense of what was right. Perhaps he foresaw the consequences of his actions; I do think he expected more federal support. Certainly, he was led by his superiors to believe that support would be forthcoming. I doubt his story is not typical; most federal officials were slower to react to changes in federal policy and less thorough in compliance when they did so. The Labor Department, because the Employment Service is a state agency, possibly reacted even more slowly than did most. But it is hard to judge this behavior; it is extremely difficult to know what a proper bureaucratic response would have been.

It is easier to judge political appointees who sat at the top of bureaucratic organizations, directed changes in agency policy, and were in many ways responsible for its content. They do not, in my view, come out well. In the beginning, they were naive: They were shocked by the contrast between stated federal policy and local practice, especially in the South, and sometimes moved swiftly to impose announced standards. But they were equally surprised and shocked by the sudden, extreme reaction which these moves brought from the Congress, most of whose committee chairmen came from districts where the gap between the haute rhetoric of national policy and local bureaucratic policy was sharpest. And in their retreat—and here I think the case of the FHA loan officer is typical—they seldom gave a thought to the lives or careers of the civil servants who might have responded to initial directives.

In later years, federal administrators were much more cognizant of the political pressures that programs were capable of generating on the local and national levels and attempted more consciously and deliberately to minimize them. However, they never fully accepted political pressures as essential to the process of restructuring the labor market. They did not respond, as I think they should have responded, by attempting to *manipulate* these pressures. They were continually looking for reforms to eliminate political conflicts inherent in programs by regrouping and decentralizing authority within traditional channels of administration.

The policies of decategorization and decentralization embodied in CETA, the latest manpower legislation, are a victory for this reform movement. Politically these reforms were justified in terms of their contribution to a concept of administrative efficiency that had meaning in terms of the intellectual constructs in which the poverty program and its manpower components were originally conceived. These constructs were not consistent with the dual labor market hypothesis in any form. Nor, it seems to me, were these administrative reforms really consistent with the highly political atmosphere in which programs were conducted during the middle and late sixties. A growing general distrust of political processes surrounding social programs and the push for administrative reform, it should be noted, characterized both Democratic and Republican administrations. Indeed, political appointees in both administrations were drawn from a common source, a kind of manpower establishment, composed largely of academic labor economists with wide experience in government and neutral in labor-management relations. Most of these people sat either before or after their government service on the National Manpower Policy Task Force, and the pronouncements of that group on manpower policy, in both the Johnson and early Nixon administrations either reflected or soon became official administration policy.

It is against this background, I think, that the Employment and Training Administration Research Program must be both understood and judged. In understanding the research program, two points seem particularly important. First, research and development offices of the manpower administration have themselves been a part of the federal bureaucracy and have felt to some extent many of the conflicts permeating the poverty program. Second, the research program was tied to a cadre of academic advisors dominated by the same manpower establishment which provided the program's appointed administrative structure capable of submerging political tensions and, in so doing, resolving them in favor of the status quo. Under these circumstances, one might have expected the manpower research program to have resurrected the original structural diagnosis of poverty or, failing that, to have sponsored the development of a new intellectualization of manpower policy supportive of administrative reform and of a reconciliation between the northern and southern ideologies which the sixties brought into conflict.

In general, but particularly in the light of the foregoing considerations, I think a review of manpower research reveals a remarkable balance. A new intellectualization has indeed begun to emerge; but it grows out of neoclassical economics and the research in which it is propounded has been funded largely by the National Science Foundation. At the same time, development of radical views that conflict most directly with the original thrust of policy began in large part under the Department's own research program. The role of that research program in contributing to the development of a more realistic view of race and poverty has probably been at least as great as that of either the EEOC or OEO, both of which had a stronger incentive in terms of their missions to promote such a line of inquiry. Labor's manpower research program is not, I should add, beyond reproach. In retrospect, it seems to me that a good deal more attention should have been devoted to the determinants of the job structure and more resources devoted to sociologists and social psychologists than to economists. But the basic point is, I think, that the overall program is not open to a broad brush review at all, and that, even from a radical perspective, improvements to be suggested would be marginal in character.

One is led by this analysis not so much to question the content of the research program but to ask how it turned out to be so much more balanced than the ideological thrust of manpower programs themselves. The answer to this question—which I will not attempt to develop fully here—would, I think, recognize three factors: First, any research program closely tied to and anchored in the experience of programs actually operating in the labor markets of the mid-1960s could not help but reject the hypotheses upon which those programs were originally founded and be sympathetic to alternative labor market views. The Labor Department manpower research programs—more perhaps than those of any other agency—were closely tied to such an operating experience. This was in part because the officials who administered them thought the research agency's existence to be dependent upon its ability to justify itself in terms of practical contributions to programming, but also, I think, because these officials were committed to such an approach themselves. Second, the research agency could afford to tie itself programmatically to the rhetoric of national policy without coming into conflict with another set of values emanating from local jurisdictions; it was not, like other agencies in the Department, locally rooted. Finally, and perhaps most importantly, the manpower advisory establishment, basically conservative in its recommendations for administrative reform, took a far more liberal approach in its own research operations. The Department was able to support relatively radical research under the sponsorship of senior researchers with the best credentials. To explain that paradox, one would have to look at the dynamics of the economics profession in the 1950s and 1960s: institutional, labor economists who composed the manpower establishment were estranged from the main body of the profession and receptive to and attractive for a group of students who were themselves distrustful of the new orthodoxy growing out of neoclassical theory.

Manpower Policy and Policy Research

One might question whether it is possible to conclude this discussion with a specific research agenda. The basic lesson of the discussion is that to focus upon a research agenda is to misconstrue the whole nature of the research problem in areas of social science, such as manpower, which is intimately connected to social policy. Such research is like the policy itself—highly political. Such research takes place within a framework resembling what Kuhn calls a scientific paradigm. Each paradigm will highlight certain areas of policy concern and obscure other areas; it will bring to the fore some policies and reject others. It does these things *not* in an explicit manner, *not* in a way which is obvious to deal with and correct, but in a way that totally obscures issues and hides policy alternatives from view. In what it highlights and what it obscures, a paradigm inevitably fosters the interests of certain social groups and compromises the interests of others. There is probably no *cure* for this. The choice among social groups is inherent in any social structure in which there is a scarcity of goods, power, or prestige. Thus, the first step in the design of a research program is to select in advance the groups one wishes to favor and the kinds of paradigms toward which one wants to work.

The groups I would like to favor are ethnic and racial minorities who are excluded from the normal political process and who stand at the bottom of the socioeconomic structure. In the decades of the fifties and sixties, the most significant group of this kind was composed of American blacks. It remains to be seen how successful the reforms of the last decade have been in integrating this group into the social and political processes from which it was previously excluded. It is evident, however, that blacks no longer constitute the major excluded minority. This position is coming increasingly to be occupied by alien workers from the Caribbean and Latin America. Most of these people are here illegally; they lack political leverage, and fear of deportation places them outside the protection of much of our labor and social welfare legislation. Immigration and Naturalization Service estimates place the number of these people at over seven million (a number equal to three-quarters of the black labor force and one-third of the black population). It is quite possible that the size of this group has doubled in the last three years and that, if the economy returns to full employment, it will double in the next three or four years as well.[15] The development of a research program that illuminates the problem of alien workers and suggests policies for their amelioration is likely to require as great a revision in our current thinking as the recognition of the black problem required in the intellectual apparatus inherited from the late 1950s.

If a commitment to this revision is the first step in the design of a research program, the second step is to establish an administrative structure capable of implementing such a change. This, however, is no easy task. It seems to me that the structure for funding manpower research in the late 1960s was relatively successful in doing for blacks what I would like to see done for the new ethnic and racial minorities, revising traditional patterns of thought so as to reveal and pinpoint real barriers to upward mobility. Elements apparently responsible for the direction of that program were (1) an organization that was nationally oriented and insulated from pressures to accommodate local interest groups; (2) an organization closely connected to operating programs that felt compelled to justify its research efforts in terms of concrete contributions to policy; and (3) an academic advisory structure standing outside the mainstream of the profession which, in this sense if in no other, had a "revolutionary" orientation. One other feature seems important to note: the personnel in the organization responsible for the research program were career civil servants. As a result they had no career reasons to favor an academically orthodox program when academic orthodoxy conflicted with programmatic goals. The outcome might have been very different if administrative personnel saw their careers as dependent upon university colleagues whose research they were sponsoring.

Even if these were the important facets of the manpower research program during the 1960s—and I am by no means certain even of this—it is not clear that these same features will lead in the next decade to a desired results. Perhaps it was merely a historical accident that the intellectual constructs which stood in the way of a new social policy were the province of the university community. In other times, the academy has led the way in social revolution. Certainly, the position of the academic advisory structure was historically unique. It would be difficult to duplicate if one were starting a program anew today and, as noted earlier, its influence upon policy was in no sense as salutory as its influence upon research.

Nonetheless, I am inclined to think that certain characteristics of the operation as a source of government support in the social sciences are sound: career civil servants, closely linked to operating programs, but nationally oriented and nationally directed. It is not that the power of blacks was especially strong at the national level during the 1960s, but it was certainly stronger nationally than it was locally; it seemed easier to influence consciousness at the national than the local level. I think much the same will prove true of the alien population in the coming decades, especially since its problems also involve foreign policy concerns having no force at all locally. Moreover, national orientation on research becomes all the more important as manpower programs themselves become more highly decentralized at the local level under CETA.

This leaves open the question of links with the academic community; here I find myself at a loss to know what to recommend. I suppose that from an intellectual standpoint, what one is looking for more than anything else is diversity of ideas. One way to achieve this is to build panels of academic advisors with multidisciplinary orientation. Hopefully, this will reduce the tendency of any one discipline to foster its own orthodoxy. But it is not foolproof because academicians tend to defer to each other in their own perceived areas of competence; heterodoxy in and of itself is threatening, irrespective of one's interest in its particular content.

NOTES

1. Thomas S. Kuhn, *The Structure of Scientific Revolutions* (Chicago: University of Chicago Press, 1970).

2. Charles C. Killingsworth, "Automation, jobs and manpower" in *Nation's Manpower Revolution*, U.S. Senate Subcommittee on Employment and Manpower of the Committee on Labor and Public Welfare, Hearings, 88th Congress, 1st Session, Washington, DC, pp. 1496-1494; Barbara Bergmann, *Structural Unemployment in the United States*, (Washington: U.S. Department of Commerce Economic Development Administration, 1967); Edward Kalachek and James Knowles, *Higher Unemployment Rates 1957-1960: Structural Transformation or Inadequate Demand*, Subcommittee on Economic Statistics of the Joint Economic Committee, 87th Congress, 1st Session, 1961.

3. National Commission on Technology, Automation, and Economic Progress, *Technology and the American Economy* (Washington, DC: Government Printing Office, 1966).

4. John Kenneth Galbraith, *The Affluent Society* (Cambridge, MA: Riverside Press, 1958).

5. Michael Harrington, *The Other America: Poverty in the United States* (Baltimore: Penguin, 1962).

6. Harrington also describes cultures of poverty that have never been incorporated in our policy thinking, and, incidentally, are probably much more closely related to things like automation: derelict alcoholics, for example.

7. See for greater elaboration of this view; David Gordon, *Theories of Poverty and Unemployment* (Lexington, MA: D. C. Heath, 1972); Michael J. Piore, "On-the-job training in a dual labor market," *Public-Private Manpower Policies*, Arnold R. Weber, et al. (ed.) (Madison: I.R.R.A., 1969); "Jobs and

training," *The State and the Poor*, Samual H. Beer (ed.) (Cambridge, MA: Winthrop, 1970).

8. For the theory of this, see Gary Becker, *Human Capital: A Theoretical and Empirical Analysis with Special Reference to Education* (New York: National Bureau of Economic Research, 1964). For an example of the theory translated into policy terms, see Martin Feldstein, "The economics of the new unemployment," *The Public Interest*, No. 33 (Fall 1973), pp. 3-42.

9. Stephen A. Marglin, "What do bosses do? The origin and functions of hierarchy in capitalist production," Harvard University, February, 1971 (mimeograph); Kathleen Stone, "Labor management and the origin of job structures in the steel industry," Harvard University, 1973 (mimeograph).

10. See Marcia Freedman, *Good Jobs, Bad Jobs*, Columbia University, Conservation of Human Resources (unpublished manuscript); Michael J. Piore, "Union rules and the changing character of work," *Social Policy*, Vol. 4, No. 1 (July/August, 1973), pp. 10-16.

11. Michael J. Piore, "On the technological foundations of economic dualism," *MIT Economics Department Working Paper* No. 110.

12. Piore, "The role of immigration in industrial growth: a case study of the origins and character of Puerto Rican migration to Boston," *MIT Economics Department Working Paper*, No. 112, May 1973.

13. Piore, "The 'new immigration' and the presumption of social policy," *I.R.R.A. Series*. Proceedings of the Twenty-Fifth Anniversary Meeting, December 1974.

14. For a general view of the political nature of the programs and its relationship to administrative reform, see Parts I and III of Piore, "Jobs and training," in *The State and the Poor,* op. cit.

15. Piore, "The 'new immigration' and the presumption of social policy." *I.R.R.A. Series,* Proceedings of the Twenty-Fifth Anniversary Meeting, December 1974.

Chapter 4

Research on Labor Supply and the Demand for Labor

Glen G. Cain
University of Wisconsin

Glen Cain assesses research sponsored by the Labor Department's Office of Manpower Research and Development (OMRD) dealing with the subjects of the supply of and the demand for labor. Cain gives particular attention to work addressing the behavior of basic "microunits" in the labor market: workers and firms. That work touches upon a wide range of issues, including, inter alia, alternative formulations of labor market theory; labor supply response to changes in income and wage rates as it bears upon policies in such areas as welfare reform, unemployment insurance and retirement; problems attendant upon policy formulation and study in the areas of immigration, work scheduling, and occupational licensing; education and training as a screening mechanism in employer selection of workers; and such macroeconomic concerns as the relationship between manpower programs and the business cycle.

Similar to the companion reviews that follow regarding R&D related to labor market operations and to special labor force groups, Cain's paper does more than summarize a body of inquiry on a certain set of topics. It illustrates a distinctive approach to evaluating the products of a government R&D program. The approach employed by Cain involves three elements: First, he attempts to describe what might be termed a "peer judgment" of Department of Labor-sponsored research on labor supply and demand by contrasting its substantive coverage over several years with the coverage of articles appearing contemporaneously in leading economic journals. The details and conclusions of the

AUTHOR'S NOTE: *I gratefully acknowledge the research assistance of Bruce Kanfman in preparing this review.*

analysis reflect another view of the evolution of labor economics as a field of inquiry—a view that the reader will wish to compare with earlier discussions by Marshall and Piore. Second, Cain differentiates between various styles or types of research: theoretical; inferential empirical work; and descriptive empirical work. The applicability of these forms of research to various (and inherently different) science and policy problems is a theme pursued throughout the review. Third, Cain grapples with the amorphous notion of policy relevance—how to identify research that is potentially useful in government decision-making and how to determine when such research has been useful in fact. Overriding concern for this issue, as well as for the matter of articulating strategies for increasing the utility and use of R&D results, characterizes each assessment of the inquiry program presented in this part of the volume.

Introduction and Summary

This introductory section offers an overview assessment of research on labor supply and demand supported by the Labor Department's Office of Manpower Research and Development (OMRD). The judgments expressed here are relatively stark and unsupported by evidence so as to bring the main themes and conclusions of the review quickly to the reader's attention. In sections that follow, the subject matter is properly delineated, criteria for evaluation are established, and specific studies are discussed.

Research sponsored by OMRD in the area of labor supply and demand has shifted toward a more theoretical and econometric orientation since 1970. The work and personnel that are supported appear as advanced and respected in the area of applied labor economics as can be found in the field. Much of the recent work conforms to the established tradition of neoclassical economic analysis, although considerable support has been provided for work following other less orthodox approaches.

Pre-1970 OMRD research reflected a style and methodology of more descriptive and institutional research, an approach which has not achieved dominance in contemporary economics generally, or in labor economics. Nevertheless, earlier research was useful in several respects. First, an older generation of labor economists, whose roots were in institutional economics and industrial relations, were encouraged to turn their attention to the study of labor market problems and government manpower policies. As the federal government initiated and expanded manpower programs in the 1960s, these labor economists played important roles in shaping and improving public and private sector manpower policies. Second, support for studies that challenged the orthodox, neoclassical approach to labor market analysis attracted a younger generation of labor economists into the field; this group has continued to criticize the methodology of neoclassical theory and to emphasize empirically so-called "imperfections" in the labor market. There are differences between these two generations of labor economists, but their analyses have had similar effects on neoclassical economic thoughts, prodding it toward greater policy relevance and empirical realism.

Taking a broader view of the role of government funding in developing and expanding knowledge of labor market within the social sciences—especially economics—the Department of Labor effort has been useful and important. The agency has not, however, been a large source of support as R&D programs go, nor has it sponsored path-breaking theoretical work—at least as this can be judged by American Economic Association awards and honors. An important qualification of this last statement is that the OMRD's Doctoral and Post-Doctoral Small Grants Program has helped launch the careers of a new generation of leading labor economists (as well as persons in other disciplines), and future "prizes" for outstanding work may have their origins in this program. The small grants efforts have been notably successful in training scholars and experts in labor market analysis at a relatively low cost. That accomplishment, as distinct from the goal of the finished research product, is less preeminent (and less justified) as a characteristic of larger grants and contracts to established researchers. Nevertheless, OMRD support has helped a number of research organizations develop the capability for monitoring, evaluating, forecasting, and performing various services that are useful to government agencies engaged in social and economic programming.

A serious shortcoming in the OMRD research program is reflected in our inability to make a convincing case that it has been directly useful to the sponsoring agency or, more generally, the formulation of government policies. The fact that many research reports are virtually unread when completed is some evidence for this proposition. On the other hand, research in the social sciences, especially in a complicated field like labor economics, should probably be viewed in terms similar to research leading to the development of mechanical inventions or medicines—many trials and failures must be expected to accompany any important successes. If only a few studies have been useful in developing programs or in staving off a bad program, the whole effort may be worthwhile. Something more than hearsay and impressions is needed to make this case, however. Only rarely will either the sponsoring agency or researchers provide an independent interpretation of the policy implications of research results, or at least a basis for testing the predictive capacity of their analyses.

A second important shortcoming, related to the first, is sluggish and inefficient communication between the research community and the research-sponsoring agency. This problem is revealed in several ways. There is limited input from the research community in planning and designing research strategies and even research projects. Too often, projects have appeared to be the product of a "crisis atmosphere" within the agency—a rush for quick answers that is perhaps an inevitable condition of government research support. There is also minimal communication or transmission of completed research products, particularly those by nonacademic researchers, to the research community. This results in serious lack of evaluation of the research and missed opportunities to learn from past achievements and mistakes. To some extent this monitoring and assessment problem is the fault of the academic research community, which should take more responsibility for keeping track of government-sponsored work that does not get published. Increased attention recently given to research in the *Monthly Labor Review* and in special pamphlet publications of the Employment and Training Administration are helping to rectify this situation.

A special problem of missed opportunities with respect to completed research is the failure of either the sponsoring agency or the research community to follow up those efforts that have yielded mainly descriptive statistics by subjecting these to more rigorous analysis.

Subject Matter Under Review

The subject matter of the research reviewed in this chapter has no clear boundary separating it from other reviews which address research on labor market operations and on special groups in the labor force. Since labor economists analyze the employment and remuneration of the labor force and, given that all variables affect employment (quantities) or remuneration (wages) by affecting either supply or demand, all research in labor economics may be claimed to fall within the domain of this chapter. Moreover, research in other disciplines is often concerned with variables that the field of economics takes as "given"—for example, the preferences of individuals, the laws of society, and the technological constraints of production. Since these forces also determine the allocation and reward system for labor, not even disciplinary boundaries are warranted. Nevertheless, "supply" and "demand" are customarily thought of as general analytical concepts used by academic economists, and this description of the concepts implies a relatively restricted jurisdiction.

"Academic research" refers to a style of research and not to the employment status of the researcher. The style involves the use of explicit theoretical frameworks or models, usually within the confines of a single discipline, and usually aimed at the goals of estimating parameters and testing hypotheses. The style is more formal than historical studies, descriptive statistical studies, and case studies, none of which are covered extensively in this chapter. A university-based group within the research community tends to emphasize "academic research" more than researchers employed in government or private research organizations, but there is considerable overlap.

This chapter does not examine most of the analyses and evaluations of specific governmental programs, such as CETA, the Emergency Employment Act, or Neighborhood Youth Corps. It does, however, focus on research reports dealing with the impact on the labor market of monetary and fiscal policies and with the general effects of training and education on labor market performance. It will not cover reports dealing with the special problems of certain groups in the labor force, but will discuss research on the general topics of labor market discrimination and occupational stratification.

Research relating to labor market operations is closely related to the subject matter considered here. The labor market is, of course, no more and no less than the setting for labor supply behavior on the part of workers and for labor demand behavior on the part of employers. In general, the research on market institutions is given less emphasis in this review. Instead it will concentrate on analyzing the labor market behavior of more basic microunits: workers and firms.

Finally, it should be pointed out that because the research under review in this chapter tends to be academically oriented, its share in the agency's total budget has been small. By far the largest and most costly types of projects are the experimental and demonstration projects, survey and data gathering operations, and programs of general institutional support.

Criteria for Evaluating Research on Labor Supply and Demand

A natural starting point in evaluating research is a determination of the purposes of its sponsors. What general objectives did the Labor Department officials have for the overall research program? What were their specific objectives for each individual research grant or contract? We may look upon the Labor Department officials as the most immediate audience among the larger group of government officials, including Congressmen, who are potential users of OMRD research. The technical staff of the Employment and Training Administration in the Department of Labor may be considered the screen or filter and the "conveyer" for research, charged with translating findings into improved programs, making recommendations for new legislation, or offering general information to facilitate the workings of the economy.

It is difficult to pin down an answer to the question of the usefulness of the research to the sponsoring agency. There is often a long time-lag between the initiation of a particular research project and the submission of a completed report. Agency officials who defined the project's thrust may no longer be in the same office, or the political or market conditions that prompted interest may no longer exist. Direct evidence of the usefulness of the research to the sponsor is hard to document, but it presumably consists of program evaluations, forecasts, and assessments of new ideas. In addition, there are indirect routes to achieve usefulness in the policy arena—the training of agency personnel and the benefits of improved instruction and consulting about labor market programs and policies. The fact that there is limited evidence of direct impact of research sponsored by the Department of Labor is disturbing. It is part of what appears as the major shortcoming of the agency's research program: insufficient two-way communication between the research community and potential users of research in government. It should also be apparent that the general research community is itself another major audience for OMRD research. Given the emphasis on academic research in this review, a crucial test of its usefulness is whether the research community has absorbed it and incorporated results into the body of scientific knowledge within the disciplines that deal with labor market phenomena. This would include particularly labor economists, whose responsibility it is to develop their discipline to promote efficiency, stability, and equity within the labor sector.

There is obviously great utility in developing models or theories that describe, predict, and explain the general operations of the labor market. The pitfall in this general endorsement of theoretical research is that it may be interpreted as a justification for indiscriminate modeling or measurement of relationships among variables. At best, models refer to important problems in the labor field and measure relationships having stability and robustness with respect to the range of empirical situations to which they may be applied.

These criteria invite attention to the question of policy relevance. Clearly, some studies may be relevant to policy even though they make little or no contribution to theory. For example, forecasts of displacement of workers in a particular industry or region may involve a routine application of an established forecasting technique. Conversely, some studies may be entirely theoretical and still have some indirect or long-run policy significance. Research on the methodology of estimating production functions might be an example. Such research generally adds to the stock of "scientific," rather than "policy" knowledge, but it is clearly "useful." Thus, the issue of policy relevance is not intended to be narrowly construed and it helps to direct attention to the specific utility of knowledge generated. Such a concern is responsive to two key features of the Department of Labor as a sponsor of research: taxpayers' money is involved, the Department's responsibilities include the improvement of the functioning of the nation's labor markets.

There are enormous difficulties in knowing what research is going to be useful in itself, and further, in knowing what research will turn out to be useful for policy. There is an obligation of those researchers who receive a government agency's support to be candid and communicative about these matters. Research on labor supply and demand may meet the standards of usefulness from either the "scientific" or "policy" perspectives according to the following classification of types of research studies:

Theoretical: Studies which advance theories or construct models that provide some qualitative predictions or a framework for quantitative measurements.

Inferential empirical work: Studies which apply an existing theory or model to a body of data for the purpose of estimating some parameter of interest—e.g., a demand elasticity for unskilled labor. Hypothesis testing could be thought of either as a special type of estimation or as a technique in theory construction.

Descriptive empirical work: "Measurement for the sake of measurement"—pure data gathering and data summarization—can be extremely valuable, if the data are intended to facilitate future theoretical and empirical work.

Given this classification, we may pose the following types of questions about Department of Labor-sponsored research: What theoretical knowledge has been contributed? What important theoretical work should be done? What empirical knowledge has been contributed? Are various estimates of the same parameters in reasonable agreement? What types of descriptive statistics and tabulations of data have actual or potential usefulness, and what gaps exist in the "data base" that need to be filled?

Coverage of Topics in Research Sponsored by the Department of Labor and in the Mainstream Journals in Economics

Overview

Department of Labor research on labor supply and demand has changed over time to a point where there are an increased number of studies paralleling the "mainstream" of research, at least as reported in "mainstream" economic journals. Prior to 1970, few of the agency's research projects emphasized economic theory or econometric models of the labor market. On the demand side, the theoretical-econometric approach in the mainstream dealt with production functions at the microlevel and with various Keynesian-type macromodels. On the supply side, mainstream studies were dominated by human capital models and labor force studies derived from labor-leisure choice models. Generally speaking, such emphases were not apparent in research sponsored by OMRD.

After 1970, both the type of studies published in mainstream journals and the type of research sponsored by the Department of Labor changed in ways to bring them closer together. Labor demand studies became less devoted to production functions, shifting to models of employer demand that focused on the special topics of discrimination, minimum wage laws, turnover, and job search. Job search models have been concerned with unemployment, focusing on both labor market demand (employer search behavior) and supply (worker search behavior). Labor supply models became popular in research sponsored by the Department of Labor. In the agency and in the journals much of the reported research was directed toward the labor supply of women, blacks, and other "minority" groups and on the interaction of labor supply with various public assistance programs and welfare reform plans. Moreover, the Department of Labor supported an increasing but still rather small share of the large research effort on human capital models, emphasizing returns to education, health investments, and the like.

Prior to this 1970 shift in research support, the agency's work on supply and demand dealt more with programmatic and case study types of research. These tended to be more institutional and less theoretical; more descriptive and less related to hypothesis testing or to estimation. Support given to the institutionalist tradition in labor economics, which dominated the field during the decades of the 40s and 50s, helped redirect the concerns of its practitioners from "industrial relations" to "manpower." Attention to "structural" factors in the labor market and to institutional aspects of manpower programs were positive elements of this work. Moreover, the skepticism that institutionalists felt with respect to neoclassical theoretical models in vogue in the mainstream helped encourage the latter school in analyzing market imperfections and disequilibrium situations.

Pre-1970 agency-sponsored research also spawned a younger group of labor economists who, in many respects, carried on the tradition of the prior generation of institutional labor economists. Their work, which has acquired various adjective labels of the term "theory"—dual, queue, job competition, segmented market, and radical—has made an important and useful impact on the way those in and out of the mainstream examine labor market policy and conduct labor market research.

Another body of work receiving considerable OMRD support involved evaluation research. To the degree that it linked factors of labor supply and demand to a methodological application of benefit-cost analysis or a human capital investment approach to evaluation, it helped to examine interactions between labor market conditions and manpower programs.

Recent Trends

A list of agency-sponsored research projects contributing to the observations made in this chapter is provided in Appendix A. It is organized into somewhat arbitrary subtopics under the two general headings: demand and supply. Titles of the projects and names of principal investigators convey more information about the type of research than does a detailed general classification scheme. Only by reading and evaluating each report, preferably with the help of highly qualified referees, can we make a complete evaluation. This was not done: not all the listed projects were completed; many that had been completed were unavailable; and time did not permit a critical appraisal of all of the reports. The observations in this chapter are based on a sample of the reports and a general familiarity gleaned from other sources.

A comparison of OMRD research with the mainstream journal research is presented in Appendix B. Two tables, one for labor supply research and the other for labor demand research contain captions of titles of articles in labor economics that were reported in the 1971-1973 issues of the *Journal of Economic Literature*. The articles are classified to facilitate a comparison with the Department of Labor classification in Appendix A.

The overlap in coverage is striking, and shows that a substantial part of recent OMRD research concerning labor supply and demand is reflected in the journals, and vice versa. Indeed, we estimate that about half of the OMRD research projects have been published in the journals. More will undoubtedly be published when the more recently funded projects are completed and prepared for journal submissions. Similarity in subject matter between OMRD research and the journals would be enhanced if a listing of the doctoral dissertation grant projects were included. These are conducted under the supervision of professors who themselves tend to govern journal content.

One rather unimportant reason for the overlap in coverage is that the list of subcategories was suggested by the titles of articles found in both sources. A more significant reason for the similarity between research topics in the two lists is that the area of research under review tends to be closer to academic research, and this is reflected in the selection of research reports to review. Thus, we compiled the Department of Labor list on the basis of the research orientation of the authors in addition to the titles of the research projects.

It is essential to recognize that the existing incentive system encourages academic researchers to make strenuous efforts to publish their research in the principal journals of their disciplines. Thus, while publication is an indicator of the quality of the research and denotes peer group approval, there is some amount of back-scratching involved. This is one more reason why those on the "demand side" of the market for research—OMRD, the Labor Department, other government offices, Congressmen, interested laymen, and taxpayers—need to look beyond the mere fact of publication and to the policy or practical utility of research.

Gaps in Coverage

The list of articles in the journals reveals some omissions and differences in emphasis in comparison with the OMRD list.

The journal literature reveals more substantial coverage of the following topics, which may deserve greater attention in OMRD research.

Micromodels of the hiring, placement, and promotion processes of employers. This gap reflects the fact that there has generally been less OMRD research on the demand side of the labor market than can be found in the journal literature.

Interrelations between labor supply decisions (mainly by mothers) and child care arrangements; and the effect of various types of day care on the labor supply of mothers.

The relationships between illness, various types of disabilities, and labor supply.

Models of occupational choice and the implications of occupational choice for the supply and demand of particular occupations.

A broader view of income distribution, including macromodels of that distribution.

The effects of unions on wages and employment by industry, occupation, and for various demographic groups.

The journal research is, as is to be expected, more theoretical; OMRD research includes more reports which merely present data. By itself, this difference is no criticism of the OMRD effort, although it is suggested later in this paper that the data-gathering efforts of OMRD are wasted unless they are followed with analysis or, at least, are distributed widely among analytical researchers.

Useful Results from Research on Labor Supply and Demand

This section contains assessments of several research topics and reports that offer various "lessons" for research strategy. The first topic discussed is alternative labor market theory, namely, dual and radical theory. On scientific or methodological grounds, this work represents the most ambitious undertaking since it challenges established neoclassical theory of labor markets. This challenge engaged a large number of younger labor economists and carried forward a strong tradition of criticism of neoclassical economics within the labor field.

Next discussed is research on labor supply functions. Work here deals with a relatively narrowly defined empirical problem, which has been pursued with relative success. Specifically, this research examines the question of the labor supply response to changes in income and wage rates—a question with implications for welfare reform, unemployment insurance systems, retirement plans and other important policies.

Studies that mainly yield descriptive statistics or descriptive institutional information about labor market trends or programs reflect a third type of OMRD-sponsored research. As mentioned earlier, work of this kind was generally bypassed in the selection of research reports for this chapter. Nonetheless, such research is fairly common, and it is important to realize how it can be useful to both policy-makers and those engaged in scientific research.

The final parts of this section include brief discussions dealing with macroeconomic issues, with some "vogue" topics in the economics profession, such as job search theories of unemployment and issues of "certification" and "screening," and with several topics that deserve more attention in the OMRD research budget.

Research on the Dual and Radical Theories of the Labor Market[1]

The dual and radical (D-R) theories of the labor market seek to replace the paradigm of neoclassical theory. In brief, neoclassical theory involves utility-maximizing models of microunits; those units operate in competitive markets and achieve economic equilibrium positions. The D-R theories, although lacking unity and cohesion in themselves, differ from the neoclassical approach in a number of ways: power and status are explicitly entered in utility functions alongside time allocation and material goods; coalitions of power groups and institutions replace microunits as the principal actors; monopoly structures and innumerable imperfections in the market—reflected in dual and/or segmented labor markets—are claimed to vitiate the competitive model; and dynamic change and disequilibria are emphasized instead of static equilibria. A principal impetus developing the new paradigm is an alleged inability of neoclassical theory to explain a number of market failures and empirical anomalies, particularly those concerning unemployment, poverty, worker alienation, and the segmentation of the market. D-R theory describes the market as divided into a *primary sector*, composed of "good" jobs offering high wages, good working conditions, upward mobility, and stability, and a *secondary sector*, composed of low-paying, dead-end, and unstable jobs. Drawing on the methodological treatise of Thomas S. Kuhn (1962), one D-R spokesman, David Gordon, claims that the empirical "anomalies" in orthodox analysis have led to a scientific "crisis" that can be resolved only by constructing "new paradigms to explain the basic processes of income determination in advanced capitalistic economies" (Gordon, 1972: 13).

The substance of the D-R challenge centers on three types of issues. The first concerns empirical or factual questions about market failures: is the income distribution widening? Have educational programs failed? Is worker dissatisfaction growing? The second is the rejection of the neoclassical explanations for empirical events, such as the neoclassical theories of discrimination or the human capital theories of education and training. The third is an advocacy of policies that focus on the demand side of the labor market, such as public employment programs, and on altering power relations in society more generally.

Several important achievements of OMRD research projects contributing to the fundamental reformulation of labor market theory may be noted.[2] First, attention has been directed to empirical problems that may be difficult to explain or analyze in terms of conventional analysis:

> Income distribution remained relatively unchanged and the poverty problem remained slow to diminish during the 1960s despite general affluence and a variety of government programs that aimed to eliminate poverty.
>
> Returns to education and other forms of investment in human capital can be questioned, especially for the poor and minority groups;

compensatory education programs and training programs were said to have failed.

Earnings differentials between white and black males and between men and women remain large, even after various productivity traits have been controlled for. These differentials have persisted over time, contrary to the predictions of neoclassical, competitive theories. Some related empirical issues are the relative decline in black male labor force participation, the decline in the ratio of black-to-white male income with higher educational attainment, the relatively slower growth in female educational attainment since 1940, and the relatively flat age-earnings profiles of women and black men.

Monopolies, unions, and other sources of protected labor markets have been partly blamed for the market segmentation into "primary" and "secondary" jobs. Moreover, D-R spokesman have claimed that such noncompetitive elements in the market were so pervasive as to make untenable the empirical work of orthodox labor economists which usually assumes competition.

Psychological and sociological variables have been introduced into models of employment and earnings; it has been claimed that these may be more important than "economic" productivity variables. This contrasts with the implicit neoclassical assumption that tastes, preferences, motivation, and other attitudinal variables are predetermined or exogenous.

Alienation and dissatisfaction by American workers are alleged to be growing problems, despite rising income and wage rates.

These empirical issues were not, of course, unknown to neoclassical economists, but they were seldom considered as explicitly as they have been by the D-R labor economists. Much of the recent debate has served to revive criticisms of neoclassical labor theory made earlier by an older generation labor economists, a group that I have elsewhere labeled the "neoinstitutionalists" (Cain, 1975). That group also emphasized such market imperfections or failures as segmented (or "Balkanized") labor markets, discrimination, monopoly elements, and the internal labor markets of large firms, wage diversity for apparently similar work and similar workers, and other shortcomings of marginal analysis of competitive models of the labor market.[3]

The neoinstitutionalist labor economists dominated their field during the 1940s and 1950s. The valuable attributes of study by this group include an astute focus on policy issues, knowledge of labor market institutions, attention to barriers to the smooth functioning of labor markets, and recognition of power relations and bargaining by groups. These attributes also characterize the best work by the D-R economists. Nevertheless, the theoretical challenge, first of the older group in the period from 1940 to 1960, and now by the younger group has not replaced or even seriously modified the neoclassical theory. It has, however, influenced the practice of empirical research by the neoclassical economists.

During the late 1950s and particularly during the 1960s, neoclassical labor economists experienced a resurgence. They engaged in abundant empirical work, while at the same time improving the rigor and flexibility of their theoretical models. They expanded their models to deal with discrimination and to accommodate nonmarket activities, developed investment models for human capital acquisition, and confronted unemployment as well as job and wage diversity in the labor market in addition to their customary attention to labor demand and labor supply functions. It would be too exhaustive as well as exhausting to develop fully the neoclassical response to D-R and neoinstitutionalist criticisms; I have elsewhere suggested that the neoclassical treatment of many of the empirical challenges is far from fully satisfactory (Cain, 1975). Attention to one useful and relatively successful body of what is essentially neoclassical research on labor supply occupies the next part of this section. Before coming to that subject we might note that although OMRD did not support early breakthroughs in the resurgence of neoclassical research, the agency has given increased emphasis to such work in recent years. Not coincidentally, more recent neoclassical efforts have taken on a more applied and policy-oriented focus.[4]

Example of Useful Research: Labor Supply Functions

During the late 1960s and through the early 1970s, a number of research studies appeared in which the relation between labor supply and wages, income, and other variables were analyzed. To some extent this activity reflected the long-standing interest of economists in the response of leisure "consumed" (or, conversely, labor supplied) to changes in wage rates and income. Economics as an empirical science is precisely concerned with behavioral responses to price and income changes (and, in turn, with the effects on prices and incomes of changes in behavior).

Two subjects of policy concern were covered by these studies: the effect of positive income (and wage) taxes on labor supply and the effects of welfare reform—income maintenance programs and the various schemes of "negative taxation"—on labor supply. Indeed, research on labor supply functions was directly stimulated by the decade of policy debate about welfare reform—expanding coverage, income supplementation, and incentives regarding work by welfare recipients.

Empirical research on labor supply functions examines the incentive question by focusing on the income and wage rate effects on labor supply. Any income maintenance legislation may be described by the amount of an income guarantee (the transfer payment the family unit would receive in the event of no other income) and by the rate at which this guarantee is reduced as the family receives income from other sources (a rate which need not be constant).

Earnings are the main source of the nontransfer income of eligible families, and the reduction in transfer payment in effect lowers the earnings (or wage) rate for the working members of such families. The question of how such legislation would alter work behavior involved estimating the effects on labor supply of variations in income and wage rates observed by means of survey data. Actually, these variations were deliberately selected so as *not* to reflect on-going income maintenance programs. Among welfare recipients the work (or nonwork) decision, voluntary or involuntary, tended to precede the receipt of transfer payments. By contrast, to measure the disincentives of an expanded negative income tax program, the work decisions were assumed to be *responses to* eligibility for transfer payments that precede the work responses. The direction of causation is the opposite of that revealed by people actually receiving welfare. Thus, the empirical work on estimating labor supply functions generally selected persons who were in the labor force, so that covariation in time worked and income and wage rates was limited to whatever the ordinary operations of the labor market produced.

Research on labor supply was well-received in the economics profession and contributed to policy discussions of welfare reform in several ways. The findings regarding labor supply tended to predict a rather small work disincentive among male heads of households in response to a negative income tax program. In addition, a good deal was learned about the design, administration, and coverage of welfare laws. Much of this research, including several costly "negative income tax experiments," was sponsored by OEO, HEW, and President Johnson's Commission on Income Maintenance. However, OMRD sponsored a number of important studies and continues today as a major sponsor of research on labor supply.[5]

The value of the research should be assessed cautiously. Most of the work, like nearly all empirical research in economics, has used nonexperimental data. However, the "natural" experiment that the labor supply has performed to generate the observations for the user of survey data—assuming that the "experiment" of conducting household interviews faithfully records the operation of the labor market—is not the same as that which would occur if a negative income tax plan ever became law. There are, therefore, severe difficulties inherent in attempts to use such survey data to make inferences about the sorts of income and wage rate effects that apply to people eligible for coverage in welfare programs. Coping with these difficulties involves the following questions of research design: What sample of observations should be included? Should disabled people, rich people, and welfare recipients be excluded? What selection of wage and income variables and what other "control" variables should be included in the model? What is the appropriate definition of labor supply? The choices the investigator made to these questions of research strategy generally affected the parameter estimates and proved to be a source of a disturbingly wide range in the estimates. Finally, the studies were aimed at measuring a labor supply response; they did not investigate the full general equilibrium outcomes that would have involved the demand function for labor. Nor did the studies examine the diverse provisions of welfare reform legislation which affected many other matters, such as family composition, day care, and labor market services.

Despite these limitations, the research was worthwhile. In the context of a review of the "state of the art," the studies deserve attention because they represent a serious effort to use economic theory and econometric estimation of empirical relationships to illuminate debate on an important economic policy issue. The studies had a specific purpose—to assess the labor supply impact of income maintenance laws—and they can be evaluated in the light of that purpose. Vague references to "qualitative" relationships with "theory" and the proliferation of statistical relationships among seemingly arbitrarily selected variables—the bane of so much research in the social sciences—were held to a minimum in this work.

The lessons for the future are relatively straightforward. New legislation and reforms in existing legislation will affect occupational safety and health, the provision of day care, and tax incentives affecting the use of labor and/or capital in production. These effects can and should provide a concrete focus for empirical research. These issues, like those of welfare reform, are "perennial." Even if fundings come too late to aid in evaluating a particular bill in Congress, the issues will remain and the research can become useful.

Descriptive Research Studies

Immigration

In recent years immigration has become an important topic for labor market analysis for several reasons, some of which are mentioned in the North-Weissert report (II.C.5): (a) the large number of immigrants in certain labor markets, particularly within coastal states; (b) the growing fraction of population growth in the United States that is composed of immigrants, partly a result of the slowdown in the natural rate of population growth; (c) the increasing number of illegal aliens; (d) the role of immigrants in so-called "critical" or "shortage" occupations, such as the health occupations; and (e) the potential unrest that immigration may spark in an economy beset by high unemployment. Labor economists have not been fully aware of these trends and, in any event, have not examined the immigration question beyond the attention given to the special case of Mexican farm workers. Given this research gap, the North-Weissert study is a welcome contribution even though it was essentially a descriptive study. However, the study was not designed in light of a theory of the determinants of immigration nor of the labor market's adjustment to an influx of immigrants.

Consider that immigrant workers are substitutes for certain types of native workers and complements for others. Within the production process, therefore, some native workers are hurt and some, presumably a lesser number, are helped. Some employers are helped while those who compete with "aided" employers are hurt. Ripples of wage, employment, price, and profit adjustments to immigration are set in motion. None of these issues is spelled out, let alone analyzed in the North-Weissert study. Perhaps an empirical study would reveal that the ripples are so slight that they can be ignored. The statistics reported suggest otherwise, but a firm judgment is unwarranted. The claim by North and Weissert that immigrants are having "a substantial impact" on the American labor market is, in fact, not backed up by any hard data on what labor market variables have been substantially changed. If there were a more systematic procedure by OMRD for evaluating completed research projects, the needed follow-up analysis might be achieved more readily. In this instance the Labor Department is only partly responsible for the gap, since the Employment and Training Administration published and circulated a summary of the North-Weissert study in a pamphlet (North, 1973). To my knowledge, no one in the research community has shown compelling interest in pursuing the analysis, and the agency has not sought a follow-up analysis.

Work Scheduling

Another example of a descriptive report having no subsequent analysis is the Glickman-Brown study of changing work schedules (I.G.12). This report is useful for its historical account of work and nonwork time-and-activity trends. It projects a continuation of reduced hours of work and greater flexibility in work schedules. The report outlines potential individual psychological problems and organizational problems in adjusting to these anticipated changes in time and schedules. The most interesting questions raised, however, remain unanswered and no research method is suggested to obtain the answers. As examples:

> Is any future increment in nonwork time likely to be qualitatively different from that experienced in the past because it will be devoted to "pure" leisure (e.g., recreation) as distinct from nonmarket work chores like shopping, home repairs, or commuting? The authors imply that the answer is yes, but offer no evidence. Nor do they spell out why the question is important beyond references to unmeasured psychological effects. Presumably, the change in leisure habits could have implications for adult education, the recreation industry, and other elements of society.
>
> What are the effects of government regulation on the ability of firms and workers to devise work schedules to meet their preferences? Glickman and Brown list a number of legal and institutional (e.g., union) impediments to flexible work schedules, but their remarks are very general, and there is no evidence of what industries or occupations are affected.
>
> What has been the experience of firms and workers who have adopted a nonstandard work-week? Glickman and Brown suggest that studies to pursue this very general question be made, but present no ideas for research design or for tests of specific hypotheses. There have been a number of journalistic accounts of the effects of flexible schedules on productivity and on worker satisfaction, but little systematic work has been done. It is a difficult problem because the experience is likely to be transitory and impermanent or to involve highly unusual, self-selected firms and workers. Given these characteristics of the sample of available observations, inferences about the long-run effects for the work force in general are suspect.
>
> Finally, the Glickman and Brown study did not consider that the business cycle might influence work schedules, facilitating "moonlighting" or work sharing depending on the state of the economy.

Economists have devoted a good deal of study to the hours-of-work question and are increasingly examining the allocation of time to nonmarket work activities.[6] Presumably, the analytical tools and previous work by labor economists would contribute to answering the questions raised by Glickman and Brown, but their study has not been extended in these directions.

Occupational Licensing

Another excellent study that succeeds in every respect except that of achieving *quantitative estimates* of the effects it sets out to examine is the study of occupational licensing by the Educational Testing Service (II.E.4), later published as a book by Shimberg, Esser, and Kruger (1972). This project examined the impact of occupational licensing legislation on the workings of the labor market. It reviewed the composition and powers of state licensing boards, eligibility requirements for applicants, various fees that are charged, licensing of practioners from other states, and the amount of public information made available by the licensing boards. The main hypothesis of this project is that occupational licensing is used to restrict entry into occupations and to protect the economic interests of the members of that occupation. Several specific difficulties were identified: (a) many licensing boards are composed of practitioners of the very occupations being controlled; (b) licensing boards are frequently insulated from legislative oversight; (c) most licensing boards administer oral or written tests, and there is tremendous variance in the level of difficulty from one test to another; (d) the detailed nature of tests often makes formal educational training in the occupation mandatory, eliminating some applicants due to high financial or time costs.

The conclusion of the study—"that licensing boards in their requirements, practices and procedures may restrict the supply and inhibit the mobility of workers in licensed occupations"—can only be regarded as contingent. The researchers offer no quantitative estimates of the effects of licensing on employment, the geographic distribution of practitioners, wages and salaries, or the prices and quality of the services. Again, it should be pointed out that economists have developed methods of analyzing the effects of unions and of regulations on these types of variables. Statistical evidence is badly needed to determine whether the effects of licensing are actual rather than potential.

Several descriptive research studies have proven useful for subsequent analysis, indicating that the standard I have posed is not impossible to meet. Outstanding in this regard are the careful collation of the Labor Department's Dictionary of Occupational Titles and the Census occupational data by Ann Miller and associates (I.G.3 and II.E.3), along with related work by Stanley Greene (II.E.2). This work has provided essential ingredients to the dissertation and subsequent publications of Robert E. B. Lucas (1972); specifically, the latter's work on nonpecuniary aspects and compensating wage differentials of occupations. A study by John Bishop (I.A.2) is also using Miller's data, and the work is promising in terms of its theoretical basis, thorough empirical work, and policy relevance.

Two examples of descriptive studies that have been extended to fruitful analysis by the original authors may also be mentioned. James Scoville's work on occupational classification systems (I.G.4 and I.G.13) is thorough, historically well grounded, analytically oriented, and useful for prescribing changes in current methods of occupational data gathering and description. His OMRD studies and some further analysis are contained in a well-received book (Scoville, 1972). A second data collection, on minority employment patterns, by Orley Ashenfelter (I.E.9) has resulted in several articles on economic discrimination that stand as landmarks in the literature (Ashenfelter, 1970, 1972; Ashenfelter and Heckman, 1974).

Fringe Benefits

An example of a subject requiring more detailed and refined measurement is fringe benefits. The trend toward a larger fraction of individual remuneration going to wage supplements or fringes has reached a point where a close look at its causes and consequences should be a high priority. The first task is simply measuring the heterogeneous types of fringe benefits in ways that permit them to be compared and aggregated. A conventional approach is to calculate the money equivalence of the fringe. But should the money cost to the employer or the money value to the employee be the basis? Only in perfect markets, with full information and costless mobility, would the two bases be equal. Clearly, the money value of such benefits as pensions and health insurance depend on unknown probabilities of behavior as well as on subjective evaluations. Sheer measurement is a difficult task and must precede the analytical work.

The principal analytical problem is that of predicting the effects of fringe benefits on the demand for and supply of labor. How, for example, are labor productivity and labor mobility affected? Fringes differ from purely money wages in that the same fringe benefit will vary in costs and value for different employers and employees. Presumably, pension plans will affect and be affected by the age distribution of the work force. The same two-way relation applies to maternity benefits and the age-sex marital status composition. Will, for example, employers shun potentially high-fertility female employees in the face of mandatory maternity benefits? Similar questions arise in connection with every type of fringe benefit. Moreover, high levels of fringes, particularly those that affect the "fixed costs" of employment, can lead to hiring policies that effectively exclude lesser skilled and disadvantaged workers.

Understanding the reasons for the growth over time in wage supplements would presumably contribute to understanding their effects on behavior. Among the reasons that might be analyzed are the following:

> progressive income taxes, which may make the fringe benefits worth more to employees than their equivalent cost in the form of wage gains;
>
> economies of scale, which may make employer provision of fringes cheaper than the same benefits when purchased by individual employees;
>
> increased incentives of employers to reduce turnover (the reasons for this would need to be explored, since fringes can be a *cause* of the higher fixed costs per employee that makes turnover more expensive); and
>
> unions, which perhaps use fringes to extract higher "wage" gains in a form that disguises their size or perhaps as a way of promoting union security.

The essential process of outlining such concerns illustrates how the important—yet still preliminary—measurement task might be approached in light of a relatively explicit theoretical framework and with an eye toward follow-up analyses.

Education and Training as a Screening Device in the Labor Market

The prominent place of formal education in the human capital literature presents an inviting target for criticism. Two types of counterarguments to the claim that human capital investment yields high (or "competitive") rates of return seem inevitable; but they are almost impossible to test satisfactorily: (1) personal ability is not adequately controlled in human capital models, and (2) the "screening" or "certification" function of education allows a favored class to get the best jobs. As mentioned earlier in this review, dual and radical labor economists have emphasized screening and certification. Thurow (1972: 68) states: "The function of education is not to confer skill and therefore increased productivity and higher wages on the worker; it is rather to certify his 'trainability' and to confer upon him a certain status."

The screening hypothesis raises three questions: Does the "screen" reveal true productivity differences? If not, then the employer who pays more for the more educated worker is not maximizing profits; instead, he must be exercising his tastes for discrimination. If the screen has some value in revealing productivity differences, are these differences reflecting the education in itself, or are they independent of the education? In its pure form, the screening hypothesis infers the latter. If a pure screen hypothesis is not accepted, how much of the return to education is due to education in itself and how much to its screening value? Presumably, the "screening hypothesis" generally claims that there is a *substantial* screening effect.

While a number of OMRD research projects have touched upon these questions, we are far from resolving them. Bowles (I.G.7) and Thurow (I.D.3) state the case for the dual and radical position most explicitly. Indirect support for their view is provided by the ETS study on occupational licensing (II.E.4). Nonetheless, as I have already noted, empirical evidence on the quantitative importance of such screens is lacking. Several studies of "labor market information systems," by Ginzberg (I.G.6), Kaufman and Stevens (II.B.4), and Thal-Larsen (I.G.5) mainly deal with other issues, and their attention to the screening question serves only to confirm that the question is important. Outside OMRD, several neoclassical economists representing the human capital school have attempted rebuttals, but their arguments are largely speculative and their empirical evidence is too indirect.[7]

Macro-Labor Market Research in OMRD

There is definitely an underemphasis on macrooriented research projects in the OMRD output, an underemphasis which may be justified. First, responsibility for macroemployment policy rests with such federal agencies as the Federal Reserve System, the Treasury Department, the Office of Management and the Budget, and, most notably for economists, the Council of Economic Advisors. Second, the universities and organizations such as the Brookings Institute also seem heavily engaged in policy-related research on macroproblems. Nevertheless, there are a number of issues of particular interest to the Labor Department and to the traditional study of labor markets that call for a closer attention to macroissues. Three such subjects are theories of unemployment, the related theory of job search, and the interrelation of manpower programs and macropolicies.

The "Phillips Curve" and the "Natural Rate" of Unemployment

The Phillips curve refers to the negative relationship between (usually) the rate of unemployment and the rate of change in prices or wages; it characterizes for both laymen and economist the much-discussed trade-off between unemployment and inflation. The customary theoretical and policy interpretations of the Phillips curve have, however, been challenged in recent years by "monetarist" economists. Most notably, Milton Friedman has proposed a theory of a "natural" or "equilibrium" rate of unemployment that is invariant to the rate of inflation in the long run. As part of this monetarist countertheory, Friedman and others (Phelps, 1970) claim that the short-run Phillips curve is highly unstable and, to repeat the earlier point in different language, that the long-run Phillips curve is a vertical line at the "natural" unemployment rate. The policy implication is that macromeasures to induce inflation by expansionary monetary and fiscal policies will only postpone the rise in unemployment that will occur when the expansion levels off.

While the Friedman position has been challenged by most leading macrotheorists (Tobin, 1971; most issues of the *Brookings Institute Papers on Economic Activity*), there are many research questions for labor economists and policy questions for government agencies in this area that can be pursued without its resolution. Consider, for example, unemployment insurance: whether it should be liberalized is probably more a political decision than an economic one, but the labor economists have a responsibility to investigate the effects of liberalized unemployment benefits on the number of persons who experience unemployment and on the duration of unemployment (Feldstein, 1973). Another issue raised by the advocates of a natural rate of unemployment is that minimum wage laws, including the Walsh-Healy and Bacon-Davis laws, create wage floors that increase unemployment, particularly among so-called marginal workers, like teenagers. Most of these studies, including the few supported by OMRD (I.B.3, I.C.1, and I.C.2), have not given explicit attention to these wage-fixing laws during business cycle fluctuations.

In a more positive vein, Holt and others (I.B.2) have argued that an improved employment service, manpower training, and other manpower programs can shift the Phillips curve and permanently lower the unemployment rate at some given rate of inflation. To date, the Holt studies have been mainly theoretical and prescriptive, and no benefit-cost evaluation of the prescribed policies has been undertaken.

Job Search Theories of Unemployment

The microneoclassical theory of unemployment—sometimes linked to the monetarist macrotheory—is generally referred to as a "job search" theory of unemployment. The OMRD projects have, except for Holt's (I.B.2) and a substantial number of Ph.D. dissertations, almost ignored the developments in this area. (The reports of Brechling (I.B.2) and Myers (I.G.10) are indirectly related to the issue.) Again, however, justification may be found in the abstractness of this work and in its remoteness from empirical analysis suitable for policy application.

Briefly, job search models postulate uncertainty and ignorance among workers in knowing their best wage offer (particularly when "best" is defined for the long-run future) or among firms in knowing their best hirings. Uncertainty is exacerbated when the cost of living (inflation) is fluctuating. The job search models begin with the quasi-tautology that search continues as long as the marginal benefits of further search exceed the marginal costs. As already noted, such costs are affected by one's alternative income, including unemployment insurance, and by the best alternative wage available in a "sure" job. In fact, these factors mainly determine the opportunity costs of search, whereas the direct costs—such as employment agency fees and travel costs—remain largely unmeasured but are, perhaps, small.

Unfortunately, little information is available about the benefits of job search. Casual observations suggest that the pay-off of job search for young people—and, indeed, the pay-off of a trial and error system in job taking— is higher than for older workers who are more sure of their abilities and preferences. Similarly, since employers usually know more about experienced or older workers, there may be less variability in job offers to them. Certainly, young people usually have lower opportunity costs when they are unemployed. These considerations thereby predict and rationalize higher unemployment rates among young people. Similar arguments are made about women workers relative to male workers.

But these are only off-hand observations. Data requirements for empirical estimation of the formal job search models are quite stringent. The model builder must know something about the distribution as well as the mean of the potential remuneration available to the searching worker. Another crucial consideration in search behavior is whether job offers that are "sampled" must be chosen or foreclosed completely or whether two or more chances are available. Adding to the difficulties of empirical specification of these models is the fact that the benefits of job search are largely dependent on an unobserved variable—"efficiency" of job search, (search efficiency may be positively related to educational attainment) and it is probably correlated with the mean expected wage; mean expected wage is obviously correlated with the opportunity cost of search. Further unobservable variables include the worker's attitude toward risk and his subjective discount rate. The discount rate, in fact, may be the one new variable brought into job search models that was not already present in previous discussion of unemployment and the reasons for its duration. However, one may question the importance of discount rates given the brief nature of most spells of unemployment. The notion of the "efficiency" of search represents an important assumption of the job search models: efficiency of search is improved when the worker is unemployed and is able to "specialize" in search activity. As Tobin has noted (1972), this crucial assumption has not been supported by any empirical evidence.

Thus, it is apparent that economists' job search models of unemployment are not yet very useful. There are gaps in the theoretical structure, but the main shortcoming is their intractability to empirical work. Such work is needed to remove the ambiguities about signs of certain variables and to provide quantitative measures of the effects under study. Too many of the variables in the models are unobservable; enough relationships are mutually causal that identification of the model would be difficult.

Manpower Programs and the Business Cycle

One important problem that connects micro- and macro-issues in labor economics is the evaluation of manpower programs during different phases of the business cycle. Manpower training efforts illustrate the problem. The traditional approach to evaluation adopts a micromodel—specifically the human capital model—to measure the costs and benefits of the investment in training. Several questions involving macroeconomics are usually ignored: Does money spent on this program mean less money spent on another program? Is there any change in net aggregate spending? Are trainees employed in place of other workers? These macro-effects could be viewed as externalities or third party effects.

A second problem area in which macroconsiderations connect with traditional micro-cost-benefit analysis emerges when we focus solely on the trainee. How do the trainee's opportunity costs while in the training program and his earnings gains in the posttraining period vary over the business cycle? Is the return to the training program likely to be higher or lower during periods of high or low unemployment? This important question has not been well analyzed, probably because the appropriate design to obtain an empirical estimate of the effect of the business cycle is extraordinarily difficult to achieve. It calls for the analysis of otherwise similar training (or other manpower) programs that differ only in an indicator of the business cycle, such as unemployment conditions. For example, in a cross-sectional study the "same" program could be analyzed among regions of labor markets with varying business conditions. In a time-series study, the same program could be evaluated over an extended period to observe how the program performs during different phases of the business cycle. Unfortunately, the implicit assumption that the programs are otherwise similar is usually untenable.

Most evaluations have looked at programs that were confined to a single area or region (Hardin and Borus, 1973; Somers, 1967). Where several areas have been examined, variation in business conditions was (apparently) not sufficient to permit generalizations about this interaction. (Olympus Research Corporation, 1971.) In any case, the more important difficulty is the likelihood that other differences in the training programs—the type of program, the administrators, the clientele, or the structural (as distinct from cyclical) conditions in the labor market—are the dominant sources of varying performances in training efforts. Moreover, policy concerns about the timing and scope of manpower programs usually arise in connection with economywide business cycle changes. For this reason, the time series design to study the interaction of the cycle and program performance is preferred. However, training programs cannot be expected to remain unchanged over the five years or so that constitute the full amplitude of a business cycle.

A final comment concerns the analysis of business cycle interactions with training programs that are based on theoretical models, rather than on empirical research. Ordinarily, theories are too weak to provide much more than some common-sensical qualitative predictions. Perhaps we could learn something about this problem if more effort was devoted to reviewing the many existing case studies to determine if a "business cycle effect" might be discerned.

Suggestions for Future Research Strategy

There are two serious criticisms of a general nature to be made of OMRD research on labor supply and demand—suggestions for change in the ways in which research funds are allocated are aimed at dealing with these difficulties. First, there appears to be insufficient communication between the research community and government policy-makers. Communication exists at the first stage of study, when problems are formulated broadly and research is initiated. From that point on, however, two-way communication bogs down. When research is completed, there tends to be a rather perfunctory review, neither researcher nor policy-maker takes responsibility for any one of several ways of following up on the research: (a) analyzing its application, if any, to concrete policies; (b) evaluating its predictive ability in varying contexts; (c) determining how it could be used to provide a base or point of departure for future research—making sure that the proposed future research includes a design for evaluating its contribution.

Only by following through with this sort of critical evaluation can the agency and the researcher learn what is and is not useful. We should probably expect that many, perhaps most, research projects will turn out not to be very useful: perhaps the original question posed for study lacked precision or was aimed at an irrelevant issue; perhaps the environment changed so markedly that the findings became irrelevant; perhaps the research proved faulty because of some design defect or data inadequacies. These and many other reasons for research areas of social science inquiry such as labor market analysis.

A second and related criticism is the limited circulation of research results within the research community, contributing to an insufficient response by researchers to these results. It is unrealistic to expect that government policy-makers study, evaluate, and either apply or reject the large array of research findings received by the agencies. Given that much (perhaps most) research will not prove directly useful to policy-makers, the transmission of research results to the social science research community outside of government needs to be facilitated. Simply relying on publications appears suboptimal.

NOTES

1. This section draws upon an unpublished paper by the author (Cain, 1975).

2. These projects include the following listed in Appendix A: Barrett (II.D.1); Bluestone, Ferman, et al. (II.G.3); Bowles (I.G.7); Doeringer (II.G.5); Doeringer

and Piore (I.G.8) and (I.G.15); Edwards, Gordon, and Reich (II.G.7); Friedlander (II.D.2); Harrison (I.E.8); Thurow (I.D.3); and Weiskoff (I.A.7). In addition, an OMRD-supported dissertation by Lucas (1972) has made a notable contribution and appeared in a widely cited paper by Thurow and Lucas (1972). Further contributions to the debate by the younger group of labor economists, but not themselves D-R spokesmen, are Flanigan (II.B.3) and Hall (II.B.2).

3. Among OMRD projects by this group, see especially Ginzberg (I.G.6), Heneman (II.D.4), Marshall (I.E.7), Stern and Johnson (II.C.4), Wallace (II.D.3), and Wolfbein (II.A.7).

4. Some representative projects are: Easley and Fearn (I.G.2), Ehrenberg (I.D.1 and I.D.2), Fearn (II.C.13), Fleisher (II.A.10), Kalachek (II.A.2 and II.A.3), Matilla (I.C.1), Reder (I.G.1 and II.D.5), and Welch and Kosters (I.B.3).

5. Eleven OMRD-supported studies are listed in Appendix C as published articles or dissertations, rather than as OMRD grants (with one exception). Their published citation emphasizes the impact on the profession of these studies. Indeed, nine of the authors—Boskin, Cohen, Hausman, Heckman, Hill, Kesselman, Lerman, Parker, and Rea—did their work on these studies as part of their OMRD dissertation fellowships.

Except for one paper, by Fleisher, Parsons, and Porter, none of the works listed used the Ohio State University National Longitudinal Study. This data source offers a time-series dimension to a large cross-sectional set of observations, and it is currently probably the best data source available for labor supply studies. (See Andrisani, 1973; Hall and Kasten, 1973; and Mincer and Polacheck, 1974.)

6. A well-known paper by Becker (1965) has been influential in this respect.

7. See Chiswick (1973), Layard and Psacharopoulos (1974), and my discussion of the debate in Cain (1975).

REFERENCES

ANDRISANI, P. J. (1973) "An empirical analysis of the dual labor market theory." Ph.D. dissertation, Ohio State University.

ASHENFELTER, O. (1970) "Changes in labor market discrimination over time." *Journal of Human Resources* (Fall).

______(1972) "Racial discrimination and trade unionism," *Journal of Political Economy* (May/June).

______and HECKMAN, J. (1974) "Measuring the effect of an anti-discrimination program." *Working Paper* No. 50. Stanford, CA: National Bureau of Economic Research.

BECKER, G. S. (1965) "A theory of the allocation of time." *Economic Journal* (September).

CAIN, G. G. (1975) "The challenge of dual and radical theories of the labor market to orthodox theory." Unpublished manuscript. Institute for Research on Poverty, University of Wisconsin.

_____(1973) "Review" of D. Hamermesh, *Economic Aspects of Manpower Training Programs*, in *Industrial and Labor Relations Review* (April).

CHISWICK, B. R. (1973) "Schooling, screening, and income." In L. Solomon (ed.), *Does College Matter?* New York: Academic Press.

FELDSTEIN, M. (1973) *Lowering the Permanent Rate of Unemployment*, A Study Prepared for the Use of the Joint Economic Committee, U. S. Congress. Washington, DC: Government Printing Office.

FRIEDMAN, M. (1968) "The role of monetary policy." *American Economic Review* (March).

GORDON, D. M. (1972) *Theories of Poverty and Unemployment*. Lexington, MA: D. C. Heath.

HALL, R. E. and KASTEN, R. A. (1973) "The relative occupational success of blacks and whites." *Brookings Papers on Economic Activity* 3.

HAMERMESH, D. S. (1971) *Economic Aspects of Manpower Training Programs*. Lexington, MA: D. C. Heath.

HARDIN, E. and BORUS, M. E. (1971) *The Economic Benefits and Costs of Retaining*. Lexington, MA: D.C. Heath.

KUHN, T. S. (1962) *The Structure of Scientific Revolutions*. Chicago: University of Chicago Press.

LAYARD, R. and PSACHAROPOULOS, G. (1974) "The screening hypothesis and the returns to education." *Journal of Political Economy* (September/ October).

LUCAS, R. E. B. (1972) *Working Conditions, Wage-Rates, and Human Capital: A Hedonic Study*. Ph.D. dissertation, Massachusetts Institute of Technology.

MINCER, J. and POLACHECK, S. (1974) "Family investments in human capital: earnings of children." *Journal of Political Economy* (March).

NORTH, D. S. (1974) *Immigrants and the American Labor Market*, Manpower Research Monograph, No. 31. Manpower Administration, U. S. Department of Labor.

Olympus Research Foundation (1971) *Total Impact Evaluation of Manpower Programs in Four Cities*, Summary Final Report, prepared for the Office of Evaluation, Manpower Administration, U. S. Department of Labor. Washington, DC: Olympus Research Corporation.

PHELPS, E. S. [ed.] (1970) *Microeconomic Foundations of Employment and Inflation*. New York: W. W. Norton.

SCOVILLE, J. G. (1972) *Manpower and Occupational Analysis: Concepts and Measurements*. Lexington, MA: D. C. Heath.

SHIMBERG, B., ESSER, B. F., and KRUGER, D. H. (1972) *Occupational Licensing: Practices and Policies*. Washington, DC: Public Affairs Press.

SOMERS, G. G., [ed.] (1967) *Retraining the Unemployed*. Madison: University of Wisconsin Press.

THUROW, L. C. (1972) "Education and income." *The Public Interest* (Summer).

_____and LUCAS, R. E. B. (1972) "The American distribution of income: a structural problem." Committee Print, U. S. Congress, Joint Economic Committee.

TOBIN, J. (1972) "Inflation and unemployment." *American Economic Review* (March).

Appendix A: List of Recent Demand and Supply Research Projects, 1970-1973

I. Demand

A. INFLUENCES ON THE DEMAND FOR LABOR: JOB CREATION, JOB DEVELOPMENT, WAGE SUBSIDIES

1. "Alternative Forms of Public Service Employment," R. A. Gordon, Bent Hansen, Lloyd Ulman, contract no. 81-06-72-01.
2. "The Potential of Wage Subsidies," John Bishop, contract no. 51-55-73-04.
3. "Employment Expansion in a Dynamic Economy," study no. 2, "Good Jobs, Poor Jobs, and Search for Shelters" by Marcia Freedman as part of a number of studies by Eli Ginzberg, contract no. 21-36-73-51.
4. "A Conceptual Framework for Measurement of the Impact of Foreign Trade on Workers," Robert Schwenger, contract no. 91-09-70-61.
5. "New Businesses and Urban Employment Opportunities," Kenneth McLennan and Paul Seidenstat, contract no. 81-40-60-20.
6. "The Employment Impact of Multinational Corporations," Alan Madian, contract no. 92-36-72-38.
7. "A Multi-Sector Simulation Model of Employment, Income, and Economic Growth in Puerto Rico," Richard Weiskoff, contract no. 91-09-71-03.
8. "Stability and Real Economic Growth: An International Comparison," Neil Palomba, grant to Iowa State University.
9. "Employment Creation Effects of Negro Businesses, with Particular Emphasis on Negro Teenage Employment," David and Alice Kidder, institutional grant to Atlanta University.

B. MACROMODELS OF EMPLOYMENT, UNEMPLOYMENT, AND INFLATION

1. "The Relationship Between Regional and Overall Employment," Frank Brechling, contract no. 91-15-70-07.
2. "Labor Markets, Inflation, and Manpower Policy," Charles Holt, Ralph Smith, Richard Toikka, and William Scanlon, contract no. 92-11-72-36.
3. "An Analvsis of (1) The Cyclical Stability of Aggregate Employment and (2) the Effects of Federal Minimum Wage Legislation on Teenage Employment," Finis Welch and Marvin Kosters, contract no. 91-34-70-58.
4. "Methods of Forecasting Short-term Unemployment Change," Stanley Lebergott, contract no. MDTA 33-64.

C. MICROMODELS OF THE EFFECT OF MINIMUM WAGES ON EMPLOYMENT AND UNEMPLOYMENT

1. "The Impact of Extending Minimum Wages to Private Household Workers," J. Peter Mattila, contract no. 91-39-71-44.
2. "Minimum Wage and Unemployment of Teenagers," James Easley and Robert Fearn, grant to Iowa State University.

D. MICROINDUSTRY STUDIES OF THE DEMAND FOR LABOR

1. "An Economic Analysis of Municipal Government Employment and Wages," Ronald Ehrenberg, contract no. 91-25-73-09.
2. "An Economic Analysis of the Demand for State and Local Government Employees," Ronald Ehrenberg, contract no. 91-17-71-26.
3. "Wage Versus Job Competition," Lester Thurow, contract no. 21-25-73-36.
4. "Short-Run Fluctuations in Employment in Public Utilities," D. J. Smyth, contract no. 91-06-7245.

E. THE DEMAND FOR PARTICULAR GROUPS

1. "Private Household Employment in the U. S.: An Exploratory Project," David Chaplin, contract no. 91-53-69-03.
2. "Professional and Supporting Personnel," Frank Pierson, contract no. 81-40-66-24.
3. "Study of Casual Labor Patterns in Selected Geographical Areas," Charles Kim, contract no. 82-11-72-26.
4. "Survey of Recent College Graduates," Sophia Travis, contract no. 81-11-71-18.
5. "An Analysis of Nonfarm Employment Problems of Farm Laborers," Paul Sultan, contract no. 92-06-72-14.
6. "Effects of Background, Personality, College and Postcollege Experience on Women's Postgraduate Employment," Sandra Tangri, contract no. 91-34-71-02.
7. "Negro Employment in the South," F. Ray Marshall, contract no. 81-19-68-13.
8. "Employment of Ghetto Residents," Bennett Harrison, contract no. 91-11-71-05.
9. "Minority Employment Patterns, 1966," Orley Ashenfelter, contract no. 81-09-67-13.

F. PRODUCTIVITY AND TECHNOLOGICAL CHANGE

1. "Comparative Total Factor Productivity," Dale Jorgensen and L. Christenson, contract no. Ilab-73-6.
2. "Technological Advance in an Expanding Economy: Its Impact on a Cross-Section of the Labor Force," Eva Mueller, contract no. 81-24-67-02.

G. DEMAND-SIDE MEASUREMENT IN THE LABOR MARKET; LABOR MARKET INFORMATION SYSTEMS

1. "A Pilot Study of Response to Job Offers as an Index of Labor Market Conditions," Melvin Reder, contract no. 91-05-70-44.
2. "Experimental Study of the Relationship Between the Growth of Employment and Migration, Utilitizing the Retrospective Data from the 1970 Census of Population," Ann Miller, contract no. 21-42-73-41.

3. "Occupations of the Labor Force According to the Dictionary of Occupational Titles," Ann Miller and Susan Klepp, contract no. 81-40-69-13.
4. "Concepts and Measurements for Manpower and Occupational Analysis," James Scoville, contract no. 81-23-67-23.
5. "Requirements and Design of a Labor Market Information System for a Large Metropolitan Area," Margaret Thal-Larsen, contract no. 71-05-70-03.
6. "The Conceptual Foundations of a Labor Market Information System," Eli Ginzberg, contract no. 71-34-70-04.
7. "Implications of Labor Market Stratification for the Labor Market Information System," Samuel Bowles, contract no. 71-36-71-03.
8. "Internal Labor Markets and Manpower Analysis," Peter Doeringer and Michael Piore, contract no. 81-23-66-22.
9. "Time Series Analysis of Relationships Between Selected Economic and Social Indicators," M. Harvey Brenner, contract no. 81-07-69-22.
10. "Job Vacancies in the Firm and the Labor Market," John Myers, contract no. 81-34-66-13.
11. "An Investigation of the Stability of Hours of Work per Week in Manufacturing, 1947-1969," Ethel Jones, contract no. 91-13-72-36.
12. "Changing Schedules of Work: Patterns and Implications," Albert Glickman and Zenia Brown, contract no. 81-11-72-11.
13. "The Job Content of the U.S. Economy," James Scoville, contract no. MDTA 29-64.
14. "Survey of Employment and Unemployment in Slum Areas," William Milligan, contract no. 81-09-67-10.
15. "Internal Labor Markets, Technological Change, and Labor Force Adjustment," Michael Piore and Peter Doeringer, contract no. MDTA 38-64.

H. MANPOWER PROGRAMS AND LABOR DEMAND

1. "Some Aggregate Effects of Manpower Programs on Long-Run Economic Growth and on Short-Run Fluctuations in Employment," Leonard Hausman, contract no. 51-25-71-05.
2. "Second Year Report on Systems Analysis and the Labor Market," Orley Ashenfelter, contract no. 81-23-67-19.

II. Supply

A. LABOR SUPPLY FUNCTIONS AND LABOR FORCE BEHAVIOR

1. "The Emergence of a Service Society: Demographic-Sociological Aspects of the Sectoral Transformation of the Labor Force in the U.S., 1940-1970," Harley Browning, contract no. 21-48-73-45.
2. "Static and Dynamic Labor Supply Functions and Public Policy Models," Edward Kalachek, contract no. 21-29-73-49.
3. "The Youth Labor Market," Edward Kalachek, contract no. 81-09-66-31.
4. "Transition from School to Work in Selected Countries," Franz Groemping, contract no. 81-09-68-08.

5. "Determinants and Consequences of Modes of Entry into the Labor Force," Peter Rossi, contract no. 91-24-71-01.
6. "Youth in Transition," Jerald Bachman, contract no. 81-24-68-33.
7. "The Emerging Labor Force," Seymour Wolfbein, grant to Temple University.
8. "Development of Stochastic Labor Force and Working Life Models," Haskel Benishay, contract no. 91-34-67-07.
9. "Entry into the American Labor Force," Michael Ornstein, contract no. 91-24-71-01.
10. "Dynamic Analysis of the Labor Force Behavior of Men and Youth," Belton Fleisher, contract no. 91-39-71-43.
11. "National Longitudinal Studies of the Labor Force Behavior of National Samples of Men (45-59), Women (30-44), and Male and Female Youth (14-24)," Herbert Parnes, contract no. 82-39-72-21.
12. "Population, Labor Force, and Long Swings in Economic Growth: The American Experience," Richard Easterlin, contract no. MDTA 20-63.
13. "Labor Force and School Participation of Teenagers," Robert Fearn, grant to North Carolina State.
14. "An Analysis of Forces Underlying Decisions of Potential Workers to Refrain from Labor Force Participation," E. E. Liebhafsky, contract no. 81-42-04.

B. JOB SEARCH, JOB TURNOVER STUDIES

1. "Job Search Survey," Sophia C. Travis, contract no. 20-11-73-04.
2. "Exploratory Empirical Research on the Pathology of Secondary Labor Markets," Robert E. Hall, contract no. 91-05-70-37.
3. "Labor Turnover, Racial Unemployment Differentials, and the Dual Labor Market Hypothesis," Robert J. Flanigan, contract no. 91-17-72-32.
4. "Supplemental Labor Market Information as a Means to Increase the Effectiveness of Job-Search Activity," Jacob J. Kaufman and David Stevens, contract no. 81-40-67-09.
5. "Bridging the Employment Gap, Strategies for Success and Causes, Consequences and Cures for Labor Turnover," grant to Norfolk State College.
6. "Racial Differences in Job Search Patterns," William Pace, grant to North Carolina State.

C. LABOR MOBILITY AND MIGRATION

1. "Labor Mobility and Income Change," George Delahanty, contract no. 91-15-70-12.
2. "The Relationship Between Unemployment and Commuting Within Geographical Areas," Louis H. Stern, contract no. 91-46-68-48.
3. "Relationships Between Changing Residence Location and Labor Performance for Black New Resident Households in an Inner Suburb," Sara Smith Sutker, contract no. 91-29-71-29.
4. "Blue to White Collar Job Mobility," James Stern and David Johnson, contract no. MDTA 14-63.

5. "Immigrants and the American Labor Market," David North and William G. Weissert.

D. UNEMPLOYMENT—SUPPLY-SIDE STUDIES

1. "Why Do Blacks and Women Have High Unemployment Rates?" Nancy Barrett, contract no. 91-11-72-40.
2. "Strategic Factors in Urban Unemployment," Stanley Friedlander, contract no. 81-34-68-44.
3. "Unemployment Among Black Teenage Females in Urban Poverty Neighborhoods," Phyllis Wallace, contract no. 41-0-004-34.
4. "Youth and Unemployment: Frictions in the Threshold of the Work Career," Herbert Heneman, contract no. 81-22-01.
5. "Unemployment Among New Labor Market Entrants," Melvin Reder, contract no. 91-05-68-34.
6. "Unemployment Rates and Employment Characteristics for Scientists and Engineers," Robert Cain, contract no. 82-11-71-28.

E. OCCUPATIONAL MEASUREMENT AND OCCUPATIONAL CHOICE

1. "Occupational Choice," Michael Boskin, contract no. 91-06-72-28.
2. "Preparation of CPS Schedules for a Comparative Analysis of Occupations Under Census Bureau and DOJ Classification Systems," Stanley Greene, contract no. 20-11-73-05.
3. "Analysis of Occupational Mobility Through Use of Longitudinal Surveys Data, with a Supplementary Analysis of Response Variability," Ann Miller, contract no. 21-42-73-05.
4. "Occupational Licensing and the Supply of Nonprofessional Manpower," Educational Testing Service, contract no. 81-32-69-32.

F. HUMAN CAPITAL AND WAGE DETERMINATION MODELS

1. "Returns from Investment in Human Capital," Thomas Johnson, grant to Iowa State University.
2. "Racial Relative Incomes," Alice Kidder, Orley Ashenfelter, and Flourney Coles, grant to Atlanta University.
3. "Occupational Education as a Source of Economic Growth," August Bolino, contract no. 91-11-72-25.

G. LABOR SUPPLY AMONG LOW-INCOME GROUPS

1. "Public Transfer Payments and Labor Force Participation," William Carter, Joseph Eichenholz, et al., contract no. 91-09-70-03.
2. "Labor Force Nonparticipation of Males in Urban Poor Areas," Karen Koziara, contract no. 91-40-68-08.
3. "Welfare Careers and Low Wage Employment," Louis Ferman and Joe Miller (Final Report: "Low Wages and the Working Poor," Barry Bluestone, William Murphy, and Mary Stevenson), contract no. 51-24-69-05.

4. "The Labor Supply for Lower Level Occupations, 1960-1980," Leonard Lecht, contract no. 21-11-73-02.
5. "Service Employment, Collective Bargaining, and the Low-Wage Labor Market," Peter Doeringer, contract no. 81-23-70-08.
6. "A Study: Those not Working in a Tight Labor Market," Arthur Greenleigh, contract no. 81-34-66-33.
7. "Labor Market Segmentation," Richard C. Edwards, David M. Gordon, and Michael Reich, contract no. 71-36-71-03.

H. WORKERS' ATTITUDES

1. "The Work Attitudes and Early Occupational Experiences of Young Men—Analysis Based on a 4-Year Longitudinal Study," Jerald Graybill, contract no. 81-26-72-05.
2. "Effectiveness in Work Roles," Stanley Seashore, contract no. 92-26-72-35.
3. "Technology, Division of Labor and Alienation from Work," John Shepard, contract no. 91-23-69-34.
4. "The Job Attitudes of Workers from Different Ethnic Backgrounds," Raymond Katzell, Robert Ewen, and Abraham Korman, contract no. 41-8-006-34.
5. "Influence of Psychological Attributes, Employment Search Patterns, Vocational Choice, and Demographic Characteristics on Earnings of Workers Terminated in a Plant Closure," James Stern, contract no. 91-55-73-04.

Appendix B: A Classification of Topics of Published Articles Listed in the Journal of Economic Literature, *1971-1974, Dealing with Labor Demand and Supply*

The separation of articles into two categories, labor demand and labor supply, is inevitably somewhat artificial, if not outright misleading. The operations of the labor market and the outcomes we observe—wages, employment, unemployment, occupational and industrial allocations of numbers and types of workers—are defined by economists to result from the interaction of supply and demand forces. Thus, most articles about labor market processes and labor market outcomes analyze both supply and demand factors. The separation is one of convenience and is based on my understanding of an uncodified tradition in labor economics about which topics are predominantly examined from the perspective or the context of the demand or supply side of the labor market. An additional and probably large source of error in our classification results from the fact that we read or were familiar with only a small fraction of the articles.

The subtopics are also only crude designations. Each article was listed in only one category, which is another limitation on the scope of coverage. The captions of the articles were listed separately unless the titles were so similar that we simply added numbers in parentheses to indicate several articles on the same topic.

Table 4.1: A Classification of Topics of Published Articles Listed in the *Journal of Economic Literature*, 1971-1974, Dealing with Labor Demand

Demand		
Employment Models of Firm Behavior	firm labor hoarding model effects of work training programs employment response with supply constraints concentration and employment fluctuations elasticity of subst. between different types of labor	effects of multinationals on labor demand optimal control model of labor demand do employers of trainees gain the most from manpower training role of overtime hours wage differentials in dynamic theory of firm
Employment-Unemployment, and Inflation (macro)	optimal stabilization paths foreign trade effects (3)* discouraged workers and unemployed (2) effects of labor misallocation welfare costs of unemployment shifting the Phillips curve through manpower policy effect of labor force structure effects of unemployment structure inflation vs. unemployment (3) regional unemployment effect	structural unemployment reconsidered employment in cities with different industrial structures spectral analysis of unemployment spatial distribution of unemployment by occupation seasonal components of unemployment secondary labor and seasonal unemployment natural rate of unemployment unemployment dispersion effect Phillips curve vs. accelerationists unions' effect on Phillips curve unemployment and inflation
Industry Specific	construction (3) elasticity of demand for farm workers manufacturing	service industries impact of state and local government spending
Occupational or Demographic Group	engineers and scientists (4) min. wage effect on household maids min. wage effect on low-wage labor min. wage effect on farm labor production vs. nonproduction workers	determinants of unemployment in 6 occupations employment of urban poor min. wage effect on teenagers (4) employment of school age youth determinants of labor market success of young men

*Numbers in parentheses refer to the number of different articles apparently dealing with the identical subject.

Table 4.1 (cont.)

Job Creation/ Development Wage Subsidies	job creation vs. welfare	public employment and economic stability
	taxes and subsidies effect on employment	employment subsidies
	work for relief recipients	use of bonuses and quotas
Wage-Income Differentials	wage differentials—North-South	wage difference and unemployment
	regional difference in wages	
Technological Change	effect on composition of American labor force	technical progress and wage differentials
	technological absorption and unemployment	
Discrimination	wage	model of disc. with interdependent utilities
	use of wage bonuses to remedy	in public service employment placements
	stochastic model of	managerial disc.
	against women (2)	blacks in building trades
	decline of	tech. progress and wage differentials
	in apprenticeship programs	in labor markets
	of employers against disadvantaged applicants	industry wage
	occupational	sex and income inequality
	in construction	racial earnings difference
	wage disc.-employment segregation	sex and pay difference
		labor market changes for blacks
Dual Labor Markets Segmented Labor Markets	dual labor market and manpower policy	dual labor market and urban blacks
	segmented markets (2)	
	low-wage employment	
	dual labor market model	

Table 4.1 (cont.)

Data Generating and Measurement	measuring subemployment in urban areas improving wage index surveys measurement of human capital in U.S.

Table 4.2: A Classification of Topics of Published Articles Listed in the *Journal of Economic Literature*, 1971-1974, Dealing with Labor Supply

Supply		
Job Search	absenteeism	index of effectiveness
	job search theory (4)	effect of unemployment insurance
	quit rates analysis	time series analysis of lay-offs
	unemployment and vacancies	
Unemployment (micro)	youths (2)	urban
	college grads	urban blacks
	by household relationship	personal attributes and duration of unemployment
Labor Mobility	college grads	migration of professionals
	returns to Southern outmigration for blacks	rural urban for blacks
	interstate migration	occupational mobility in central cities
	in times of high demand	industry mobility and income
	of unemployed engineers	determinants of household migration
	mobility and interregional differentials	upward mobility of low-income workers
	migration of college students	occ. mobility and income
	effects of welfare	
Occupational Choice	women's choice	standing of blacks by area, industry
	bariance of discrimination between occ.	spatial distribution of occ.
	black-white differences in occ. in Southern cities	of low-income workers
	impact of defense expenditures	occ. employment differences of black-white teenagers
	of urban workers	
Labor Force Composition	characteristics of entrants, leavers, and job losers	changing composition of the unemployed
	marital and family characteristics	

Table 4.2 (cont.)

Labor Supply Functions	preference orderings as determinants for women's	optimal lifetime pattern
	effect of children on women's	health impact
	dynamic analysis for women's	for welfare mothers
	disabled men	for secondary workers
	expectations effect	effect of rate of inflation
	value of housewife's time	impact of fiscal redistribution
	married women (2)	probability model of labor supply
	assets effect	availability of empl. effect
	analysis of LFPRs	aggregation functions
	for self-employed proprietors	estimation of substitution and income effects in LFP
	effect of day care availability on women's	in ghetto
	family life cycle allocation of time	effect of education and underemployment
	changes in LFPRs	income redistribution effect
	retirement decisions effect	commuting distance effect
	location of industry effect	taxes effect on labor supply
	women in professions	incentive effects of negative income tax plans
	decline in male LFPRs	
	Keynsian supply function	
	transfer payments effect (3)	
Human Capital	voc.-tech. training benefits	schooling and socioecon. background
	minorities in construction apprenticeship prog.	social returns to quantity and quality of schooling
	adults back to school	foregone earnings effect on demand for schooling
	optimal h.c. investment path	schooling as a screening device
	choice between investment and income	impact on income distribution
	rural high school production functions	earnings of low achievers

Table 4.2 (cont.)

	rates of return for women	specific training and quit rates
	education and econ. growth	elasticity of substitution between educ. groups
	black-white differences in returns	black-white returns from college
	dist. of educational resources in cities	measuring human capital returns (2)
	college enrollment rates of high school grads	and interindustry wages
	skill obsolescence	effect of high school graduation and occupation
	in North-South migration	education and income distribution
	education, learning, and productivity	labor subst. and its implications for educ. planning
	comparative costs of manpower training	
Unions	wage differentials and unions	unions and racial disc.
	unions and quality of labor	
Sociopsychological Factors in Labor Supply	why employees stay?	4-day week
	working conditions	unions view of job redesign
	alienation	employee background and job satisfaction
	job redesign	helping hard-core unempl. adjust to work
Forecasting	month to month labor force changes	racial integration of empl.
	sensitivity analysis	education of workers to 1990
	employment and growth	

Appendix C: OMRD-Supported Research on the Question of Labor Supply Responses to Income, Wage, Rates, and Welfare Reform Plans

1. ASHENFELTER, O. and HECKMAN, J. "The estimation of income and substitution effects in a model of family labor supply." *Econometrica*.
2. BAWDEN, D. L., CAIN, G. G., and HAUSMAN, L. J. (1971) "The Family Assistance Plan: analysis and evaluation." *Public Policy* 19 (Spring): 323-354.
3. BOSKIN, M. J. (1973) "The economics of the labor supply." In G. G. Cain and H. W. Watts, *Income Maintenance and Labor Supply*. New York: Academic Press.

   ______(1967) "The negative income tax and the supply of work effort." *National Tax Journal* 20 (December): 353-367.
4. BOWEN, W. G. and FINEGAN, T. A. (1967) *The Economics of Labor Force Participation*. Princeton, NJ: Princeton University Press.
5. COHEN, M. S., REA, S. A., Jr., and LERMAN, R. I. (1970) "A micro model of labor supply." U.S. Department of Labor, *Bureau of Labor Statistics Staff Paper* 4. Washington, DC: Government Printing Office.
6. FLEISHER, B. M., PARSONS, D. O., and PORTER, R. D. (1973) "Asset adjustments and labor supply of older workers." In G. G. Cain and H. W. Watts, *Income Maintenance and Labor Supply*. New York: Academic Press.
7. HILL, C. R. (1973) "The determinants of labor supply for the working urban poor." In G. G. Cain and H. W. Watts, *Income Maintenance and Labor Supply*. New York: Academic Press.
8. JONES, E. B. "An investigation of the stability of hours of work per week in manufacturing, 1947-1969." Contract no. 91-13-72-36.
9. KESSELMAN, J. (1969) "Labor-supply effects of income, income-work, and wage subsidies." *Journal of Human Resources* 4, 3 (Summer): 275-292.
10. PARKER, C. D. (1971) "The determinants of hours of work of low-income family heads: a statistical analysis." Ph.D. dissertation, Oklahoma State University.
11. REA, S. A., Jr. (1971) "The supply of labor and the incentive effects of income maintenance laws." Ph.D. dissertation, Harvard University.

Chapter 5

Labor Market Operations: A Review of Research

Peter Barth
University of Connecticut

Research regarding the operation of labor markets covers a substantial range of manpower policy concerns. That research must consider how employing and employment-promoting institutions, public and private, and workers and worker organizations, influence and are influenced, in turn, by market structure, dynamics, and effectiveness. Peter Barth examines OMRD activity directed toward understanding these issues with respect to five topics: the firm, the worker, labor market intermediaries, labor market imperfections, and the interrelations of manpower and macroeconomic variables.

This review emphasizes the assessment of individual research studies on their own terms: whether the methods selected by the researcher illuminate fully the problems giving rise to the research; whether findings or other evidence generate support for stated conclusions; and whether the undertaking suffers from any internal inconsistency. Barth also recognizes the need to evaluate labor market research efforts as indices of OMRD performance in providing guidance for manpower policy and program decisions. First, he relates findings that have emerged from one area of labor market research to those derived from other areas, highlighting a significant integrative function that an R&D agency such as OMRD must constantly pursue. Second, he illustrates the various ways in which the institutional location and setting of an R&D office can affect its coverage of a broad subject area. Overlaps among Labor Department units interested in various aspects of employment and training policy—and a desire to minimize the potential for conflict in such a situation—have helped produce patterns of labor market research that may or may not be entirely logical.

Finally, Barth gives numerous examples—summarized in a concluding section of findings and recommendations—of promising new lines of inquiry opened by previous research. Comparing these possibilities to the labor market research interests apparent in the OMRD program at its inception in the early 1960s should give the reader another good general perspective on progress and progression in the field over a decade's time.

Behavioral and social scientists often speak of the cumulative effects of their efforts, particularly in the sense that past research constitutes a foundation for future study and continually revises and strengthens the knowledge base in a discipline or field. No less important is the fact that an R&D agency itself can have cumulative effects in preserving and expanding an area of essential policy study, as OMRD appears to have done with respect to the study of labor markets.

Introduction

The purposes of this report are to review the research sponsored by the Office of Manpower Research and Development (OMRD) of the Manpower Administration and to indicate those areas in which future study may be pursued profitably. Although I have formed certain impressions about the average quality of the work, this paper is not meant to grade the Office on its efforts. While criticism and praise of both individual projects and Office practices do emerge, my principal aim has been to put past research into a perspective that will allow the Office to generate important, useful, and sound research in the future.

A review of the research can be approached in a variety of ways. One of these is to identify subject areas that have received relatively more or less attention in the past. Because the area of labor market operations is extremely open-ended, it would be impossible for a single reviewer to fully summarize or encapsulate all the knowledge generated. Thus, this review will focus on major subjects; it will not analyze every topic within the field of labor market operations. In places I shall attempt to assess in general terms the level of understanding that research has disclosed. Doing this unavoidably means taking subjective positions regarding the worth of particular research projects. The point of such an approach is not to criticize or to praise specific researchers, but to seek generalizations about past efforts that may lead to a higher rate of consistency in the quality of work commissioned in the future. Specifically, in what areas has the quality of research been consistently good or regularly poor? What patterns, if any, emerge from an examination of the previous question? Finally, how might research program production be strengthened?

By what standards can the quality of a set of research projects be judged? There are a number of criteria that might be employed. Surely, the costs of the research must be considered, and contrasted with the costs of alternative ways of achieving comparably convincing findings. This is usually more feasible than quantifying the benefits derived from research findings. Even in the absence of an explicit calculus, it is clear that the decision-maker can often have an implicit valuation in mind. The more basic or abstract the research, for example, the greater the tendency to assess it in terms of originality or inventiveness. Research may also be evaluated on the basis of its timeliness; how well it fits with a continuing stream of information emerging from the entire research community. The relationship of research to policy formulation has also been used to judge the caliber of research products. However, it seems to make no sense at all to judge research solely on the grounds that it has been useful in policy formulation. While strong support can be given to the concept of "practical" or "useful" research, research that is meant to aid policy-makers ought to be evaluated with regard to how specifically it contributed to the success of a particular policy. It is not enough to say that research was an input in decision-making.

While all of these previous criteria could legitimately be employed in evaluating the research efforts supported by OMRD, the standards involved in this review will be somewhat less ambitious and, hopefully, more practical. They include the following: Does the research technique or methodology selected by the researcher allow him to address the essential problem(s) that gave rise to the research effort? Do the findings or evidence presented warrant the stated conclusions? Does the work suffer from any internal inconsistency? In short, the bulk of the work reviewed here will be judged on grounds established by the researchers themselves.

While individual projects can be readily and fairly objectively assessed in these terms, the more challenging task will be to determine whether OMRD has supported a program of research that is in some sense appropriate to both the short- and long-run needs of the Manpower Administration. I admit ruefully that this larger issue of a proper research strategy is never directly confronted in the balance of the paper. Ideally, we ought to evaluate both the merits of an articulated strategy as well as past success in meeting the goals implied by that strategy. Instead, I shall limit the review to identifying certain areas of neglect, to fitting together wherever possible findings and conclusions from related studies of significant topics, and to observing certain patterns that appear to have developed.

Coverage of the Report

OMRD Programs

The entire body of work sponsored by OMRD with respect to labor market operations includes several hundred projects, ranging in size from multivolume reports to brief summaries of research findings. Although I began with some familiarity with the subject matter and had previously read a number of these reports, it quickly became apparent that a review would need to be based on a sampling of previous work rather than the entire literature. This review, then, is based on an examination of a substantial sample arbitrarily drawn from completed R&D reports. Most of the work reviewed involved research, although some experimentation and demonstration (E&D) projects were examined because they were or appeared to have been linked to the research effort. Indeed, to completely divorce a review of research from a review of experimentation and demonstration might suggest that E&D projects do not have a substantial research component or that these modes of inquiry are not often intimately related. Such perceptions are incorrect; an important outcome of a research project may be an experiment or a field demonstration to test some kind of programmatic change.

For several reasons, doctoral and postdoctoral research inducted under the Department's Small Grants Program was not considered at all in this review. First, I have been involved in the past with this program, and my unqualified enthusiasm for it could be construed as bias. Second, a goal of the Small Grants Program is to enlarge and strengthen the community of scholars involved in manpower research. Such an end is entirely appropriate, but ought not be evaluated alongside research that has been generated for purposes that do not include the expansion of the stock of human capital. A final reason for excluding products of the Small Grants Program from the review is that grantee selection is made primarily by a panel of nonagency staff persons and the agency does not monitor intensively a grantee's substantive performance after that point. Thus, the quality of individual projects will vary for reasons largely beyond the control of agency staff.

Research generated specifically under OMRD's Institutional Grants Program was not examined for similar reasons: it has generally been institution-directed rather than agency-directed. Nor, with rare exceptions, were proceedings of conferences sponsored by OMRD generally reviewed. Conference planners, not OMRD staff, generally chose reports to be included in such proceedings; many of the presentations are based on research that has not been sponsored by OMRD.

Selection

National Academy of Sciences staff prepared a listing of research (and to some extent E&D work) sponsored by OMRD since its inception that dealt with labor market operations. When Small Grants projects were eliminated, approximately 500 projects remained. I asked to examine about 110 of these reports, selected on the basis of several criteria. If a title appeared to summarize or evaluate a body of research, I requested it. Work that had received some substantial attention by researchers in the professional literature was also requested (Marshall and Briggs, 1967; Sheppard and Belitsky, 1966; Doeringer and Piore, 1966, 1970). I attempted to get reports covering the entire range of subjects I was examining within the field of labor market operations. I also sought a balance between recently supported projects and earlier funded ones, between work done at universities and that done by contract research firms, between research undertaken by persons whom I regard to be prominent in the field and that conducted by less well-known authors, and between studies that I knew to be relatively loosely monitored by OMRD (in a substantive sense), and those projects to which close guidance and supervision had been given. Additionally, staff at OMRD suggested ten projects that they believed should be incorporated in this review.

For a variety of reasons only about half of the 110 reports were obtained. Thus, my views are based on my reading of somewhat over 50 reports prepared from OMRD.[1]

Topics

I interpreted labor market operations to include research (and E&D) that examines the *processes* whereby workers and employers are brought together and are maintained together in the employment relationship. The primary problem I encountered in defining the scope of my study was not so much the vagueness of its boundaries, but rather that my area so clearly crossed the jurisdictional lines set for other reviews in this volume. I have excluded reference to studies that specifically relate to labor supply or demand and have given little attention to discrimination and other problems that can be discussed in terms of research focusing on special groups in the labor force.

There are additional reasons why this review may not cover the entire area of labor market operations. First, certain subjects fall largely under the purview of agencies in or outside of the Department of Labor *other than* OMRD. For example, since the Fair Labor Standards Act is administered by the Employment Standards Administration, it is this agency that has generally taken the lead for the Department of Labor in studying the effects of the minimum wage on employment and earnings.[2] Second, in some instances, in OMRD research projects may have helped set in motion other, more extensive, undertakings that may or may not have been sponsored by OMRD. For example, it is increasingly difficult to catalog the proliferation of studies using data from the National Longitudinal Surveys sponsored by OMRD. Conversely, on some occasions, OMRD has published work that it did not commission or continued projects that other agencies or sources had begun. Another caveat that the reader—and this writer—must bear in mind is that this overview is based only upon a sample drawn from a large and heterogeneous set of projects; these employ techniques and terminology drawn from the full range of the social sciences, and from disciplines such as engineering, computer sciences, business, education, and health sciences.

Finally, the framework that I have developed to evaluate work done for OMRD is not totally satisfactory, but I have found no better one. It suffers as a classification scheme in that a number of studies might as readily have been considered in other categories and contexts. Moreover, where a research report covered several groups of issues under separate headings, arbitrary decisions had to be made regarding presentation. Essentially, the review examines OMRD research in terms of five major categories:

(1) the employer or the firm;
(2) the worker;
(3) labor market intermediaries;
(4) labor market imperfections; and
(5) manpower in terms of macroeconomic variables

And since so much of the research sponsored by OMRD has dealt with the first two of these subjects, this report will concentrate on those areas.

Research Focused on the Employer

Research that sheds light on employer behavior includes the economist's concept of the demand for labor, but it is also far broader. From the vantage point of labor market operations, such research would examine and attempt to explain the process of recruiting labor, the use of advertising and other techniques to increase the pool of talent from which an employer draws, the testing and screening practices employed by the firm, and the utilization of labor by firms after the individual becomes an employee. Included under the heading of utilization of labor would be the practices of the internal labor market as well as employer training efforts; manpower planning by the firm; and the analysis of turnover ranging from a purely economic treatment of vacancies, separations, and accessions to institutional problems posed by collectively bargained arrangements regarding such turnover.

There is no a priori reason to suppose that research attention ought to be balanced between the subject of employer behavior and the subject of the employee. Still, I am struck by the vast difference between these two areas in the amount of support given by OMRD over the years. The office's preponderant concern with the employee (the supply side) may closely parallel the interests of researchers, judging at least from the general literature. Yet, it seems appropriate to inquire whether OMRD ought to have helped tip the scales toward a more even approach. This is not to argue that no work has been done on the employer side—but rather that far less has been supported than that which explores the employee side.

Employer Hiring Requirements

An important concern high on any future research agenda, is to explain fully how industry sets hiring requirements. The literature on this subject is thin, including various contributions by economists. While economists have given some limited attention to the *changes* in hiring standards over the business cycle and how this may relate to productivity changes, very little attention seems to have been given to the setting of qualitative standards by the employer. Significant questions remain unanswered: under what circumstances do employers become more flexible in their demands? how much do they experiment with standards? what trade-offs in employee characteristics are they willing to consider? what role does a labor organization play in setting these standards? These questions lend themselves to both theoretical and empirical analysis.

An attempt was made to examine several such issues in the work of Diamond and Bedrosian (1970). This study probed hiring patterns in industry by looking at ten occupations, including white- and blue-collar ones, in New York City and St. Louis. Data were sought not only on employer requirements but on hiring procedures and experience after hiring. Information was provided mainly by employers and employment agencies.

Diamond and Bedrosian (1970: 3) found that overblown hiring requirements appeared to be a major source of costly labor turnover. They also suggested that such standards contribute to the "labor shortage which existed in virtually all of the occupations." Seemingly unrealistic or unnecessary standards hurt the disadvantaged worker who, typically, did not meet the requirements set by the firm. Why should employers deprive themselves of necessary labor and thereby forego profits? Diamond and Bedrosian found that although employers asserted that high standards were necessary to identify workers with high potential for promotion, few of the workers hired were vertically mobile. The authors also found little correlation between measures of job performance and age, sex, education, or experience among workers.

On the basis of the findings, Diamond and Bedrosian recommended that employers be educated as to the negative consequences of overly stringent hiring criteria; once employers become aware of their seemingly irrational behavior, they would modify practices accordingly. Although such a suggestion is naive, this is the type of research project that can lead to the formulation and testing of other hypotheses and policy prescriptions through experimentation or demonstration efforts. Employers with similar occupational needs might be "educated" in a variety of ways while others were held as a control group. Comparative experiences in terms of productivity, turnover, and future hiring patterns could then be observed. My own view is that we still do not well understand the ways in which employers set hiring standards, jeopardizing themselves by overpaying labor relative to their marginal products. Further, if Diamond and Bedrosian are correct, costly turnover also results from such practices. Their position, however, leaves unanswered the question of why more rational employers do not enter the picture, hire according to more realistic standards, avoid such unreasonable costs, and drive from the market less efficient competitors.

Another striking finding in the Diamond and Bedrosian study (1970) is that few firms have written statements outlining hiring requirements. Surely, this is enlightening to agencies charged with promoting equal employment opportunity and deserves some further attention in that vein. It would be useful to learn if this pattern of employer behavior has shifted with wider enforcement of equal employment laws.

The role that potential upward progression plays in the hiring process also warrants further inquiry. Do employers set standards for entry level positions on the basis of the immediate or short-run needs to fill those positions or are entry level job standards related to future needs defined by progression ladders within the firm? Do collective bargaining rules that apply to advancement in the firm affect hiring requirements? Why do some firms attempt to attract high quality (and relatively high wage) labor while competing firms in the same industry prefer to hire less skilled (and relatively low wage) employees? In either case, wages may equal marginal products, but the quantity of labor per unit of output will vary. What kinds of employers seek to develop reputations as high wage firms? What is the relationship between the quantity and the type of capital employed and the quantity of labor sought? In the past, economists have been interested primarily in the quantitative and not the qualitative dimensions of the demand for labor. Yet, the implications of such qualitative issues for manpower problems ranging from automation to the employment of the disadvantaged worker are obvious. The importance of such issues also tends to belie the main Diamond and Bedrosian prescriptions of educating employers as a substantial new direction for manpower policy.

A different view of the employer is developed in the significant work of Doeringer and Piore (1970) on internal labor markets, as are different policy prescriptions. Their work refines and extends studies originated earlier at Harvard University, for example, those by Dunlop and Livernesh. It can be suggested that internal labor market theory represents the first major attempt in the post-World War II era to overhaul the neoclassical view of the labor market. As such, OMRD's investments in refining this approach have been absolutely appropriate.

The Doeringer and Piore report (1970) was an effort to define internal labor markets, and to explain how they function, how they originated and how the concept can lead to a better understanding of how manpower programs might succeed. To the extent that it blends theories drawn from a variety of disciplines in the social sciences the work is truly innovative. It is also unlike many other studies prepared for OMRD and for that matter unlike the professional journal literature on this subject in that it explicitly accepts elements of neoclassical analysis in some places, while rejecting the use of that traditional economic framework in others. Where the study concentrates on assertions based upon some personal and limited observations, rather than upon analysis yielding testable hypotheses, it is somewhat unconvincing. At the same time, because it is so full of assertions, the study can be seen as an important point of departure for other researchers. While

OMRD has supported some later research, such as Flanagan (1973) and Edwards, Gordon, and Reich (1973), which have built upon the dual labor market hypothesis, these extensions or modifications have not dealt directly with the central issue of existence of an internal-external dichotomy and with problems surrounding the manner in which firms recruit, retain, and reward, and advance their work force.

While the comprehensiveness of the Doeringer and Piore study prevents a complete review here, several points should be highlighted. The authors begin by categorizing internal and external labor markets. They do not, however, make clear the conditions for predicting which jobs are to be within the external labor market—where competitive forces contribute to the setting of the wage and the allocation of labor—and which are within the internal labor market—where workers are largely insulated from the vagaries of market forces. Indeed, it appears in this and particularly in subsequent related work on segmented labor markets that for every factual observation that is not in accordance with a propounded theory, the theory is modified or qualified. Nevertheless, the widespread attention that the early work by Doeringer and Piore has received suggests that it be tested empirically and on that basis further developed or rejected. While two excellent recent reviews (Cain, 1975; Stigler, 1972) examine the cases for the "dual-radical" or the segmented labor market hypotheses, further descriptive work, hypothesis formulation, and empirical testing of models of the internal labor market are needed to follow-up in the area of thought.

Turnover in the Labor Market

OMRD has not supported a significant share of the growing body of literature in the area of labor market turnover. Specifically, a number of economists have attempted to develop models or to measure correlates of the components of labor turnover, including quit rates, lay-off rates, discharges, new hires, and vacancies.[3] Although such work is relevant to the mission of the Manpower Administration, it may have been given limited attention because of its tenuous relationship to operational aspects of manpower training programs and because of its complex connection to manpower policy. Still, many turnover studies do not involve the generation of new bodies of data and therefore would not be expensive to fund. Detailed job histories developed in the National Longitudinal Surveys will allow some analysis of turnover, but only from the perspective of the worker. Employer behavior will still be inadequately understood.

An interesting publication along different lines was supported by OMRD at a time when the ability of government to collect vacancy rate data was uncertain. The study by Myers and Creamer (1967) of the National Industrial Conference Board was not financed by OMRD, but the volume presenting their finding was. Their work represented a somewhat different approach than that taken by the BLS to determine if job vacancy statistics could be collected; as such, it was a productive follow-up to the Gordon Report of 1962. Myers and Creamer concluded that such data could be collected, that the costs of procuring such data were not high relative to benefits, that the quality of the data made them superior to other alternatives such as help wanted indexes as an indicator of employer behavior, and that there was no reason not to proceed to a regular national survey.

Although the study by itself may not have persuaded the Manpower Administration to support the collection of such data, the project was a useful supplement to other work being done on this problem. Though OMRD's support was apparently limited to having the study published, such dissemination efforts are often inexpensive ways to bring significant fundings to the attention of the research community. OMRD should be encouraged by this project to pursue similar, inexpensive kinds of efforts. It is also important to note that this study was one of the few instances where OMRD supported work of a largely, if not exclusively, methodological character. This reviewer at least found that virtually no attention has been given to research whose sole end is to improve techniques, data, or instruments that are potentially employable by researchers in the manpower field.

Summary

Research focusing on employers has generally dwelled upon the hiring process or, to a lesser extent, on worker separations. Perhaps this orientation derives from a predisposition of the Manpower Administration to view the "manpower problem" largely in terms of unemployment and the inability of some workers to retain jobs. Yet, from the perspective of either the individual worker or the economy as a whole, I believe there exists a host of difficult and poorly understood issues that extend well beyond matters usually associated with being cyclically or structurally unemployed. Specifically, I suggest that some attention can and should be given to the following: the quality of work as viewed by the employee in terms of safety and health, fringe benefits, job security, the personal sense of worth or satisfaction emanating from the work process or from its setting, the ability to adjust the hours one works, and a host of other issues. Each of these issues ought to be evaluated in terms of labor turnover and employer recruiting practices. These matters all represent important characteristics of the employment taken by a worker. As such, they must be considered in an assessment of the success of our various training programs. Because so little is known about them, they are usually not explicitly considered in such evaluations. Typically, economists have tucked them away from consideration by incorporating them into the wage. This splendid cop-out allows a limitless range of significant questions to be ignored.

From the perspective of the employer, we know precious little about how he views such variables, under what circumstances he manipulates them, and the extent of variability in them that exists within the firm and across firms. For example, a study is badly needed that will integrate and evaluate the various techniques that quantify the value of fringe benefits on an interindustry basis. While different agencies of government have worked with such estimates—as have a host of private groups—a methodological and quantitative reconciliation is badly needed. Such a piece of research would be a service to the labor economics research community.

Another interesting area of inquiry that has not been addressed is the wage-setting behavior of unorganized firms. Although modern job search literature along with a volume of previous research of a less sophisticated sort gives very close attention to workers' reservation wages (the lowest pay a person will accept to take work). I know of no analog on the employer side. Thus, unemployed workers may not find work because employers maintain sticky wage rates rather than dropping them—at least at the entry level for new employees—at a time of substantial surplus labor. Since so much attention has been given to the reluctance of workers to lower their reservation wages, it is surprising that parallel behavior of employers has not received at least some attention. Certainly, wage cutting is a phenomenon that occurred with some regularity during recessions and "panics" of the 19th century and the early years of the 20th century. It is by no means clear what rigidities, aside from collective bargaining agreements, have caused such behavior to disappear. Possibly, it still exists in a form that is not readily identifiable. Yet, with more than three-quarters of the labor force outside of trade unions, one might expect to find more examples of wage cutting than appear to exist during periods of recession.

Finally, very little attention has been given to manpower planning and human resource development by the private sector. Here, too, the issue is not employment or unemployment but, rather, the utilization of factors after they are employed. Does an apparent growth of interest in manpower planning and human resource accounting within the private sector suggest that labor will be utilized more efficiently in the future? How serious is the interest, overall? In what ways might the public sector help support programs undertaken largely through private initiative? The only study of the sort I describe here that has been supported by OMRD was prepared in 1968 as an "exploratory probe" by Heneman (1968). Unfortunately, that study was based on a very limited nonrandom sample and many of the findings are based on cell sizes of three or four observations. The study was not intended to be an in-depth analysis, and little attention was given to the costs or benefits of manpower forecasting. The report does note, however, that the process of forecasting was rapidly becoming more common, at least in firms with 500 or more employees. It is surprising that no follow-up was done to this preliminary inquiry.

Research Focused on the Employee

Compared to the volume of research on employer behavior, far more work has appeared in the professional literature and has been supported by OMRD dealing with workers (or potential employees). This subject area includes all dimensions of labor supply as well as issues related to labor market information, labor mobility and occupational choice, job search techniques and behavior, training and the worker, upgrading of employees, special occupations and their special labor markets, and the activities of labor organizations as they affect the rank and file. Clearly, some of the projects reviewed under these headings could easily be fitted into other sections, but the significance of any individual project is not affected by my choice of classifications.

Labor Market Information

Until the early 1960s, economists generally paid little attention to the issue of labor market information. In neoclassical analyses, information was "perfect"—it could be acquired at no cost by firms and by workers who could accordingly make decisions appropriate to profit and utility-maximizing behavior. Models that incorporated the presence of some imperfections generally dealt with the existence of labor organizations or with product markets that were not purely competitive. Beginning with Stigler's classic piece, "Information in the Labor Market"(1972), neoclassical theorists began incorporating imperfect information and job search costs into their models in order to help reconcile them with observed behavior. Critics of this approach argued, in turn, that the neoclassicist was now able to explain away all phenomena that previously had seemed irreconcilable with the theory, but without necessarily explaining them. In any case, interest in the subject was further heightened in the early 1960s by the apparent inability to reduce unemployment quickly for certain classes of workers despite the obvious existence of areas of labor shortage in some sectors. Perhaps this less than satisfactory merging of supply and demand forces was a result of inadequate information on the part of firms and workers about their mutual availability. One result of these factors was a growing awareness of the need for more and better information on the labor market. Such information could assist the parties directly involved as well as interested groups such as policy-makers, planners, and educators. By 1968, the Manpower Development and Training Act was amended to direct the Department of Labor to set up a comprehensive labor market information program. Thus, a significant amount of research dealing with labor market information has been generated by OMRD.

USE OF AVAILABLE DATA

A number of studies supported by OMRD in this area are outstanding. One of these was a project by Malcolm Cohen et al. of the University of Michigan (1972). Its purpose was to evaluate the need for new labor market information, as well as to develop methods for better employing currently available statistical and administrative data. Not only was the contractor charged with these tasks, he was also asked to demonstrate various information technologies which might improve the delivery of labor market information. Cohen and his colleagues did not restrict themselves to a single methodology; indeed, the variety of approaches used by them is one of the interesting and valuable features of their work. They developed computer programs to allow local employment service personnel and others to readily access existing information. They also developed sophisticated econometric models to allow planners to forecast labor supply and labor demand in order to help estimate a "universe of need" for training or to project the level of benefit expirations under the unemployment insurance program.

A remarkable aspect of this project is that although the report contained elaborate and sophisticated work, the day-to-day problems of both the planners of a labor market information system and the ultimate users of such a system seemed to be explicitly recognized. Indeed, perhaps the most laudable aspect of this document is that it begins by formulating the questions that program people ought to ask; it then sets about to answer them in ways that can be readily understood and applied by them. The authors not only posed alternative methods for dealing with policy questions, they costed these out, providing planners with an entire package—a rarity in the contract research field generally. This kind of report helped clarify why so few policy decisions appear to result from governmental R&D findings. Unless a researcher is able to place himself in the position of the decision-maker, he may not be able to identify *all* questions that will necessarily arise in the process of instituting a policy or policy recommendation. For example, Cohen and his colleagues spelled out how access to more information would help staff in the field. Beyond specifying those additional data too costly to collect relative to their use, and those that need to be obtained, the researchers evaluated the desirability of doing this on a statewide basis. They found that regional information centers ought to be promoted rather than the less efficient, but more traditional way of generating and analyzing data—on a state-by-state basis.

COUNSELING AND PLACEMENT AGENCIES

An equally comprehensive study focusing on substantially different questions regarding labor market information and the process involved in its dissemination and use was conducted by Thal-Larsen et al. (1970). The report's scrupulous attention to detail and technique also suggest that Thal-Larsen's substantial list of findings and recommendations be subjected to serious and widespread attention. The purposes of the Thal-Larsen study were to examine the processes of counseling and placement provided by private employment agencies and by the public Employment Service, the counseling provided by local schools and their efforts at preparing students for the world of employment, and labor market information needs of various potential users. That this study was limited to California's Bay Area does not diminish the importance of its findings or conclusions. Although many new data were generated through interviews of school, Employment Service and employment agency personnel, some useful information also was drawn from an earlier study by Gordon and Thal-Larsen (1969).

The following represents a very brief summary of Thal-Larsen's findings and conclusions. Both the Employment Service and local schools were badly undersupported in terms of their respective missions. Resource inadequacies were particularly acute in the Employment Service as it was expected to maintain its traditional labor exchange function at the same time that it acquired responsibilities as a manpower-antipoverty agency. The growth of private employment agencies during the 1960s was attributed by Thal-Larsen to this growing burden on Employment Service operations. The quantity and quality of counseling in the local schools was also judged to be poor. The increased scarcity of resources in both the Employment Service and in schools contributed directly to the problem of inadequate counseling of both students and workers.

The Employment Service focused more on the disadvantaged, while the private agencies specialized largely in the placement activity of the "advantaged." Thal-Larsen notes that a significant number of persons were not attractive to either type of agency and "fell between the cracks." These persons generally were least able to afford to pay for the services of the private agencies. For this reason, possible strategy of narrowing further Employment Service responsibility for assisting the disadvantaged, leaving all other placement activities to private agencies.

In most states including California, private sector employment agencies are subject to some public regulation. Thal-Larsen warns that continued rapid growth of the private agencies could weaken monitoring, opening the door to such abuses as existed in preregulation days. The author mildly endorses state licensing of private placement agencies as one means to maintain their integrity.

Thal-Larsen's findings also suggest that the proliferation of manpower programs for special groups has undermined the efficiency of all Employment Service programs. She recommends, as many others have, an end to expansion of the number of categoric programs that the Employment Service must administer. She also recommends several other approaches to improve the delivery system of the Employment Service. Interestingly, she found that successful private agencies gave considerable attention to the personality traits of their counselors. No such emphasis was found to exist in the public sector. Thal-Larsen suggests that this could have contributed to problems there of dealing with clients. Additionally, she tentatively reiterates a familiar theme—greater division of labor among Employment Service staff, particularly as it might apply to worker counseling. Along these lines, she speculates that counseling for the disadvantaged might be moved out of the Employment Service into another agency or branch not responsible for the placement of workers in jobs.

Such issues and prescriptions have been debated and acted upon frequently since the passage of MDTA. Thal-Larsen's contribution to the debate emerges from her apparent objectivity in analyzing not only the Employment Service, but in studying sources of guidance, counseling and placement assistance that supplement the work of the Employment Service. The comprehensiveness of this study permits recommendations that treat the schools, the Employment Service, and the private employment agencies as a system having certain overall capacities—where the status and capabilities of each element of the system should be viewed in relation to those of other elements.

This is only a very brief assessment of a very rich report. Like the Cohen study, Thal-Larsen's deserves a great deal of credit for integrating an academic and a "practical" perspective, leading to policy recommendations that must be considered seriously by the entire community of manpower specialists.

A different overview of the role of the public sector in generating a more comprehensive labor market information system was attempted by Yavitz, Morse and Dutka (1973). Unfortunately, the effort does not provide that at all. While there are typically incisive comments in the introduction by Eli Ginzberg, the book does not contain any articulated theory, testable hypotheses, new data analysis or manipulation of data. As such it must be viewed as a highly speculative "think-piece," intended to provoke or stimulate others in their own research on labor market information problems. Few references to this study, however, have been found by me in other literature on the subject.

NEW DATA AND DATA SOURCES

Another study, "Supplemental Labor Market Information as a Means to Increase the Effectiveness of Job Search Activity" by David Stevens (1968) is a novel effort to test whether greater knowledge will assist workers in their own (self-) placement activities. In some ways, the work deserves substantial attention by the community that performs experimental and demonstration work, the effort provides a model, methodologically, of what an experimental or demonstration project should contain in operation and in its subsequent documentation.

Stevens begins with a set of related questions from which he derives certain testable hypotheses. He then argues that a controlled experiment will best serve to examine these hypotheses. The experiment seems well designed and contains experimental and control groups of adequate size to allow sufficient data to be generated to provide reliable measurements. The author avoids costly recreation of prior study by carefully searching and reviewing relevant literature. A theoretical section precedes the empirical portion of the work, allowing Stevens to anticipate how various potential outcomes of the experiment might be interpreted. The host of operational decisions made in the process of carrying out the experiment are explained in helpful detail. Data generated are well manipulated—the techniques used to analyze the data are appropriate. By contrast, some researchers tend to use highly sophisticated and even pretentious techniques when working with very crude data, while others have underutilized their data by applying superficial or elementary analysis when more refined techniques would be appropriate. Stevens acknowledges that his findings are relatively modest; he clearly notes the shortcomings in his own study. This description of the Stevens piece suggests some rudimentary and minimal criteria for undertaking or evaluating future E&D work.

Substantively, Stevens's project attempts to determine if supplemental labor market information helps increase the effectiveness of job search behavior. Seven hundred seventy-seven male registrants, clients of a single Employment Service office in Pittsburgh who fell into a single broad occupational category, were divided at random into an experimental and a control group of comparable size. The experimental group was given supplementary information about job opportunities and their subsequent experience was compared to that of the control group on the basis of several variables, including the length of time taken to find work and the number of employer contacts made. Black workers in the experimental group had more success in finding work than did blacks in the control group, but the former did not attribute their good fortune to the supplemental labor market information they received. No comparable findings were apparent among the white workers. The finding with respect to the number of contacts made by the experimental and control groups is somewhat more ambiguous.

If the Stevens study has a flaw, it rests with the basic question raised, rather than with the way the work was carried out. Few persons would argue against the proposition that additional information about available job openings, together with information about location, terms of employment, conditions on the job, advancement opportunities, and employer requirements would serve to reduce unemployment for some workers. Thus, Stevens's findings do not mean that supplemental or additional job information does not help people find work more rapidly.

Rather, what we need to know and do not learn from this study are the *kinds* of information that workers need in order to improve the process of job search (to reduce the time it takes to find work of the sort that would have been found without such information or to find "better" employment within a given amount of time) and the most cost-effective way of delivering that knowledge to workers. Stevens was apparently not asked to pursue either of these matters. The first issue lends itself to further controlled experimentation, while the second may, I believe, be probed more profitably by demonstration or research than by experimentation. For example, demonstration-research projects could be designed that used different modes of information delivery to unemployed or underemployed persons. Strategies for transmission might center—in various combinations—on (closed-circuit) television programming, civic groups, labor unions, religious organizations, private employment agencies, schools, and special newspaper supplements.

While the Stevens study focused on the information needs of workers, a recent report by the Olympus Research Corporation (1973), "A Study to Test the Feasibility of Determining Whether Classified Want Ads in Daily Newspapers Are an Accurate Reflection of Local Labor Markets and of Significance to Employers and Job Seekers," attempted to examine the quality of that traditional economic indicator as a source of labor market information. The study reports that the usefulness of labor market information in newspaper help wanted advertisements is very limited. Ads placed by private employment agencies are largely "come-ons"—primarily a form of advertising for the agencies. Few firms used such advertising; not surprisingly, those that did found it useful. Some inverse correlation was found between unemployment rates and help wanted advertising. The report asserts that want ads, could be made more useful to the "hapless job seeker," although it does not make clear how such an outcome might be obtained. Job seekers are said to have a low opinion of the ads. Unfortunately, problems in the conception and development of this project, as well as certain methodological difficulties, suggest that the research issues involved here are treated lightly.

The study is limited to two cities, selected on the rather unrepresentative basis that ORC has offices in both of them. Though the title suggests that daily newspapers will be scrutinized, only Sunday issues are examined. Moreover ORC finds that a major change in the advertising format by the Salt Lake City newspaper during the time period under study rendered any time series data for that paper unusable. Thus, the only major Sunday newspaper studied was in San Francisco.

Only persons who reported using want ads and who were present at the Employment Service were surveyed. Persons who do not use the Employment Service are in many respects, at least according to the Thal-Larsen findings, a different class of worker than those who do; a sample drawn from that group would have been instructive. Additionally, want ads serve as a source of information for persons not unemployed but contemplating either changing jobs or entering the labor force; they also provide individuals, firms, and others with data on prevailing wage levels. These aspects of employment advertising are not confronted in the report. More significantly, data that are developed need to be analyzed in terms of multivariate analysis to allow for the presence of trends, seasonality, and other factors. Only some simple correlations are presented in the report, rendering the conclusions regarding the value of such advertising as an indicator of labor market conditions highly suspect. Better analyses of this question have already been done by both the Conference Board and the National Bureau of Economic Research. The usefulness of newspaper advertising to a variety of persons is a very important matter that unfortunately has received only scant attention by the research community thus far; further inquiry by OMRD is surely warranted.

SUMMARY

To summarize OMRD's contributions to the subject of labor market information it is essential to delineate the various users of such information. The kinds of information sought by policy-makers at the national level, CETA planners locally, program managers, employers, (potential) employees, labor organizations, local government policy-makers, the Employment Service, and others are quite different. Research into this subject should shed some light on the public and private costs and benefits of acquiring and transmitting such information to each of these various potential users; in so doing it can begin to set a framework for establishing priorities information collection. Malcolm Cohen's study fits nicely into such a research strategy since it deals with the needs of local and regional government operatives. Margaret Thal-Larsen's work evaluates the ability of the school system, the Employment Service, and private employment agencies to use such information. Nonetheless, it is fair to conclude that research has only barely begun to fill out this framework. Global questions remain, such as the extent to which more and better labor market information can contribute to reducing structural unemployment, increasing lifetime earnings, stimulating or inhibiting labor mobility, and raising the productivity of labor. Stevens's work is a possible point of departure on some of these issues. While OMRD has given considerable attention to the matter of labor market information, needs in relation to the state of knowledge in this field are very great. Some of the work supported by OMRD enhance the knowledge base substantially, but much more could be done before diminishing returns occur.

Processes of Job Search

OMRD has shown far less interest in the subject of job search, closely related to the area of labor market information. While the literature in this field is burgeoning, it must be treated dichotomously; aside from the shared term "job search," there is virtually no commonality between two currently popular approaches to the subject. One approach is epitomized by the introduction and Part I of a volume edited by Phelps (1970), which rationalizes the process of job search and explicitly incorporates it into the supply side of (usually) dynamic models of the labor market. In the Phelps volume (but not in all of the work of this genre) macroeconomic phenomena are studied by elaborating and embellishing a modified neoclassical microeconomic framework: workers and firms are treated as pursuing (maximizing) behavior according to rational economic principles. OMRD has not been supportive of such work—except, perhaps, through the Small Grants Program.

The other approach explores empirical dimensions of job search. Where theoretical discussion is involved, it is typically neither neoclassical nor dynamic. In some instances, pyschological or sociological variables are introduced. Although both approaches are valuable and potentially very rewarding areas for the future communication between the two sets of literature is minimal. (One of the rare exceptions is Holt, pp. 53-123 in Phelps, 1970). Useful cross-fertilization could be supported by OMRD, so that the empirical findings of Sheppard and Belitsky (1966), Sobel and Folk (1965), the National Longitudinal Surveys, Wilcock and Franke (1963), and others might be integrated or reconciled with the largely, though not exclusively, theoretical contributions of Phelps, Alchian, Mortenson (all in Phelps, 1970), Stigler (1972), and others. A paper along these lines should be inexpensive to commission and it might well serve a synergistic purpose.

One of the better studies in this field, *The Job Hunt,* by Sheppard and Belitsky (1966), was sponsored by OMRD. Their report describes the results of interviews with 450 blue-collar and 90 white-collar unemployed workers in Erie, Pennsylvania in 1964. Among these subjects, reservation wages, the lowest wage that a worker would accept to take a job, tended to be substantially lower than the wage actually earned upon reemployment. Additionally, the authors found that no correlation exists between high reservation wages and the probability of remaining unemployed; prolonged unemployment, however, tended to reduce a worker's reservation wage. In line with results of virtually every other study of this kind, the bulk of labor market information was transmitted informally—through friends and relatives and to some extent by newspapers (this seems to be at odds with the Olympus finding). While male workers tended to use visits to the gates or personnel offices of factories and firms, females were more likely to use the Employment Service. Many unemployed who were inactive in search reported they were waiting to be recalled, but only 80% of that group actually were rehired by their former employers. Similar to the findings later reported by Stevens, we learn that the number of firms contacted was positively correlated with the probability of becoming reemployed.

Sheppard and Belitsky's study is based on a relatively small sample, drawn from a single locality at one time. The findings are presented in simple tabular form, although multivariate analysis could have been usefully employed in places. This was still an excellent start by OMRD and could have led to more extensive longitudinal work. As OMRD's National Longitudinal Surveys continue, perhaps a follow-up of this sort will be possible; it should. The Stevens study represents only one of a number of E&D projects that might logically have been spun off from this early contribution. Stevens's acknowledgement of *The Job Hunt* illustrates some continuity in OMRD's concerns about the job search issue. It also neatly demonstrates how a research product can lead to an E&D effort.

Empirical attention to the process of job search has tended to concentrate on mature, male workers, frequently emphasizing the unemployed. Much less attention has been given to job search processes among females and youth. For females a critical period would be reentry to the labor force after early child-rearing years. Although a substantial amount of attention has been given to problems of younger persons and the period between school termination and maturity at work, job search practices of youth are not well understood. Even the Thal-Larsen work gives this matter little direction attention. At the conference sponsored by OMRD that resulted in the excellent volume, *The Transition from School to Work* (Department of Labor, 1968), I find almost no mention of the job search process (except very briefly on pp. 241-242). Better resource allocation in manpower programming and service delivery might occur if we understood more fully how such processes actually operate.

Mobility in the Labor Market

A substantially complete and recent review of the literature on labor mobility is found in Herbert Parnes (1970). The over-all volume of research on the subject is so vast as to be intimidating. OMRD's efforts alone are formidable, particularly in light of the Manpower Administration's early mobility demonstration projects and the stream of findings emerging from OMRD's National Longitudinal Surveys. I will therefore limit my observations to a very small part of the research that OMRD has supported over the years in this field.

SEVERANCE PAY AND MOBILITY

One such study was prepared by the Bureau of Labor Statistics (1966) and was one of the first projects undertaken by OMRD. At issue was the operation of severance pay plans and their implications for labor mobility. It is one of the few pieces of research commissioned by OMRD that deals with the relationship between manpower questions and collective bargaining.

In this study firms with collective bargaining contracts covering 1,000 or more workers that also contained severance pay provisions were surveyed by mail. Based on over 400 responses, the BLS reported that such provisions may have their greatest impact by providing workers with some sense of security. According to the BLS, during all of 1962 only about 2 percent of the workers covered received severance pay benefits; for the three year period 1960-1962 about 30 percent of the plans made no severance payments at all. Although severance pay was estimated as approximately .002 of payrolls covered, net benefits to workers were even less because such pay was subject both to income taxes and, in almost one-half the states, affected the size and availability of unemployment compensation.

One reason that severance pay provisions had a negligible impact on geographic mobility was that about one-half of the workers receiving severance pay had recall rights to their jobs, encouraging continued attachment to an employer and a location. Further, benefit payments were usually small, eligibility provisions were fairly restrictive, and benefits were often delayed. Not surprisingly, employers reported that workers did not bypass other jobs offered in order to receive severance benefits.

To acquire information on how workers used their severance pay, five case studies were undertaken. A significant finding, that workers did not ordinarily use benefits for training or to otherwise enhance their employability, was based on these very limited inquiries. Moreover, it was derived primarily from interviews with Employment Service staff, union officials, and employers rather than with the workers involved. It is only a very tentative conclusion. Thus, in general, the study dealt with a very precise kind of question and might have allayed any fears about the possibility that such plans represented an impediment to mobility. The major finding appears to be how seemingly unimportant severance pay provisions actually are.

URBAN IN-MIGRANTS

A more significant effort, by Laure Sharp of the Bureau of Social Science Research (1970), examined Experiences of 1300 in-migrants to Cleveland from the South and a control group of 400 long-term Cleveland residents. While the findings are interesting, the procedures employed are troublesome and tend to undermine the strength of the results and conclusions.

Sharp states that Cleveland was selected for the study because it is a typical, large, diversified urban area in the North which has received many in-migrants in recent years. The last assertion is challenged directly by one of the study's findings. Other descriptors —for example, that Cleveland is diversified and typical of other northern urban areas—are only asserted and not proven or explained. The typicality of a single city or area is a difficult matter that warrants some serious discussion. Many studies of geographic movement indicate the existence of well-established trails; persons locating in specific parts of northern cities have frequently been drawn in clusters from particular points in the South or from rural locations. Thus, home areas of migrants to Cleveland are not likely representative of those who have settled in many other northern cities. The extent to which this is a serious problem depends upon the kinds of data sought, and the degree to which findings will be generalized.[4] Moreover, migrants to parts of Cleveland not included in the sample of 60 low-income census tracts, migrants to the target area who had since moved, and migrants who were not members of the labor force or who were female heads of households were not included in the survey. These sampling characteristics diminish tremendously the value of the entire exercise.

The report does indicate that virtually all of the migrants moved for job-related reasons, that half of them had less than $50 at the time of their move, that the bulk of the migrants were young but had some work experience prior to their moves, and that many had been unemployed just before migrating. The report concludes that migrants do not need special program treatment. Instead, they could be served adequately by the provision of counseling and orientation (for example, with respect to the availability of public transportation) by the Employment Service. Since the small number of migrants seeking long-term training were women, the report concludes that the government should reassess its practice of placing males into the bulk of long-term training program slots. While this and the other recommendations are (or were at that time) quite pertinent to manpower officials, the wisdom of acting on the basis of a puzzling sampling scheme would be highly questionable.

MOBILITY RESEARCH ASSESSMENTS

The National Manpower Policy Task Force, through OMRD support, commissioned a study along lines comparable to Sharp's work: *Rural Worker Adjustment to Urban Life: An Assessment of the Research* by Varden Fuller (1970). Such examinations of prior research can be enormously valuable to both government staff and the research community. Regrettably, Fuller's book did not fully achieve its potential. It provided only the sketchiest guidance for the development of future research and it contains no bibliography. Surprisingly, almost no attempt was made to systematically report on the status of work in the field. Fuller warned researchers and other users of existing studies that most past work on the subject has been so aggragative as to be misleading or even wrong. He complained, further, that too little interdisciplinary work had been done, and that most data were no longer useful by the time they became available.

Another review prepared for OMRD on mobility was *Worker Relocation: A Review of U.S. Department of Labor Mobility Projects* by Charles Fairchild of E. F. Shelley and Co. (1970). Again, such a review could be extremely valuable as a means of piecing together various threads emerging from many separate mobility projects. Unfortunately, the project was far less than that. This was due partly to the unavailability of some of the project findings. But more significantly, the report assiduously avoided criteria of some apparently very poor projects, and one of its stronger recommendations appeared at best to be self-serving. The Fairchild piece not only failed to evaluate and synthesize results of demonstration projects, it did not provide OMRD staff with a sense of what was not known, did not outline what might have been learned despite the fact that many projects had failed to meet specified programmatic goals, and did not even indicate where such efforts had gone awry. Moreover, there was no guidance on how future projects could be designed to assure a more fruitful experience. The report complained that insufficient resources were allocated to research measuring demonstration project effects—less than 3 percent of overall program expenditure. Yet the outlay was over $300,000, not an inconsequential sum. That various demonstration projects were apparently less than successful is no reason to accept a conclusion that experience cannot be constructively appraised so as to avoid previous errors and to minimize unnecessary redundancy.

SUMMARY

While much research has been done on the subject of labor mobility, there remain some areas of considerable ignorance. In particular, the employment experience of illegal aliens has recently become a highly visible issue. The movement of persons between Canada and the United States will almost certainly reflect very different qualitative characteristics than other forms of U.S.-foreign migration and is another subject worthy of attention. Further, aside from a few theoretical and even fewer empirical pieces done in the latter half of the 1960s on the "brain drain," there has been little study of international mobility, particularly of persons who are not engineers, scientists, or physicians. Nor am I aware of work in the area of out-migration from the United States, either during periods of "normalcy" or during recession.

Just as the massive long-term shift of people away from the South has slowed inexplicably in recent years, the net flow of Puerto Ricans migrating to the mainland has been sharply reduced. Reasons underlying such changes may provide clues regarding factors to be monitored in order to anticipate and understand future changes. The continuing stream of longitudinal data from the National Longitudinal Surveys will allow researchers to explore further, at little expense, some of the more traditional issues in this field. Aside from such work, however, and despite unanswered questions, the very substantial attention already given to this subject might justify giving it low priority status over the next several years.

Labor Markets in Specific Occupations or Industries

This area includes studies that have dealt with the operation of specific labor markets encompassing a related set of occupations or industries. While OMRD has commissioned several such studies, concentrated attention has been given to at least two labor markets—the health services industry and the construction sector.

In these, as well as in other categories, some of the research has been highly instructive.

AUTOMATION

One early general study reflecting initial and widely held concerns about the impact of automation on employment was *Mechanization and Manpower in Gray-Iron Foundries* by Dean S. Ammer (1965). That work is interesting and, for the most part well-done. Ammer selected 15 firms to comprise a sample containing large and small firms, northern and southern establishments, and companies that had "automated" and several that had not. The bulk of the report is descriptive. The purpose of the study was to learn why firms automated in the particular industry, to examine the operating results of such a change, and to determine impact on wages, job mix, and other labor market variables.

While Ammer found no purely automated establishments, he did observe examples of "Detroit-style" automation. Where some automation occurred, skilled workers were almost entirely replaced (with the exception of electricians in maintenance departments). In unautomated plants, a serious shortage of skilled molders, coremakers, and patternmakers prevailed. Indeed, Ammer speculated that some firms might be pressed to automate in the face of continued labor shortages among the skilled, citing the example of a German foundry that had already done this.

Within unskilled occupations in plants studied, involving very poor working conditions, many of the workers were black. In New England, even in the presence of reportedly high rates of unemployment, foundries were having serious difficulties recruiting labor, particularly young workers. Ammer found that some of those firms were having sufficient recruiting problems to consider altering their production processes.

The Ammer report is limited to a small sample of firms in a single industry and relies only upon a single source of information —the views of employers. Nevertheless, as a case study the work seems extremely well done. Ammer errs, however, when he reports that it is major technological change that explains the industry's 32 percent decline in employment from 1947 to 1963, in the face of no growth in output over the period. Since such a change can be readily explained in terms of a productivity change of about 1.5 percent per year, well below the overall U.S. experience during that period, *major* technological change almost certainly contributed little to the employment decline. His finding that labor shortages existed despite substantial unemployment attests to the presence of structural problems. That labor shortages could stimulate the adoption of more automated processes should be a source of concern to those researchers who would conclude that causality is clear in situations where unemployment and technological change are found concurrently.

Similar kinds of findings are included in the massive (3 volumes, 1,250 pages) report edited by Cargill and Rossmiller, *Fruit and Vegetable Harvest Mechanization* (1969a, 1969b, 1970). Volumes 1 and 2 are reports drawn from a conference that examined the status and future of mechanization in particular fruit and vegetable crops and the manpower implications of apparent trends. Volume 3 is a summary with policy recommendations. Unfortunately, several of the recommendations do not seem to be derived from any of the findings, others are rather general if not vague (employers, for example, are warned "to create a more positive work environment"), and a number seem somewhat unrealistic (terminating the migratory farm labor system without suggesting how this might be done or what would be needed to replace it). Still, these comments should not detract from the worth of the entire report; it is often highly revealing. Moreover, the thrust of the conference was to warn the government that although few production problems existed at the time, serious changes were emerging in the industry. The conferees suggested it would be easier to deal with forecasted problems before they became serious than to react to them when they occurred in full force.

When we piece together parts of the Cargill and Rossmiller volumes, a situation like that found in the gray-iron foundries becomes evident—labor shortages are forcing employers (farmers) to mechanize. In large measure the labor market for harvest labor is as "unstructured" as the California market described 25 years earlier by Lloyd Fisher (1953). But as the price of labor increased relative to that of capital, mechanization was introduced for several crops. This caused changes in the pattern of mobility of migrant labor. As such labor ceased to be able to work its way through a region, unmechanized farmers there no longer had adequate numbers of workers to harvest their crops. This tended to hasten the process of mechanization overall. Again, as in the gray-iron foundry case, a researcher examining this phenomenon after the fact might mistakenly conclude that reduced levels of employment were caused, simply, by technological change. In the dispassionate aftermath of the great automation scare, it would be useful to review what we learned from such studies as these in the early 1960s, why some forecasts proved to be near the mark and others did not, and to use such a review to allow us to think through where we may be going in terms of technological shifts and their impact on the labor market. A decade's research effort since the time when the subject was so controversial would make such a study both feasible and enlightening.

THE CONSTRUCTION INDUSTRY LABOR MARKET

An industry given special attention by OMRD is construction. This interest is probably attributable to several factors. Very rapid rise of wages in construction during the 1960s caused the industry to receive substantial attention from the government and from the labor department in particular. The general inability of blacks and other minority groups to find work in the industry brought it even more attention. Shortages of labor in some occupations and regions characterize another set of concerns for the construction labor market. Whether it was ever hoped explicitly within the department that a significant number of poor and minority persons could find employment there, eliminate bottlenecks caused by labor shortages, reduce upward pressure on the wage rate, *and* not cause some workers already in the industry to become disemployed is unknown.

Once interest in the construction labor market was triggered, it soon became evident how little was actually known of practices there, how few data existed that were reliable, and how few researchers had experience in the subject field. Baseline work was needed to deal with the apprenticeship system (where OMRD made considerable efforts, not examined in this review), the utilization of labor in the industry, and the availability of usable data. Some of the early work by Howard Foster (1972) and by D. Quinn Mills helped to provide this necessary background. On the basis of Mills's previous work, including his doctoral dissertation,

OMRD commissioned a study of utilization of labor in the industry, focusing partly on problems of seasonality. Mills (1969) reported (relying to a degree on an earlier survey by the BLS of 13 crafts in four areas) that the average hours worked by construction industry workers was well below the average in most other industries—though great variance existed within and among crafts. He found that the industry went through sharp, periodic swings of substantial labor surpluses and shortages. In consonance with the findings reported in Cargill and Rossmiller for harvest labor, Mills reported that there was substantial movement of labor into the industry during periods of high unemployment in the rest of the economy. This explains the very high positive correlation between national unemployment rates and those in construction sector. During periods of tightness in the construction labor market—when a net outflow of labor from the industry occurred—employers operated with a less pronounced seasonal pattern. When slack markets existed and employers did not anticipate shortages of labor their pattern of building became much more seasonally sensitive. Mills concluded by observing that the industry had been geared historically to periods of looseness in the labor market; adjustments to labor scarcity had occurred only with considerable delay and increasing costs. The problem of seasonality in construction was pinpointed as a "major element of underutilization of a largely skilled labor force." Mills found that the problem existed throughout the country and had survived in its current form for many years.

Mills's findings cast doubt on certain governmental policies which posit the relatively high wage rates and annual incomes in the industry as a powerful attraction for some workers. The fact that workers leave the construction sector during the periods of expanding general employment opportunities should raise questions about the attractiveness of that sector as compared to others. Movement out of the sector during periods of low unemployment suggests that other sectors may have more appeal for many workers, possibly on grounds of safety, working conditions, fringe benefits, job security, opportunities for upward mobility, regularity of hours of employment, transportation expenses, or other variables.[5]

OMRD commissioned John Dunlop and Mills to develop further this study. While their report, *Manpower Development and Utilization in the Contract Construction Industry* (1971), contains no new data, it does provide a helpful summary of the authors' impressions and experiences. Paralleling the findings of Ammer, Cargill and Rossmiller, and others, Dunlop and Mills note that labor shortages in certain crafts—in specific regions—often exist side by side with substantial labor surpluses. Business cycle patterns contribute to sequential occurrences of serious shortages and surpluses in the industry. To temper these sharp swings, Dunlop and Mills urge that greater use be made of forecasts of the supply of and demand for construction labor, by craft, on a localized basis. They also present a brief section on techniques for accomplishing this, warning of their limitations. I am unaware of any follow-up to demonstrate such techniques in the field.

Dunlop and Mills also criticize academics (and presumably others) who assume apprenticeship and other formal training programs are the sole points of entry to the construction crafts. They also criticize researchers who treat the U.S. apprenticeship system as a monolith, arguing that the substantial variation across programs undermines generalizations about all apprenticeship.

Several policy recommendations contained in the Mills and Dunlop and Mills reports have already been adopted. OMRD could play a role in following up on the recommendation on local forecasting. Indeed, the whole area of forecasting labor supply and demand—and not simply in the construction sector—deserves consideration in future research. One major possibility would be to evaluate past forecasts—and the techniques used—by the Department of Labor. An obvious starting point in such a review would be past projections found in the Occupational Outlook Handbooks of recent years. My own small random sampling of projections in a handbook less than ten years old shows a batting average that may be unacceptably low.

Research on both current employment practices and the development of techniques for forecasting labor needs in the construction industry could be pursued simultaneously as a logical follow-up of the Dunlop and Mills report. However, the recent report, *A Feasibility Study of a Computer-Based Manpower Information System for the Construction Industry"* by Markowitz, Mills, and Dunlop (1973), should not be regarded as such a study. Although it took a year to prepare, that piece appears hasty and superficial. Part of the problem may be that the study does not rely on persons drawn from the computer and information sciences or on any systems specialists. No cost data are presented or even outlined, nor is any effort made to guage or quantify the benefits of a construction labor market information system. Little consideration is given alternative ways of providing the services desired. There is no mention of how such a system would be integrated with or incorporated into the job matching program of the Employment Service. Although a stated purpose of the project was to survey the literature, there is no bibliography. While this clearly inadequate work does not undermine the important contributions of the previous studies by Mills and Dunlop, it does illustrate the need for a more specialized selection of technicians and experts from outside the customary community of manpower researchers where a problem warrants it.

A useful inquiry by Theresa R. Shapiro (1972) adopts an approach quite different from that of Mills and Dunlop. In *Negro Construction Craftsmen in a Southern Labor Market* Shapiro addresses the somewhat vague and ambitious problem of predicting what will happen to black workers who succeed in entering the construction crafts. The study is limited to experiences of black and white, union and nonunion workers in two crafts, carpentry and roofing, in New Orleans (although no white roofers were found in that city). Whether the New Orleans construction labor market is representative of a larger universe is unknown, nor is the typicality of carpentry to other building trade work discussed. Nevertheless, some of the results of this case study are interesting.

Shapiro finds that "the most common path of entry into the craft was by picking up skills on the job." Apprenticeship was the second most prevalent path of entry. Shapiro reported evidence of substantial movement by workers between union and nonunion status. Unionized workers usually faced more unemployment that nonunion members of the same craft, creating a much narrower earnings differential than would be implied by wage rate differences alone. Black union members seemed to experience more unemployment than did whites (but only carpentry was available for comparison). Shapiro concluded, somewhat arbitrarily, that this could not be explained by discriminatory practices on the part of the union. Still unionism was not necessarily a ticket to higher earnings in construction; Shapiro found that nonunion carpenters regularly earned significantly more than did unionized roofers.

While the Shapiro study was a solid, professional piece of work, the purpose of the undertaking remains a bit vague. If OMRD was seeking to anticipate the effects of successful integration of the construction industry, the appropriateness of the case study approach must be questioned. The peculiarities of any single city and any two crafts suggest that a much wider set of case studies be employed—if a case study approach itself is deemed to be the most potentially enlightening.

THE HEALTH SERVICES INDUSTRY LABOR MARKET

Health services has been the other major occupation industry receiving substantial attention in OMRD research. Indeed, this sector has in recent years attracted the attention of many government agencies because of alleged manpower shortages, extremely rapid rate of growth in health service costs, the presence of artificial barriers to occupational entry, and actual and forecasted expansion of employment opportunities.

OMRD commissioned a valuable overview of a significant portion of the health services field in *Allied Health Manpower: Trends and Prospects* by Harry Greenfield, with Carol Brown (1969). Attention in that study was limited to the 1.2 million health workers, who typically had less than the baccalaureate degree. The training, supply, and utilization of such workers were explored, along with the characteristics of their labor markets and the existing battery of federal programs that apply to them. Greenfield found that roughly 80 percent of these persons were females, mostly in their late teens or in their late 30s and above. Their training had been of short duration and of indifferent quality. Unionization was rare (this may no longer be true) and wages were extremely low. Employment growth in the sector had been very rapid, providing substantial employment opportunities for minority persons. Occupations were rather specialized, creating a rigid separation among types of workers and impediments to advancement. Workers often found that they had to quit their jobs and relocate in order to gain promotion.

Even though several of the conclusions and policy recommendations are not derived from the analysis, they are reasonable. For example, Greenfield argues that these workers should be covered by workmen's compensation and unemployment insurance (and coverage has been expanded substantially in both areas in recent years). While I fully concur with this view, the recommendation is not supported by Greenfield's direct observation. Similarly, when Greenfield argues that better methods of collective bargaining are needed in this sector, that more minority employees should be recruited, and that federal support for schools in allied health professions should be increased, the recommendations are generally not derived from analysis contained in the study. Nevertheless, the piece remains a useful point of departure for more specialized research pursued in more recent years.

An imaginative type of study was commissioned to learn if the skills of allied health personnel trained in the military are transferable into the civilian sector. Robert R. Nathan Associates (1970a, 1970b) was asked to determine why persons with such training did not flock into comparable occupations—allegedly experiencing serious shortages—upon their return to civilian life. The military at that time released over 30,000 such persons annually.

The study is well designed, and its findings are persuasive.[6] It reports that the inability to match this group of veterans with employers stemmed primarily from the inflexibility of employers. They were unwilling to waive (or substitute for) formed educational requirements, offered rigid pay scales, and were hesitant to provide small amounts of training. A logical sequel to this study would trace through the experience of veterans who did manage to become employed as civilians in allied health occupations for which they had received military training. Much to OMRD's credit, precisely this kind of thing was done by Nathan Associates in a demonstration project, *Project VEHTS.* Unfortunately, only a first, interim report of the project was available for me at the time of this review, and the preliminary findings are not highly instructive. Still, the model—a good, instructive research project followed up by a demonstration program implementing research recommendations and aiming to learn more—provides desirable linkage and should be pursued more regularly in the future.

The finding by Nathan in its original research that former military personnel were not able to shift early to civilian allied health occupations is at odds with findings reported in *Hiring Standards for Paramedical Manpower* by Horowitz, Goldstein, and Rodwin (1968). They observed that Navy trained technicians were readily employable by civilian hospitals. This conclusion, however, was based on very fragmentary evidence based on the experiences of workers in 22 occupations, in 20 hospitals (of six different types) in the Boston area. The purpose of the study was to explore the duties performed by employees in selected paramedical occupations and the characteristics and skills that hospitals required of them. The study attemped to test the hypothesis that hiring standards are higher than needed, making it difficult to fill many paramedical jobs. Like the Diamond and Bedrosian report, this research does not suggest why hospitals might pursue a policy so deleterious to their own interests.

The study is a very brief one,[7] and the conclusions and policy recommendations offered do not seem to follow from the text, so the reader is handicapped in attempting to evaluate them. The difficult task of evaluating the describing job characteristics and employer requirements in so technical an area would have benefited from the contribution of specialists in personnel evaluation drawn from the health field. This omission created some substantial problems. Moreover, the almost unique setting (Boston) of this case study of hospital practices meant that generalizations could not readily be drawn from such a project.

SUMMARY

While the concentrated attention given to the health services and construction industries seems entirely warranted for reasons noted earlier, it is surprising that some other labor markets were only minimally examined despite important changes occurring within them. Some of these gaps in OMRD research can be explained by the presence of other federal agencies interested in research—elementary and secondary education sectors have been addressed by the Office of Education, and later the National Institute of Education; DHEW has an Office of Health Manpower. Still, other large labor sectors experienced (or may experience in the future) significant quantitative or qualitative manpower shifts, including railway labor, county and municipal nonprofessionals, higher education, farming, information processing and business machinery, and "finance, insurance and real-estate." Undoubtedly, inattention to such sectors is partially a reflection of the overall inadequacy of manpower research resources. Indeed, the OMRD may have consciously decided to specialize in a few sectors rather than to spread itself more thinly. Nevertheless, continuing rapid changes in the sectors noted and in others where signs of change may just be emerging should be monitored carefully by the research community so as to alert policy-makers to both growing worker needs and employment opportunities.

Research on the Upgrading of Employees

The approach taken by the OMRD to the subject of upgrading has been more balanced than most other areas of inquiry in terms of the relative expenditures on research and experimentation and demonstration. Moreover, the subject matter itself represents a qualitatively different area of concern for OMRD. While a preponderant interest in preventing or ameliorating unemployment underlies a great deal of the work of OMRD, upgrading recognizes other kinds of employment problems. Upgrading emphasizes the improvement of the terms of employment, improvement that presumably benefits the establishment where the worker is already employed. I will briefly summarize some of OMRD's work on this subject.

In an evaluation of private sector effort designed to provide adult basic education to workers in the southern paper industry, Rowan and Northrup (1972) examine the experiences of five companies (seven sites), which conducted three different types of programs. Relying on two sets of criteria—program effects on test scores in reading and mathematics and the impact of programs and learning outcomes on progression through the firms—the authors found that the programs were not effective. Even though the standards for success employed in the study may possibly have been set too high, the evaluation was straightforward and professional. While the authors found a correlation between certain demographic characteristics and nonlearners, they could not explain why the programs were ineffective. They speculated, however, that the paper industry was probably "representative," and that other industries would fare no better with similarly designed programs.

Perhaps the most interesting portion of the Rowan and Northrup report dealt with the question of employer hiring standards, discussed earlier with respect to reports by Diamond and Bedrosian and Horowitz and Goldstein. According to Rowan and Northrup, the progression of workers in the paper industry follows a tenure principle. Longer-term employees have more responsible positions; they are more likely to be handling sophisticated equipment. Thus, hiring the entry-level positions must proceed in light of the tasks that eventually may have to be learned. While employer requirements may be "unrealistic" in terms of entry-level skills, they might be considered quite rational in terms of expected future responsibilities. Even if only a small fraction of those at the entry level ever achieve full advancement within the firm, the employer responds to a need for self-protection, particularly where promotional practices based strictly on tenure are rigorously applied under collective bargaining agreements or by tradition. If this concern among employers reflects widespread response to institutionalized practices, public policy that incorrectly views this as irrational behavior—subject to modification by employer education programs—is naive and bound to be unsuccessful. The Rowan and Northrup results need to be tested in other sectors to learn how widespread the phenomenon is.

In related a effort, the National Restaurant Association (1971, 1973) undertook a study of upgrading practices within that industry. First, it helped to prepare a piece of research on career paths in the food service industry, a sector characterized by a tremendous volume of employee turnover. As a result of this study, a career ladder was defined to provide advancement for workers employed in what formerly might have been dead-end jobs. Following the research report, a handbook was developed describing that career path concept; this was widely disseminated among member firms in the industry.

Unfortunately, I know of no follow-up or analysis of the impact of this type of approach: who used the handbook, and why? what were the results of the project? was the handbook ever modified? did other industries emulate the food services sector in preparing analogous studies? and how might the Department of Labor support future efforts like this one? An evaluation of this sort could provide guidance on a future research strategy. That may have happened here, though I found no clue that it did.

By contrast, an outside contractor, Greenleigh Associates, was asked to prepare an evaluation of a demonstration project undertaken by the Medical and Health Research Association of New York City (1970), dealing with the upgrading of nurses' aides to positions as licensed practical nurses. Regrettably, I could not locate the Greenleigh study though I was able to review the original report of the project. While the program was exceptionally expensive,[8] the project demonstrated that over a 14 month period a work-study program was capable to upgrading nurses' aides to become practical nurses. The program showed that a traditionally dead-end job in the health field need not be a terminal position, and that upgrading could occur even while the trainee continued to work at the hospital. The sketchiness of the final report, particularly in terms of possible ways to reduce the costs of providing such upgrade training, should not diminish the significance of the project. I hope, however, that the Greenleigh study would involve follow-up on the trainees to learn how many remained practical nurses, whether those who failed the licensing examination took it at a later date and passed, whether the program survives at its original site and whether it has been replicated elsewhere, whether the upgrading can be done more cheaply in the future, and whether the increased costs over more traditional methods of preparing licensed practical nurses can be justified.

To provide a badly needed overview for a perspective on the state of knowledge regarding upgrading programs, OMRD engaged E. F. Shelley and Co. to prepare *Upgrading the Workforce: Problems and Possibilities* in early 1971 (E. F. Shelley, 1971). The report stated that its intention was "to fertilize the thinking of decision-makers about the problems and possibilities in providing greater opportunities for non-supervisory workers." However, the analysis was based largely on a sample of only 20 firms engaged in upgrading activities. Shelley acknowledged the problem: "the sample was too limited and the data too uneven to allow developing strongly supported arguments."[9]

The report observes that no single model or upgrading technique can work successfully at all companies. Unions can play a significant and positive role where upgrading provides clear benefits to the workers and the union's authority is not threatened by such training. Basic educational deficiencies—not the lack of manual skill—have been a prime obstacle to upgrading the underemployed. Upgrading programs tend to be casualties of economic downturns. The Shelley report finds that the most lasting and beneficial efforts "are those which strive for a total work environment of openness and opportunity deriving from management's broad interest in the needs of its employees." This environment is best developed, according to the report, through two-way internal communication.

The report does not provide a needed perspective on the costs of such programs, nor does it give much hard or even soft data on their benefits. Quantitative findings along those lines are essential. Government needs such guidance in deciding how much to invest in related programs. More importantly, a primary stumbling block in gaining wider acceptance for upgrading efforts appears to be fear or uncertainty among employers that such programs are not worth undertaking. Given the OMRD's considerable effort in demonstrating various upgrading models, it is important to examine more carefully the costs and benefits of those approaches. If some models appear to be worthy of replication, dissemination to trade organizations, chambers of commerce, the National Commission on Productivity, and other interested parties should follow. And since a substantial portion of the upgrading effort has occurred in the public sector, perhaps a next step ought to be a conference developed around the various models tried there. With growing attention being given to problems of public employment, such a conference aimed at describing what we know about upgrading in the public sector could be immensely useful.

Labor Market Intermediaries

Historically, economics has been the discipline involved most intensively in research on the labor market. Economists studying the market have tended to concentrate on aspects of labor supply, although their attention has turned increasingly to the subject of the demand for labor. Possibly because of obvious parrallels to research done on product markets, where price theory gives scant recognition to the process of interaction between supply and demand, economists in general have avoided study of this dimension of the labor market. So long as analysis rested on a traditional mode of comparative statics, this neglect was hardly problematic. As labor economics advanced towards dynamic analyses, as research was less consistently centered on the concept of equilibrium, and as demands for more pragmatic, policy-oriented inquiry developed, the oversight became more evident. We know very little about the process whereby employers and employees meet in the labor market, exchange demands, and set conditions of employment. We do know, however, that the process involves certain frictions which impose transaction costs. Our society has sought in a variety of ways to reduce these costs as they affect individual workers, attempting to shift this burden elsewhere, or to reduce it through scale economies. There are also private arrangements designed to lower transaction costs to workers and, occasionally, to employers. I have labeled one class of institutions serving to reduce the frictions generated in bringing together labor supply and demand labor market intermediaries.[10]

Employment Service

Probably the largest and certainly the most visible intermediary in the labor market is the federal-state Employment Service. While there are innumerable studies on the Employment Service, I have been unable to locate a sufficient sample of material to comment on this body of work. Further, even if I had a larger number of studies prepared under the auspices of OMRD, it would only be appropriate to review that work in light of R&D activities conducted directly under state and Employment Service auspices. Those agencies have primary responsibility for generating information about their own programs.

Such a review—a massive undertaking and heavily dependent upon the active support of many separate agencies—could prove enormously helpful to the states, the Manpower Administration, and the research community. While researcher needs are secondary, there appears to be so little reporting in the professional journals (at least in economics and business) on the Employment Service as to suggest that academics have had little contact with the agency or its operations at either the federal or state level. If a review of research in this area were commissioned, the matter of testing would have to be treated separately since the disciplines and perspective involved would almost certainly differ from those underlying matters such as placement, job development, and a wide range of other labor market activities.

Other Public Intermediaries

The Employment Service may not be the only significant labor market intermediary in the public sector. Thal-Larsen and several others have begun to examine the quantity and quality of counseling in the high schools; the booming interest in "career education" has reinforced this concern. However, no comparable attention has been given, so far as I can determine, to counseling and placement in the nation's public and private colleges and universities. We do not know what resources these schools devote to assisting school leavers (especially that significant proportion of students who leave school before graduation) what techniques have proven effective, or how more current (timely) labor market information can be transmitted to counseling and placement staff. Other public sector labor market intermediaries include corrections and parole personnel, the military system, and agencies such as rehabilitation centers. I have not found a body of literature that documents counseling, placement, and follow-up activities in such organizations. If it exists, it has not been approached within a framework of economics. While the activities involved may be small by comparison to the Employment Service, these other intermediary complements to it, and their role should be better understood. Moreover, the resources now committed to their activities may be quite large.

Private Intermediaries

The role of private employment agencies also has been barely explored (the Olymus project [Olympus Research Corporation, 1973] is an exception to this), as has the placement function within the private school system. Placement services provided by the private trade schools should be of special interest. Many of those schools must assure placements for graduates in order to maintain a continuing stream of students. In a somewhat different vein, private firms have emerged in recent years, especially in the major cities, that are related to but are not actually employment agencies. These firms do not provide direct placement services but rather counsel persons—usually white-collar workers—on how to seek (better) employment, on how to prepare resumes, on employer screening procedures, and on job search strategies. Some of these organizations also administer tests to their clients. So far as I can tell, the scope of such agencies, the quality of their services, their track records, and their fee practices have not been studied by anyone.

Unions

OMRD has given surprisingly little attention to the role played by labor organizations in a wide range of manpower issues. Perhaps, the subject has been avoided primarily in deference to a sister agency within the Department of Labor, the Labor-Management Services Administration. But since that agency is a far smaller operation that OMRD, the relationship between unions and manpower programs has been barely studied by the Department (exceptions are Marshall and Briggs, 1967; and Lowenberg, Koziara, and Koziara, 1973). Therefore, in the context of labor market intermediaries, we should determine the ways that successful unions have helped to place or counsel their unemployed rank and file. What role can government play to assist interested unions in better servicing their members? Can labor organizations serve to provide early warnings to the Employment Service in the event of impending layoffs? The obvious political concerns about sensitive labor-management relationships ought not to prevent OMRD from exploring some of these questions. However, I am not aware that this concern alone has caused the subject and related issues where collective bargaining and manpower interact to be given so little attention.

Labor Market Imperfections

The neoclassical model generally describes the labor market in terms of perfectly competitive economic conditions. Those imperfections incorporated into the textbook models still do not fully reflect the myriad factors that prevent the labor market from allocating resources in a frictionless and idealized manner. Some of the impediments to perfectly competitive labor markets include licensing practices, discrimination, dual (or segmented) labor markets, capital market imperfections, credentialism, risk, uncertainty and costs of information, collective bargaining, nonprofit employers, legislation affecting minimum wage, pension, health and safety, and the presence of alternatives to work that provide income and support. A number of these matters have received some attention by OMRD. Some of the research involved was described in previous sections.

Licensing and Credentialism

The question of credentialism was raised in connection with the Diamond and Bedrosian (1970), Horowitz, Goldstein, and Rodwin (1968), Nathan Associates (1970b), and Rowan and Northrup (1972) reports.[11] Licensing practices were the subject of a projects by Shimberg, Esser and Kruger (1972). Their book, *Occupational Licensing,* grew out of separate work conducted at Michigan State University and at the Educational Testing Service. The Michigan State effort was methodological, seeking to devise procedures to collect quantitative data on licensing; the ETS effort involved visits to 23 cities in eight states to examine how licensing practices were related to manpower shortages. Although they did not advocate abandonment of occupational licensing, the authors found the system "riddled with faults." While the ostensible purpose of licensing is to protect the public, the system actually insulates those with licenses, or access to them, from the pressures of substantial competition.

The study is well done; it is only weak in proposing a number of potentially corrective policy recommendations with little likelihood of being adopted. Since the negative effects of licensing can be attributed largely to the political strength of interest groups, proposals to open up the system must identify pressure points and techniques to overcome the certain potency of forces that will resist proposed change. The volume does not provide such guidance. A useful follow-up to *Occupational Licensing* might be done by a political scientist or a public administration specialist who would be sensitive to these types of issues.

DUAL LABOR MARKETS

Some of the issues pertaining to dual labor markets have been studied by OMRD. A summary paper by R. C. Edwards, D. Gordon and M. Reich (1973) redefines the area in terms of labor market segmentation, since the authors find more than two distinct labor markets. Segmented labor market theorists deserve credit for attempting relatively broad analysis; their work represents an amalgam of sociology, personnel administration, psychology, economic and political history, and, of course, economics, and is filled with explicit recommendations for manpower policy officials.

It is not possible to summarize and evaluate the dual (or segmented) labor market hypothesis in the course of this chapter. Two excellent efforts recently prepared by Michael Wachter (1974) and Glen Cain (1975) should be brought to the attention of the OMRD. While Cain appears to be somewhat more unconvinced of the case presented in the "dual-radical" literature, he does suggest four areas of research "that stem from the D-R challenge and neoclassical response": (1) to examine more fully the nonwage dimension of remuneration; (2) to conduct longitudinal research on occupational promotion paths; (3) to explore the role of psychological variables in the performance of workers in the labor market; and (4) to undertake a greater number of benefit-cost analyses of government intervention. The first two of these areas were also recommended earlier in this chapter; the final subject is more typically associated with OMRD's counterpart, the Office of Evaluation.

Wachter is also critical of the dual approach; still he finds that some of its elements represent positive contributions to our understanding of the labor market. His work is replete with areas of theoretical and empirical inquiry that need further study. Similar to comments made earlier in this report, he finds that virtually no empirical attention has been given to questions relating to the internal labor market within the primary sector since the work of Doeringer and Piore (1966, 1970). Most contributions by the dualists explicate problems of unemployment and underemployment of the secondary market.

MINIMUM WAGE

The minimum wage law has received almost no attention by OMRD. Funding through OMRD is small grants program, however, allowed Peter Mattila (1973) to prepare an excellent paper on the effect of extending minimum wage coverage to domestic workers. By estimating equations for labor supply, demand, and labor force participation functions, Mattila assessed the quantitative impact of such a change in the law. A paper by Seidman (1971) simulated an antipoverty program that depended heavily on substantial increases in the minimum wage. This report appeared as part of a series done by students and faculty in the Department of Economics at the University of California, Berkeley.

OMRD's handling of the minimum wage issue raises a tricky question. The Fair Labor Standards Act is administered within the Employment Standards Administration of the Department of Labor. That agency has primary responsibility for conducting research on the minimum wage and for preparing annually the so-called 4-D reports for the Congress. These reports evaluate the impact of the law. Another agency in the Department, the Bureau of Labor Statistics, has also conducted research on this subject and its report on youth unemployment and the minimum wage (Bureau of Labor Statistics, 1970) has been one of the finest studies of the subject available. Thus, OMRD's "inattention" to the subject can be attributed to recognition of these other vested interests within the Department. Since the area is obviously significant to a host of manpower matters, one should either detect substantial OMRD support or none at all. The presence of some interest, albeit small, is therefore puzzling. Similar areas of overlapping interest between OMRD and other parts of the Department of Labor outside of the Manpower Administration exist—for example, questions relating to job satisfaction, to international trade and unemployment, and to discrimination in employment. Jurisdictional uncertainties also exist among large numbers of federal departments dealing with manpower concerns, raising similar kinds of questions.

PROTECTIVE LEGISLATION

Until passage of the Coal Mine Health and Safety Act in 1969, and, later, the Occupational Safety and Health Act of 1970, very little policy attention was given to the interface of conditions of safety on the job and such manpower issues as labor turnover, compensation, productivity, and time loss. Similarly, research regarding these subject areas has been minimized within the Department of Labor until recently. The only work relating to worker health and safety undertaken by OMRD that I could find was a report by Ewan Clague et al. (1972) on the problems of the black-lung program. Since the Department's Occupational Safety and Health Administration has virtually no money appropriated for research—at least social science research adopting a manpower perspective—OMRD could consider the field still accessible to it. Along related lines some very interesting findings have emerged from OMRD's National Longitudinal Manpower Surveys on black-white differences in labor force participation rates due to differential health problems. Perhaps these data will eventually help to shed light on the relationship between occupation and health and the impact of the two on lifetime earnings.

COLLECTIVE BARGAINING

When we scan OMRD studies over the years that deal with labor market imperfections, the greatest gap in the entire subject matter is the dearth of research on collective bargaining as it affects manpower questions. Collective bargaining ties in with virtually all the subjects described in the previous sections. Rather than suggesting specific research topics to be studied, it seems more useful to remind the researchers to pay continuing heed to matters pertaining to labor-management relations. Any reluctance among labor market analysts to deal with such questions must be overcome through continuous prodding.

Macroeconomic Variables and Manpower Issues

Almost without exception OMRD has avoided studies of macroeconomics and its relationship to manpower. In particular, the role of manpower programs in relation to the Phillips curve is not understood. Other aggregative issues—the sources of change in long-run movements in productivity, the secular drift upward in unemployment and the changing composition of the labor force, the qualitative and quantitative effects on employment of international capital flows, the impact of environmental and safety legislation on employment patterns, the factors that influence average working hours and what this may suggest for the future—have received surprisingly little attention, except in a few instances of Small Grants Program efforts and in the work of Urban Institute researchers (for example, Holt et al., 1971).

While this apparent gap may reflect a shortage of talented and interested researchers, it is also possible that OMRD has avoided such work on the grounds that it might not lead or relate directly to policy decisions. Still, it would be very helpful to the entire manpower community, including policy-makers, program managers, and researchers, to have a better understanding of interrelationships between certain structural phenomena and the existing unemployment situation.

I can suggest a few lines of study in this area that warrant consideration in developing future research plans. For example, some of the early impetus underlying passage of MDTA involved concern about labor shortages and bottlenecks. Unfortunately, interest in the issues waned before much light was shed on the subject. It would be worthwhile knowing how much unskilled labor remains unemployed where it cannot serve in a complementary way with unavailable or scarce skilled labor. How quickly and substantially do employers substitute capital for labor in the face of scarcity of skilled employees? How seriously do scarce supplies of skilled labor drive up labor costs in the presence of rapid growth of aggregate demand? What specific kinds of labor shortages take longest for the market mechanism to eliminate or ameliorate? How well can future shortages be forecast?

A wholly different line of inquiry might be to examine the issue of the efficient allocation of labor resources in the United States. While some studies have estimated the costs to our society of racial discrimination, we know little about the economic losses due to sex discrimination, underemployment, the costs and benefits of work rules or customs that affect levels of labor productivity, and the problem of labor hoarding. Moreover, achieving low unemployment rates is not the ultimate goal in assuring that human resources are efficiently allocated from a societal perspective. A wide range of questions deserve examination in terms of how well firms use workers in their employ. Simply to know more about the process of establishing working hours across industries and occupations would be valuable in this regard.

Findings and Recommendations

This review has been so lengthy and filled with recommendations that a lengthy summarization hardly seems appropriate. It may be useful, however, to reiterate the criteria that I have *not* used in evaluating the research sponsored by the OMRD. I have not examined the utilization of projects. I did not have access to project proposals that might have allowed reports to be assessed directly on the basis of the original plans and promises of the researcher. I have not had data on the costs of individual projects, Thus, individual projects have been analyzed primarily on the terms set by the researchers themselves—internal consistency and adherence to customary, acceptable criteria of research in the social sciences—and by examining findings and conclusions in terms of material actually presented.

Having read so many reports in a brief period has provided me a good perspective of the status of research flowing out of OMRD. In general, the work has been good; it has been balanced and basically free of political and ideological overtones, and it has been spread widely in personal and disciplinary senses over the research community (although noneconomists might readily dispute this final point). In general, the work has been empirically oriented; there has been a distinct tendency by OMRD to avoid supporting theoretical work. OMRD's setting within an agency with a programmatic mission explains this predilection. Nevertheless, for the empirical research to maintain its vitality and direction, some theoretical work must be supported, if not in OMRD then in other places. Even strictly empirical work has some dependence upon its theoretical underpinnings, though no explicit reference be made to any theory.

I have found no bunching of research that suggested a tendency to pursue research fads, though the subjects of reports of recent vintage are quite different from those generated in the earlier days of OMRD. Concern about automation, labor shortages, and mobility have given way in later years to some other interests. Model building has never been a prominent part of OMRD's program, but the Small Grants Program allows some work along these lines to be supported.

One of the most striking features of the OMRD record is that so much useful research has been developed even though the agency is without a staff that can boast very much technical training. As the size of the staff has declined substantially in recent years, and as some of the most experienced research and development personnel have left the Office, it may be an appropriate and necessary time for the OMRD to alter some of its past practices in priority setting, project selection, and monitoring. While there is no evidence that responsibilities or mission have been reduced, the OMRD is apparently being asked to continue as always with a smaller staff composed more of talented generalists than of technicians.

Past Research

Some general observations about past research efforts emerge from this overview. Where applicable these comments should be thought of as guidelines, over and above those currently employed, in the commissioning of future projects. Examples to support these observations can readily be cited, but considerations of space suggest that such specific references not be used.

All research projects and experimental and demonstration projects should contain a review of existing, relevant literature. In those rare cases where no such literature exists, the author should assert that. This practice should rarely, if ever, impose a significant burden on the researcher or require additional funds from OMRD, since such a review ought typically to be a part of the project proposal process. A review will typically prove useful to both readers or users of the reports and persons who intend to pursue more research in the area.

A significant number of the reports I read contain policy recommendations that are naive, poorly conceived or developed, and/or not drawn from the research actually discussed. In many instances interesting and outstanding pieces of research conclude with short sections of policy recommendations that appear to be afterthoughts by the author. The point is simply that not all reports should contain policy recommendations. Since the OMRD staff are much closer to policy-makers and current issues, it would seem reasonable for them to develop the policy recommendations on the basis of research for them to develop the policy recommendations on the basis of research findings. Staffers might "bounce" such prescriptions off the researchers in some instances. This is not to suggest that researchers be precluded from making policy judgments; rather, OMRD might drop its apparent insistence that all reports contain such recommendations. The prescriptions would almost certainly improve, on average, if staffers saw this as one of their own responsibilities.

OMRD should be alert to a special problem detected in this review. In some instances, researchers who have done splendid work previously—possibly for OMRD—have become involved in projects involving different kinds of skills than those earlier demonstrated. These are researchers who subsequently work in different subject areas, or utilize different approaches, or switch from research to the experimentation or demonstration project area. The caution—perhaps an elementary one—is that where such a change occurs, the researcher's prior performance should be disregarded. This implies that the relevant proposal be fully spelled out, just as would be the case in the event the researcher were not known at all to OMRD.

Since many of the case studies have provided such limited and intuitive kinds of evidence, I recommend that this technique be dropped *except* where (a) there is a clear plan indicated as to how findings might be integrated together with other related research, and (b) an explicit argument is presented as to why that particular case was selected for study. I should add that this reflects no personal distaste for the case study approach to research. But the use of this technique should be limited to instances where no alternative methodology exists; readers should be repeatedly warned about the problems of generalizing from limited samples; and case studies should be systematically clustered so that a compendium of integrable projects results. Such a package of projects requires careful design so that the costs of needless duplication are minimized, while the ability to generalize to something broader than a particular set of facts is enhanced. Thus, the sites selected for examination in a case study must be carefully screened and not chosen simply to accommodate the convenience of the contractor.

I would suggest that a propitious strategy to be followed where staff has been reduced is to opt for fewer, but larger-scale projects. This recommendation, however, derives not simply from staffing problems. Rather, a significant number of OMRD studies in the past have been undermined because funding constraints limited sample sizes and follow-up, and sometimes forced the use of procedures that raised fundamental questions about the quality and usefulness of research findings. If a project is to be so marginally funded as to jeopardize its quality—the validity or strength of its findings—it would be better to avoid the undertaking altogether and aim elsewhere for a higher quality product.

OMRD has supported some work that summarized a literature, provided a state-of-the-art review, or evaluated conflicting research findings. More work along these lines is needed, both to give direction to the research community and to provide some focus for government staff on the status of an issue or of a discipline's capacity to deal with that issue. Such studies need not be costly and can give research offices like OMRD an added sense of how to proceed in their work.

Most of the E&D projects that I read were not evaluated, nor were they systematically followed up to learn if they had been implemented in other localities or settings—and how and why they were. Such evaluations would seem to be essential to allow staff to learn how to implement and measure the viability of future projects.

Very little of the research supported by the OMRD has been methodological—designed specifically to improve the ability of the research community to do better quality research. Although OMRD is not particularly large in comparison to other government agencies, its budget has not been so inadequate as to not allow it to support this kind of work in some small measure. Obviously, such tool-building work must relate to the needs, particularly, of manpower researchers. Relevant methodological issues in this area might include: (a) the ability of respondents to estimate previous annual income; (b) the design of uniform instruments to develop work histories; (c) the measurement of the value of various fringe benefits; (d) the design of questions to analyze people's health status; and (e) the usefulness of monthly C.P.S. data for estimating unemployment rates by state or large city. These are only examples; another reviewer might select entirely different ones. Nevertheless, some small methodological research can appropriately be viewed as investments in future research quality.

Future Research

This chapter is an attempt to provide at least a cursory overview of OMRD efforts in the area of labor market operations. The subject matter reviewed is so vast as to correctly allow the effort to be critized on grounds of superficiality. Many specific research areas discussed deserve reviews that would be as long as this overview is. Moreover, since I have not examined subjects falling outside the purview of labor market operations, there is no way that a judgment can be rendered about the adequacy or the extent of past research in this area relative to that supported in other subject areas. If one asks whether additional productive research can be carried out on labor market operations, the answer is unequivocally yes. If the question is posed, however, whether more research should be done on labor market operations relative to work on some other subject, there are absolutely no grounds on which I can respond.

Throughout this chapter, a number of suggestions have been given regarding high-priority areas for the future. The following list is a partial summary of these suggestions:

- There is need for more research and data on employer hiring requirements, selection criteria, and processes.
- Substantial empirical work remains to be done on aspects of internal labor markets.
- Significant work is needed on nonwage aspects of employment conditions. The foremost need is to evaluate and reconcile disparate estimates of the values of "fringe benefits" both to workers and to employers (these can vary for a variety of reasons). The relationships of safety, quality of life on the job, security, and other conditions of work to manpower matters, such as turnover, wages, and productivity, should be seriously probed.
- Employer "reservation wages" have been neglected in the theoretical and empirical literature. We do not understand why firms do not cut wages as frequently as they once did and why some firms choose a low wage-low productivity image (compared to alternative strategies).
- Manpower planning in the firm and broadly aggregated for the economy needs to be analyzed and competing methodologies appraised and developed. Recent political efforts espousing economic planning may eventually shed light on the dearth of research on manpower planning.
- Job search has been inadequately examined. For certain groups—for example, women and young persons between school and their working careers—the subject has barely been studied.
- A range of work should be focused on aspects of international labor mobility, both legal and illegal. Emigration from the United States should also be given some attention.
- A retrospective analysis of the great automation scare, and its lessons, is now in order.
- The existence of labor shortages in the presence of recessions or sectoral unemployment problems suggests that the "structuralist"

perspective of the early 1960s ought not to be ignored. While academics may consider the issue settled, the literature emerging from OMRD abounds with observations or references to situations where labor shortages appear to coexist with redundant supplies of labor.

- There appears to be very little research on the speed with which the market mechanism can respond to ameliorate problems of sectoral imbalance. Yet, from a policy perspective the amount of time it takes to clear the market is crucial. Economists should be encouraged to go beyond simple (and uninformative) references to the short run or the long run.
- OMRD might explore forecasting and planning in specific sectors such as the construction labor market and attempt to develop experiments there on information transmission systems.
- More work can usefully be done on the transfer of skills acquired in the military to civilian occupations and industries. OMRD has done several such studies already, but potential areas for analysis still abound.
- Studies are needed of the labor markets of certain large industry-occupation groups aside from construction and health services.
- Costs and benefits of upgrading programs should be measured, probably through case studies. Methodological work is needed on how to transmit the useful lessons of such programs to employers.
- A variety of research on the Employment Service would be worthwhile even if such study did little more than generate interest in the subject among academic researchers. Reviews of past research, including research done by the states, are badly needed. Alternative delivery systems should be explored through experimental work.
- Labor market intermediaries, aside from the Employment Service, have been given inadequate attention.
- Theoretical and empirical work is needed on capital/labor substitution. The role of capital as a complement to labor and the relationship (as substitutes or complements) between classes of workers with differing skills deserves empirical attention.
- While not cited earlier, critical questions relating to the location of industry have not been given attention in the past by OMRD. For a variety of policy reasons—especially the role played by states and localities under CETA—the subject deserves quick and substantial attention to aid local manpower planners in their decision-making.

Work in each of these areas is manageable and within the capability of existing researchers. In addition to these specific areas it has also been suggested here that OMRD give increased attention to methodological or block-building research and that efforts be continued to provide support to publish and distribute important research in the field that the office itself may not have sponsored.

NOTES

1. In several cases project reports were not available or arrived too late to be used, but publications that resulted from these original projects were available and were read.

2. The office of the Assistant Secretary for Policy, Evaluation and Review (ASPER) and the Bureau of Labor Statistics have conducted research on this subject. OMRD has supported at least three related studies.

3. Examples of such work that were not done under the auspices of the Manpower Administration are Oi (1962), Burton and Parker (1969), Barth (1971), Ball and St. Cyr (1966), and Brechling (1965).

4. On the other questions relating to the generalizability of the sample the report does warn the reader of the following:

> It should be remembered throughout the discussion that the respondents in this study do not constitute a sample of any larger population, neither of all migrants to Cleveland nor of low-income migrants: not all living in low-income areas are themselves poor (p.5).

5. Another significant contribution by Mills in this report is the material appearing in a fairly long appendix, including a very useful summary of the sources of data available in this area. The author evaluates the shortcomings and the usefulness of the various series described.

6. This type of inquiry should probably be replicated in other occupational areas where civilian shortages are thought to exist.

7. The text is 51 pages with 40 pages given over to describing characteristics of 22 separate occupations. The text is followed by 128 tables!

8. $5,800 per admittee to the program and $6,800 per person passing the licensing examination (for an overall expense in excess of $2.6 million).

9. Nonetheless, the report makes some quite strong recommendations, such as the creation within the Department of Labor of an office with exclusive responsibility for upgrading programs.

10. As this paper was outlined, I intended to give substantial attention to the subject of such intermediaries. This expectation was a naive one on my part for a variety of reasons, not the least of which was the immense scope of such an undertaking. Still, the subject necessarily deserves some mention here, albeit brief.

11. The related subject of discrimination is treated in depth by several of the other papers in this volume (Marshall; Briggs). Information costs were considered briefly in the section of this paper dealing with job search.

REFERENCES

A. OMRD Projects Reviewed

AMMER, D. S. (1965) *Mechanization and Manpower in Gray-Iron Froundries: A Study of The Impact of Technological Change on Employment in an Industry Where Widely Varying Levels of Technology Co-exist.* Boston: Bureau of Business and Economic Research, September.

Bureau of Labor Statistics. (1966) "The operation of severance pay plans and their implications for labor mobility." *BLS Bulletin* 1462. Washington, DC: U.S. Department of Labor, January.

Bureau of Social Science Research. (1970) *Southern Migrants to Cleveland.* Washington, DC: Bureau of Social Science Research.

CARGILL, B. F. and ROSSMILLER, G. E. [eds.] (1969a) *Fruit and Vegetable Harvest Mechanization: Technological Implications.* Rural Manpower Center Report No. 16. East Lansing, MI: Rural Manpower Center.

——(1969b) *Fruit and Vegetable Harvest Mechanization: Manpower Implications.* Rural Manpower Center Report No. 17. East Lansing, Rural Manpower Center.

——(1970) *Fruit and Vegetable Harvest Mechanization: Policy Implications.* Rural Manpower Center Report No. 18. East Lansing, MI: Rural Manpower Center.

BROWN, D. G. (1965) *Academic Labor Markets.* Chapel Hill, NC: University of North Carolina.

COOK, P. (1971) *The Effect of Legitimate Opportunities on the Probability of Parolee Recidivism.* Berkeley: Institute of Industrial Relations, University of California.

——and FRANK, R. H. (1971) *The Inflationary Effects of Public Service Employment.* Berkeley: Institute of Industrial Relations, University of California.

DOERINGER, P. B. and PIORE, M. J. (1966) *Internal Labor Markets, Technological Change, and Labor Force Adjustment.* Cambridge, MA: Office of Manpower Research, U. S. Department of Labor.

——(1970) *Internal Labor Markets and Manpower Analysis.* Cambridge, MA: Office of Manpower Research, U. S. Department of Labor.

DIAMOND, D. E. and BEDROSIAN, H. (1970) *Industry Hiring Requirements and the Employment of Disadvantaged Groups.* New York: New York University School of Commerce.

DUNLOP, J. T. and MILLS, D. Q. (1971) *Manpower Development and Utilization in the Contract Construction Industry.* Cambridge, MA: Harvard University.

EDWARDS, R. C., GORDON, D. M., and REICH, M. (1973) *Labor Market Segmentation: A Research Report to the U. S. Department of Labor.* Cambridge, MA: Center for Educational Policy Research, Harvard University.

FAIRCHILD, C. K. (1970) *Worker Relocation: A Review of U. S. Department of Labor Mobility Demonstration Projects.* New York: E. F. Shelley.

FLANAGAN, R. J. (1973) "Segmented market theories and racial discrimination." *Industrial Relations* (October): 253-273.

FRANK, R. H. (1971) *Public Service Employment and the Supply of Labor to the Private Sector.* Berkeley: Institute of Industrial Relations, University of California.

FREEDMAN, M. and MACLACHLAN, G. (1969) *The Process of Work Establishment.* New York: Columbia University Press.

FULLER, V. (1970) *Rural Worker Adjustment to Urban Life: An Assessment of the Research.* Policy Papers in Human Resources and Industrial Relations, No. 15. Ann Arbor: University of Michigan-Wayne State University. Washington, DC: National Manpower Policy Task Force.

GORDON, M. S. (1965) *Retraining and Labor Market Adjustment in Western Europe.* Manpower Automation Research Monograph, No. 4.

GREENFIELD, H. I. with BROWN, C. A. (1969) *Allied Health Manpower: Trends and Prospects.* New York: Columbia University Press.

HENEMAN, H. G., Jr. and SELTZER, G. (1968) *Manpower Planning and Forecasting in The Firm: An Exploratory Probe.* Minneapolis: Industrial Relations Center, University of Minnesota.

HIESTAND, D. L. (1970) *Discrimination in Employment: An Appraisal of the Research.* Policy Papers in Human Resources and Industrial Relations, No. 16. Ann Arbor: University of Michigan-Wayne State University.

HOLT, C. C., MacRAE, C. D., SCHWEITZER, S. O., and SMITH, R. E. (1971) *The Unemployment-Inflation Dilemma: A Manpower Solution.* Washington, DC: Urban Institute.

HOROWITZ, M. A., GOLDSTEIN, H. M., and RODWIN, N. (1968) *Hiring Standards for Paramedical Manpower.* Boston: Northeastern University Department of Economics.

FRAZIER, K. (1967) *Computer-Based Job Matching Systems: An Exploration of the State of the Art and the Proposed Nationwide Matching System.* Cambridge: MIT.

LEVY, F. and WISEMAN, M. (1971) *An Expanded Public Service Employment Program: Some Supply and Demand Considerations.* Berkeley: Institute of Industrial Relations, University of California.

MARKOWITZ, E. A., MILLS, D. Q., and DUNLOP, J. T. (1973) *Feasibility Study of a Computer-Based Manpower Information System for the Construction Industry.* Cambridge, MA: Harvard University School of Arts and Sciences.

MARSHALL, F. R. and BRIGGS, V. M., Jr. (1967) *The Negro and Apprenticeship.* Baltimore: Johns Hopkins University Press.

MARTINEZ, T. M. *Past and Present Counseling and Placement Procedures in Private Employment Agencies: An Empirical Study.* Santa Clara, CA: Community Studies Center, University of Santa Clara.

Medical and Health Research Association of New York City (1970) *Upgrading Nurses's Aides to LPN's Through a Work-Study Program.* New York: Medical and Health Research Association of New York City.

MILLS, D. Q. (1969) *A Study of Problems of Manpower Utilization in the Construction Industry: Intermittency of Employment, Unemployment and Labor Shortages.* Cambridge, MA: Harvard University.

MORSE, D. (1969) *The Peripheral Worker.* New York: Columbia University Press.

MYERS, J. G. and CREAMER, D. (1967) *Measuring Job Vacancies: A Feasibility Study in the Rochester, N. Y. Area.* Studies in Business Economics, No. 97. New York: National Industrial Conference Board.

Nathan, Robert R. Associates (1970a) *Transferability of Military-Trained Personnel to the Civilian Sector, Appendixes.* Washington, DC: Robert R. Nathan Associates.

______(1970b) *Transferability of Military-Trained Medical Personnel to the Civilian Sector.* Washington, DC: Robert R. Nathan Associates.

______(1972) *Projects VEHTS: First Interim Report.* Washington, DC: Project VEHTS.

National Committee on Employment of Youth (1972) *Upgrading and Credentialling Paraprofessionals: Developing New Models in Human-Service Occupations.* New York: National Committee on Employment of Youth.

National Restaurant Association (1971) *Career Ladders in the Food Service Industry.* Washington, DC: Manpower Administration, U. S. Department of Labor.

______(1973) *How to Invest in People: A Handbook on Career Ladders.* Washington, DC: Manpower Administration, U. S. Department of Labor.

Olympus Research Corporation (1973) *A Study to Test the Feasibility of Determining Whether Classified Want Ads in Daily Newspapers Are an Accurate Reflection of Local Labor Markets and of Significant to Employers and Job Seekers.* Salt Lake City: Olympus Research Corporation.

REDER, M. W. (1970) *Unemployment Among New Labor Market Entrants.* Palo Alto, CA: Stanford University.

RODERICK, R. D. and KOHEN, A. I. (1973) *Years for Decisions: A Longitudinal Study of the Educational and Labor Market Experience of Young Women,* Vol. 3. Columbus, OH: Center for Human Resource Research.

ROWAN, R. L. and NORTHRUP, H. R. (1972) *Educating the Employed Disadvantaged for Upgrading: A Report on Remedial Education Programs in the Paper Industry.* Industrial Research Reports, Miscellaneous Series, No. 18. Philadelphia: Industrial Research Unit, Wharton School of Finance and Commerce, University of Pennsylvania.

ROWAN, R. L. and RUBIN, L. (1972) *Opening the Skilled Construction Trades to Blacks: A Study of the Washington and Indianapolis Plans for Minority Employment.* Labor Relations and Public Policy Series, No. 7. Philadelphia: Industrial Research Unit, Warton School of Finance and Commerce, University of Pennsylvania.

San Francisco Unified School District (1969) *A Trainee Upgrading Project for Newly Appointed Federal Civil Service Employees in the San Francisco Bay Area.* San Francisco: San Francisco Unified School District.

SEIDMAN, L. S. (1971) *The Design of a Federal Employment Program in a Strategy to Raise Low Earnings.* Berkeley: Institute of Industrial Relations, University of California.

SHAPIRO, T. R. (1972) *Negro Construction Craftsmen in a Southern Labor Market.* New Orleans: Louisiana State University.

Shelley, E. F. and Company (1971) *Upgrading the Workforce: Problems and Possibilities.* Washington, DC: E. F. Shelley and Company.

SHIMBERG, B., ESSER, B. F., and KRUGER, D. H. (1972) *Occupational Licensing: Practices and Policies.* Washington, DC: Public Affairs Press.

Skill Upgrading in Cleveland (1970a) *Final Report: SUIC Improving Opportunities Through In-Plant Training.* Cleveland: Skill Upgrading in Cleveland.

______(1970b) *SUIC: An Analysis of Some Effects of High Intensity Training in Cleveland.* Cleveland: Skill Upgrading in Cleveland.

______(1972) *Final Report-Advanced High Intensity Training (AHIT)* (by Bruce Carter, Jr. et al.). Cleveland: Manpower Development Division of Department of Human Resources and Economic Development, City of Cleveland.

STERN, J. L. and JOHNSON, D. B. (1968) *Blue to White-Collar Job Mobility.* Madison, WI: Industrial Relations Research Institute, University of Wisconsin.

STEVENS, D. W. (1968) *Supplemental Labor Market Information as a Means to Increase the Effectiveness of Job-Search Activity.* University Park, PA: Institute for Research on Human Resources, Pennsylvania State University.

THAL-LARSEN, M, CAVANA, G., and DANA, J. (1970) *Placement and Counseling in a Changing Labor Market: Public and Private Employment Agencies and Schools.* Berkeley: Institute of Industrial Relations, University of California.

THAL-LARSEN, M., LANER, S., and MAGALL, D. (1972) *Requirements and Design of a Labor Market Information System for a Large Metropolitan Area.* Berkeley: Human Factors in Technology Research Group, Department of Industrial Engineering and Operations Research, University of California.

ULMAN, L. [ed.] (1973) *Manpower Programs in the Policy Mix.* Baltimore: Johns Hopkins University Press.

U. S. Department of Labor; U. S. Department of Health, Education and Welfare: National Manpower Policy Task Force: Woodrow Wilson School and Industrial Relations Section, Princeton University (1968). *The Transition From School to Work.* Research Report Series, No. 3. Princeton, NJ: Industrial Relations Sections, Princeton University.

U. S. Department of Labor (1970a) *Dual Careers: A Longitudinal Study of Labor Market Experience of Women.* Manpower Research Monograph, Vol. 1, No. 21.

______(1970b) *The Pre-retirement Years: A Longitudinal Study of the Labor Market Experience of Men.* Manpower Research Monograph, Vol. 1, No. 15.

______(1970c) *The Pre-retirement Years: A Longitudinal Study of the Labor Market Experience of Men.* Manpower Research Monograph, Vol. 2, No. 15.

______(1971a) *Career Thresholds: A Longitudinal Study of the Educational and Labor Market Experience of the Male Youth.* Manpower Research Monograph, Vol. 2, No. 16.

______(1971b) *Career Thresholds: A Longitudinal Study of the Educational and Labor Market Experience of Male Youth.* Manpower Research Monograph, Vol. 3, No. 16.

______(1973) *The Pre-retirement Years: A Longitudinal Study of the Labor Market Experience of Men.* Manpower Research Monograph, Vol. 3, No. 15.

______(1974a) *Career Thresholds: A Longitudinal Study of the Educational and Labor Market Experience of Male Youth.* Manpower Research Monograph, Vol. 4,No. 16.

_____(1974b) *Years for Decision: A Longitudinal Study of the Educational and Labor Market Experience of Young Women.* Manpower Research Monograph, Vol. 2, No. 24.

WILSON, M. (1974) *Job Analysis for Human Resource Management: A Review of Selected Research and Development.* Washington, DC: Manpower Management Institute.

YAVITZ, B., MORSE, D. W., with DUTKA, A. B. (1973) *The Labor Market: An Information System.* New York: Frederick A. Praeger.

B. Additional References

BALL, R. J. AND ST. CYR, E.B.A. (1966) "Short term employment functions in British manufacturing." *Review of Economic Studies* 33: 179-208.

BARTH, P. S. (1971) "A time series analysis of layoff rates." *Journal of Human Resources* (Fall): 448-465.

BRECHLING, F. (1965) "The relationships between output and employment in British manufacturing industries." *Review of Economic Studies* 32: 187-216.

BURTON, J. F., Jr. and PARKER, J. E. "Inter-industry variations in voluntary labor mobility." *Industrial and Labor Relations Review* 22: 199-216.

CAIN, G. G. (1975) *The Challenge of Dual and Radical Theories of the Labor Market to Orthodox Theory.* Madison: University of Wisconsin.

COHEN, Malcolm et al. (1972) *On The Feasibility of a Labor Market Information System.* 3 vols. Ann Arbor: University of Michigan.

DAVID, M. and OTSUKI, T. (1968) "Forecasting short-run variation in labor market activity." *Review of Economics and Statistics* 50: 68-77.

FISHER, L. (1953) *The Harvest Labor Market in California.* Cambridge, MA: Harvard University Press.

FOSTER, H. (1972) *The Development and Utilization of Manpower Resources in the Homebuilding Industry: A Local Survey of Contemporary Practices.* Buffalo: State University of New York.

KUH, E. (1965) in J. S. Duesenberry et al., *Income Distribution and Employment over the Business Cycle.* Brookings Quarterly Economic Model of the United States. Chicago: Rand McNally.

GORDON, M. S., and THAL-LARSEN, M. (1969) *Employer Policies in a Changing Labor Market, Report of the San Francisco Bay Area Employer Policy Survey.* Berkeley: Institute of Industrial Relations, University of California.

LOEWENBERG, J. J., KOZIARA, K. S., and KOZIARA, E. C. (1973) *The Impact of Employee Unions on the Public Employment Program (PEP).* Philadelphia: Temple University School of Business Administration.

OI, W. U. (1962) "Labor as a quasi-fixed factor." *Journal of Political Economy* 70: 538-555.

PARNES, H. (1970) "A review of industrial relations research." Pp. 1-78 in *Industrial Relations Research Association Series,* Vol. I.

PHELPS, E., [ed.] (1970) *Microeconomic Foundations of Employment and Inflation Theory.* New York: W. W. Norton.

SHEPPARD, H. L. and BELITSKY, A. H. (1966) *The Job Hunt.* Baltimore: Johns Hopkins University Press.

SOBEL, I. and FOLK, H. (1965) in Arthur Ross, ed., *Employment Policy and The Labor Market.* Berkeley: University of California Press, 1965. Pp. 333-357.

STIGLER, G. (1972) "Information in the labor market." *Journal of Political Economy,* Supplement (October): 94-105.

WACHTER, M. (1974) "Primary and secondary labor markets: a critique of the dual approach." *Brookings Papers on Economic Activity* 3: 637-680.

WELCH, F. and KOSTERS, M. (1970) *An Analysis of the Cyclical Stability of Aggregate Employment and the Effects of the Federal Minimum Wage Legislation on Teenage Employment.* New York: National Bureau of Economic Research.

WILCOCK, R. D. and FRANKE, W. H. (1963) *Unwanted Workers: Permanent Layoffs and Long-Term Unemployment.* Glencoe, IL: Free Press.

Bureau of Labor Statistics, U.S. Department of Labor (1970) *Youth Unemployment and Minimum Wages.* Bulletin 1657. Washington, DC: Government Printing Office.

CLAGUE, Ewan, et al. *The Health-Impaired Coal Miner Under the Black Lung Legislation.* Washington, DC: Leo Kramer, Inc.

MATTILA, J. (1973) "The effect of extending minimum wages to cover household maids." *Journal of Human Resources* (Summer): 365-382.

Chapter 6

Special Labor Market Segments

Vernon Briggs
Cornell University

The review by Vernon Briggs considers a third subject area to which significant research attention has been directed: employment problems confronting certain groups in the labor force—especially so-called "disadvantaged" populations—and the impacts of manpower programs serving such groups. Briggs discusses the findings of studies relating to the influence of cultural factors on individuals' labor market experiences; the ways in which institutional practices and procedures affect these experiences; the presence and strength of different types of labor market discrimination; the special difficulties associated with the total labor force; the manpower problems of professional, managerial, and technical workers; and legal and illegal immigration.

While some study in this area involves traditional forms of empirical research, the Department of Labor has placed great emphasis on demonstration and experimental techniques which attempt to influence directly manpower program design and operation. For that reason, Briggs adopts an approach to R&D assessment somewhat different from those employed by other authors. He focuses on what has been learned about labor force segments as a result of the sponsored R&D, on methodological issues and dilemmas, and on lines of future inquiry to extend the present knowledge base in directions that would be useful to manpower policy. He is somewhat less concerned than either Cain or Barth with judging OMRD activity against an academic standard of performance.

Briggs's analysis highlights the importance for manpower policy of several factors that tend to be examined only indirectly in research concerning labor supply and demand and labor market operations. Those factors are (1) culture—personal and group norms and perceptions as these interrelate with the employment experience; and (2) institutional practices and procedures, as these impinge directly upon processes of skill acquisition and job opportunity, particularly in local labor markets. Briggs also emphasizes the fact that, at least for R&D in the manpower field, vexing methodological problems may be common to all forms of policy-oriented research, whether or not they require contact with an operating manpower program. The challenge such problems pose for a government agency such as the Department of Labor has already been discussed at several other points in this volume. The agency must work with disciplines as it finds them; the development of new, more powerful research methodologies is a long-term and usually highly speculative undertaking.

Finally, Briggs points very clearly to one of the serious substantive limitations of the federal government's manpower R&D effort to date. Manpower R&D has concentrated too intensively on disadvantaged groups, has generally neglected analysis of the problem and factors influencing employment of other labor force segments, and has failed to integrate manpower study either with research in education (especially vocational education) or with national economic and social policy and policy research as has been done in several European countries.

Introduction

The written and unwritten history of manpower policy in the United States since the early 1960s is resplendent with references to a mandate to serve a variety of labor force segments.[1] Indeed, the origin of the so-called "manpower revolution" can be traced largely to a confluence of two major developments which both emphasized the importance of labor market groups. One was an academic backlash against macroeconomics as a sufficient guide for policies to achieve full employment. The other was the growth of the civil rights movement from a crusade for political and social rights in the South to a quest for economic quality on a nationwide scale.

The academic debate underlying the emergence of manpower policy in the early 1960s was a reaction to the intellectual dominance of Keynesian economics as the exclusive diagnosis and sole remedy for employment problems. Based upon aggregate economic barometers, traditional macroeconomics was premised upon the manipulation of government spending and taxation powers (fiscal policy) to affect levels of employment and production. To the degree that macroeconomics focused upon unemployment, that problem was viewed essentially in terms of inadequate aggregate demand. Accordingly, proposed remedies dealt with ways to increase overall demand by increasing the purchasing power of society. Relatively little attention was given to the supply of labor as a significant source of labor market adjustment problems; if fiscal policy manages demand properly, supply will respond with only minor frictional difficulties.

Aggregate barometers of economic welfare, however, can be quite deceiving. They often mask extreme variations in the labor market experience of population subgroups.[2] Exclusive reliance upon fiscal policy to modulate unemployment and labor force participation may be insufficient in an era when unemployed people coexist with vacant jobs;[3] when pockets of regional poverty and high unemployment coexist with periods of national affluence and low unemployment;[4] and when rising expectations among long-suppressed minority groups focus on high quality jobs for which competition may be intense.[5] Consequently, the perspective of microeconomics (though not necessarily the neoclassical model with its debatable behavioral assumptions) was revived as an appropriate window through which to view difficulties of labor market adjustment and utilization.[6] Composition of labor supply[7] and geographic concentration of economically depressed areas[8] became objects of attention for many labor market diagnosticians and subjects of concern among policy formulators. Not surprisingly, since the early 1960s, several new theories which emphasize differential labor market experiences of workers with diverse characteristics have been posited (indeed, one such theory is known as "the theory of labor market segmentation"[9]). Likewise, this period has been marked by meteoric rise in public outlays for a proliferation of categorical manpower programs. Most of these programs zeroed in on some segment of the actual or potential labor force.[10]

Resurgence of the microeconomic perspective; disparate components of the supply of labor; and diverse regional unemployment experiences did not alone provide momentum sufficient to launch a manpower revolution. The maturing civil rights movement contributed as an ignition device. Many of the labor force segments requiring special attention had a common feature: they were composed of an inordinately high number of individuals from groups who have historically suffered from employment discrimination. In particular, interest centered upon racial and ethnic discrimination.[11] To provide equal employment opportunities for members of these groups required policy measures that might alter industrial and occupational patterns. Manpower policy was regarded as a means to enhance "employability," and manpower programs were envisioned as a possible means to create a supply of qualified minority group applicants to fulfill employment demands of business, unions, and government agencies. Antidiscrimination efforts, in turn, would help assure job selection on an equal basis. Even if discrimination could be somehow purged from the nation, the residue of stifled occupational aspirations, undeveloped latent skills and talents, limited labor market information channels, unequal educational opportunities, and geographic concentration in economically poor regions meant that little in the way of meaningful change could be expected unless needs were addressed specifically.

Manpower research, however, has not dealt exclusively with labor market problems confronting racial and ethnic minorities or only with poverty-stricken groups. As national consciousness and political concern has shifted to other segments of the labor force, the pattern of inquiry has changed. The emerging women's movement, for example, has received much attention. Likewise, labor force adjustment problems of skilled workers displaced from aerospace industries and of retired military officers have been researched. Yet irrespective of client group, most studies have shared common theme of trying to translate ideas into some operational form.

The importance of manpower research into special labor market segments involves primarily subjective notions of need for greater equity within our society. A purely objective rationale of a need to make labor markets function more smoothly has been far less important. Manpower policies since the early 1960s have reflected the idea that government *should* intervene to assist groups not participating in the general affluence of the nation. Manpower research, in general, has shared this intellectual orientation: It too *ought* to assist in the effort to design policies and programs to enhance the achievement of a more equitable society.[12] A symbiotic accord was struck between researchers seeking to influence policy, policy formulators, and program administrators seeking practical knowledge to guide policy measures.

A periodic review of some of the principal findings, methodological issues, and future requirements is essential to any subject area of applied research. This is especially true in the manpower field because research support provided by the federal government has come to dominate the total effect.[13] The Office of Manpower Research and Development (OMRD) of the U. S. Department of Labor has become a major force in determining research priorities. Foundation support has tended to favor action programs; university-financed research and individual scholarly inquiry have made relatively marginal contributions to the total store of manpower knowledge.[14] Research sponsored by the Department of Labor is, no doubt, the principal factor contributing to the pragmatic orientation of much of the work in this field.

Special Labor Market Segments

The topic "special labor market segments" is a catch-all subject. In fact, there were Department of Labor-sponsored research projects relevant to this topic for seven selected fiscal years (1963, 1966, 1969, 1970, 1971, 1972, and 1973); their total funding amounted to over $76 million. At first glance, a review of such a body of work seems overpowering; numerous segments that have been topics of numerous research investigations. Upon closer scrutiny, however, a logic emerges; designated segments share some statistically identifiable group characteristics. Two broad categories stand out: one contains segments possessing characteristics that are involuntarily acquired, such as race, age, sex, or ethnic group; the other contains segments that have a characteristic acquired to some degree by choice, chance or circumstances, such as migrant workers, unemployed engineers, veterans, rural workers, offenders, addicts, military rejectees, welfare recipients, or epileptics. Obviously, there are infinite variations and an infinite potential for overlap among the groupings. Yet the premise that underpins all research projects in this area is that the characteristics of the designated segment influence the group's labor market experience. To the degree that the premise is correct, it should be possible to identify specific policy responses to alter and improve that experience.

The Sample

Grouping diverse projects made it possible to select a sample for review. A total of 40 research reports were examined (or roughly 10 percent of those funded in the subject area during the selected years) for this review. A large number were originally sought, but it was necessary to reduce slightly the intended scope. The original selection of studies was made entirely by the author and was based upon a decision to secure a diversity of subject matter. An effort was made to avoid overemphasizing one group to the exclusion of another. The Department of Labor submitted a list of 14 projects that it felt should be considered that were not included in the initial sample. Five of these were ultimately reviewed.

In addition to subject diversity, a variety of types of research projects was chosen, including doctoral dissertations, research studies, demonstration projects, and experimental ventures. An effort was made to obtain a cross-section of academic disciplines among the chosen studies. In many cases, of course, where private counsulting firms conducted projects, it was not always possible to make a clear distinction.

Whether or not a labor force segment is in fact "special" is based upon a subjective appraisal of policy developments since the early 1960s. The list of the studies chosen for this review is contained in the references.

Emphases

What follows, therefore, are conclusions drawn from the findings of the chosen research projects. The chapter focuses on what has been learned, methodological issues that have arisen, and on implications for future research. It is not my purpose to summarize specific projects, to quarrel about methodological procedures, or to second-guess respective authors about conclusions they have drawn from their work. Rather, this is simply a general assessment of the current status of OMRD research on "special labor market segments."

Research Findings

As intuition might suggest, research findings on the subject of special labor market segments uniformly endorse the notion that special groups require special policy and program attention. Studies rarely hint that established institutions which have a broad population focus—the public employment service, schools, private industry, unions, or churches—have satisfactorily served the designated special clientele. Throughout most studies of programs designed to serve special groups, the range of the function performed is uniformly similar: outreach recruitment, intensive counseling, remedial instruction (when possible or appropriate), an array of supportive services, job development, and follow-up after placement. Generally, little in the way of occupational training was provided other than participation in existing manpower programs. Programs involved differ in activities designed to empathize with the specific needs of the client group.

Beyond a common interest in basically similar programs, the studies reviewed in this section contain a number of recurring themes. In some cases these themes were principal findings of a study, in others they were subsidiary to the major purpose of the research. Nevertheless, we can designate some overriding observations about what has been learned about special labor force segments that transcends parochial findings of individual studies.

Culture Is a Critical Factor in Labor Market Adjustment Processes

A common thread running through most of the studies is that cultural factors affect labor market experience. The implication is that far more attention should be paid to this issue in future research and program design than has been the case in the past. The finding is by no means restricted to ethnic culture; it is also a significant labor market phenomenon with respect to such diverse populations as racial groups, youth, low-income families, rural workers, welfare recipients, older workers, migrant workers, and immigrants. At first, one wonders if culture is only a researcher's "cop-out phase" to rationalize program failure or to explain all unpredicted or unexpected results. But the repetition of the topic in so many different circumstances eventually makes its impact.

Once recognized as a factor, however, there is general agreement in the research that cultural problems are not insurmountable if addressed directly in program design.

By far the most frequently cited cultural obstacle is language. Repeatedly, programs and studies of Puerto Rican migrants (Migrant Division, 1969) Indians (Miles and Henny, 1974; Schneider et al., 1972) and Chicanos (Abt Associates, 1971; McCann, 1966; Sultan and Enos, 1974) stress the magnitude of the problem. Likewise, a comprehensive study of new immigrants to the United States (North and Weissert, 1973) found that the principal predictor of job success is command of the English language. Language was a key explanation for the inability of many Chicano ex-farm workers in the Southwest to find stable and good jobs in the urban labor market (Sultan and Enos, 1974). Similarly, language is described as one of the principal factors tying many Chicanos to the migrant stream (Abt Associates, 1971; McCann, 1966; Sultan and Enos, 1974). As the migrant labor force is slowly drying up, the importance of this unattended problem is growing at a rapid pace.

For Indian youth, language barriers encountered when they enter school is severe (Miles and Henny, 1974; Schneider et al., 1972). Those Indian youths who stay in school are disproportionately old for their grade levels. The language block to education, of course, also restricts labor market opportunities. A 1970 study in Denver, for instance, showed that only 14 percent of Navajo Indians who had migrated to that city had 11 years or more of education (Schneider et al., 1972). With unemployment on their reservation exceeding 60 percent, prospects for those who stay or those who migrate to urban areas are bleak. Not surprisingly, alcoholism and suicide rates have risen alarmingly among Indian youth.

In addition to language, there are other ethnic cultural characteristics that cause serious difficulties in the labor market experience of Chicanos and Indians. The roles of family and of kinship are cited frequently in research relating to both groups (McCann, 1966; Miles and Henney, 1974; Schneider et al., 1972; Sultan and Enos, 1974). Seemingly, little parental support is given to children to excel in school; nor is encouragement given to those who wish to seek new life styles. Indians who do seek new ways are often ostracized as social misfits, "trying to live as white people do" (Schneider et al., 1972). For Chicanos, the importance of cultural factors has been recognized for some time as an issue in need of penetrating analysis. For instance, the monumental study of the Mexican-American people completed in 1970 by the Mexican American Study Project at UCLA argued that "our analysis makes it clear that ethnic culture *perhaps more than any other area* warrants continuing intensive research."[15] Department of Labor supported manpower research on the Chicano worker strongly supports that conclusion.

The problem of ethnic cultural differences poses a serious dilemma for manpower policy-makers. Research findings show that if sufficient recognition is not given to cultural differences, manpower programs will fail to accomplish their goals. At the same time, if programs try to alter cultural patterns, they are often attacked for disregarding values of individuals and groups. Perhaps the only way around this problem is to address the issue squarely in program design, but to stress repeatedly the fact that participation is always voluntary. Such a posture is conditioned upon the programs which are in fact voluntary; this has not, of course, always been the case (the WIN program, for example, was compulsory for some participants).

Cultural influences are not totally ethnic in nature. A study of participants in the Work Incentive Program (WIN) found work ethic among welfare recipients to be as strong as among the general populace, but that levels of self-confidence among black women recipients were much lower (Goodwin, 1971). Sociopsychological elements of attitude, goals, beliefs, and intentions of these black women exerted negative influence on their work orientations. An apparent cultural gap seems to develop in response to recurring failure and job discrimination experienced by this group. Under proper conditions, the gap might be reduced.

Identical conclusions are propounded in a research investigation of unemployed urban black teenage women (Wallace, 1972). These teenagers were described as having extremely low levels of self-esteem, deriving partly from their labor market experiences. In addition, the inability of parents to provide a viable image of a working adult was cited as a causal factor.

Another study, seeking to place black women into professional occupations in Atlanta (King, 1973), has uncovered another cultural obstacle influencing labor market experiences, as well as manpower program personnel. White men develop the criteria for filling vacancies at the administrative, managerial, and professional level; in the past, they have hired only other white men. The study asserts that a gap has therefore developed in perception among employers and other market institutions of what type of person can fill positions of influence and responsibility. That study also contends that, because of cultural bias, white men do not want to compete or take directions from a black woman. The same type of problem has been noted in another context. A review of various manpower programs serving rural youth in the southeastern states found extreme hesitancy among employers in accepting the idea that black men and white women could be trained to work together in the same jobs (Rogoff et al., 1972).

Institutional Practices and Procedures Dominate Local Labor Market Operations

In research examining aggregate behavior, particular labor market institutions may seem to have little influence. In reality, however, manpower programs are localized; they unite people and programs in a limited environment in which local institutional rules, personalities, political pressures, and community relationships often have greater impact than rational economic behavior.

One research project concerning training in urban ghettos adamantly maintains that institutional realities are far more significant than technical job requirements in determining who will be employed and who will not (Harrison, 1970). The study argues that urban manpower programs must be city-specific to compensate for tremendous variation in local labor market processes among cities. The Comprehensive Employment and Training Act of 1973, with its decentralization emphasis, would seem to be a step in the right direction toward meeting this perceived need.

Institutional rules have a substantial impact on the labor market adjustment experience of new immigrants (North and Weissert, 1973). In many instances, immigrants (especially those in professional and craft occupations) are bumped down the occupational hierarchy to jobs requiring less skill than jobs held by those immigrants in their native lands. Occupational licensing examinations frequently given only in English appear to be a particularly important obstacle. Also, new immigrants lack informal "networks of assistance"—friends, relatives or "grapevine" information—that citizen workers have (Judy, 1973).

Programs designed to reclaim problem drinkers also focus on insitutional factors. In fact, research shows that methods and procedures used by companies and unions to identify and to refer alcoholism employees can often play a greater rehabilitative role than actual treatment (Schramm and De Fillippi, 1973).

The influence of institutional practices appears in a study of the effects of military service on low-aptitude individuals (Beusse, 1974). The postmilitary labor experience of a group of men admitted to the military after the mental aptitude test requirements were lowered in 1966 was matched with a carefully selected control group of nonveterans of the same age, race, educational level, and geographic location. The comparison indicated that military service had a significant, positive impact upon labor market experiences, relative to that of the nonveteran group. Signs of postmilitary success were a higher rate of high school completion or equivalency, employment in higher-skilled occupations in better industries, higher incidence of union membership, and greater geographic mobility. The significant differences in employment experience between the two low-aptitude groups were attributed to institutional arrangements that accrued as a result of military service, including eligibility for G.I. bill educational entitlements; a "credential effect" (exposure to a wider and hitherto unknown world outside of the ghetto from which participants often came). Military service itself was not a major explanation for the differences between the two groups; a very high proportion of the low-aptitude military men served in combat capacities, having little transfer value to private life.

A study of minority participation in apprenticeship programs (Marshall and Briggs, 1967) exposed numerous barriers to occupational entry. Discrimination proved to be only one factor; the project showed that access processes were highly complex. Institutional barriers were almost as insurmountable as overt discrimination, including nepotism, informational secrecy, credential requirements, and union pressures to control the size of the skilled labor pool in their respective trades. The outreach program was devised partly on the basis of this project and, as of 1974, in operation in 121 labor markets was designed to overcome these institutional obstacles.

A subsequent study of dropouts of several apprenticeship outreach programs criticized the entire operation as too restricted in focus on the institutional requirements and procedures for admission into apprenticeship (Derryck, 1971). The study stated that the dropout rate of minority youth from apprenticeship programs could be lowered only if it were recognized that the unions (in this case in the construction industry) are social institutions. Customs and traditions of these unions, the study found, govern not only entry to the craft but also success in achieving long-term membership. More emphasis by equal employment opportunity bodies on retention of minority apprentices might force unions to be more supportive of minority group workers representation in their ranks. While the process of "induced social change" is admittedly a murky area of knowledge in the social sciences, time is rapidly approaching when the questions of whether and precisely how such changes should be fostered must be addressed more directly by research.

A comprehensive study of efforts to rehabilitate drug addicts to be productive workers encountered serious institutional obstacles. In one instance, the paradox confronting project administrators of the conflict between productivity and rehabilitation was documented (Friedman and Zeisel, 1973). When the project stressed job productivity as a goal (by trying to stop bad work habits), the participants lost their jobs because they could not receive the slow step-by-step assistance that successful rehabilitation required. When the program became more tolerant of bad work habits, the participants lost their jobs because they were insufficiently productive.

Research on the topic of training offenders stresses the fact that it is hard enough simply to place ex-convicts into jobs for which they were trained. But when the offender is also an ex-addict, the mission is almost impossible (Rovner-Pieczenik, 1973). Vocational preparation of prisoners is especially difficult because rehabilitative training is given a very low priority by most prison authorities. Security and custody are seen as the primary concerns. Rehabilitation has been unsuccessfully superimposed on a system designed to be purely punitive (Parker, 1972). Although research shows wide variation in the rehabilitation efforts among the states (ibid.), the findings show it matters little how well-conceived a program may be; the institutional pressures stifle results. One study suggested that it is only because there are no other available training alternatives that most federally supported manpower training programs for offenders continue to exist (Rovner-Pieczenik, 1973).

Employment Discrimination

The problem of employment discrimination is far more pervasive than most public policy-makers wish to accede. Closely associated with a discussion of the strength of institutional practices is the problem of such discrimination. Frequently, the research discussion of institutional barriers to employment is really a subtle discussion of discriminatory practices. The point, however, is usually not well developed in many of the studies. Most of the research studies are premised on the belief that the employment problems in a particular labor market rest with the participants themselves. In the jargon of labor economics, the programs typically reflect the human capital philosophy; the explanation of differential labor market experiences is alleged to be the lack of productive capacity of the people. The labor market does not want the services offered by these individuals; hence, manpower policy should try to change the productive capacities of the people.

The obvious difficulty with the logic of the human capital approach is the assumption that employers will not practice discrimination against qualified job applicants. A serious assault of this premise was made in a study of urban ghetto employment opportunities (Harrison, 1970). It found that many ghetto workers were overly qualified in terms of training and education they already possessed for the jobs they held. The study concluded that it was the types of jobs to which many urban ghetto workers are confined rather than the skills of the people that is more at fault. Frequently, the economic returns to both training and education were found to be negligible for this group.

In a related way, a study of a program to assist welfare recipients to become wage earners (i.e., the WIN program) revealed another dimension of discrimination. It found that although the participants had a strong work ethic, the staff of the program had a diametrically opposite attitudinal view of the trainees (Goodwin, 1971). The training staff tended to see the WIN participants as having both very poor work aspirations and a strong attraction toward illicit activities as an alternative life style. Given such a perception gap, the critical issue is whether the trainees really can be helped. In a more general way, one might question whether any program staffed by middle-class people can help the poor. The implication of the study was "no," but other research does not support the general conclusion.

A few of the studies pinpoint overt discrimination as a major hurdle. These encounters usually involved racial discrimination. One example involved an interstate program to assist Chicano migrant workers to leave the migrant stream (Abt Associates, 1971). The receiving states were more than willing to have Chicanos as workers but wanted no part of "Texas-Mexicans" as permanent residents. Discrimination was the principal reason for the program's failure. Another study of projects to assist youth in the rural South found that discrimination was a major reason why black youth participated in manpower programs at disproportionately higher rates than whites (Rogoff et al., 1972). Blacks had fewer alternatives in the regular labor market. To the degree this is true, it means that manpower programs in the South have tended to serve more as an income maintenance devices than as an occupational training mechanism. The same study found extensive local resistance to training black men and white women for the same jobs. It also contended that frequent encounters with job discrimination was instrumental in the decision of many black youth from the rural South to migrate to urban areas outside of the South, whereas white youngsters, having known less discrimination, were more likely to migrate to the urban South (ibid.). Still another study concluded that it was the fact that many urban black females have experienced numerous discriminatory acts that causes them to have low self-perceptions of their ability (Wallace, 1972). Military service was found to be considerably more beneficial to the postservice labor market experience for low-aptitude white men than for low-aptitude black men (Beusse, 1974).

In addition, programs that focused upon women had frequent brushes with labor market discrimination. One study of urban black women (Wallace, 1972) concluded that the job training and placement staffs of manpower programs seldom give priority to women; they are served only as a last resort. A study of WIN participants also supported this finding. While there was no evidence of racial discrimination in the use of project training funds, and while blacks and whites tended to have equal access to the same types of training, there was extensive evidence of sex discrimination. Men (who are a far smaller number of the total WIN recipients) were trained and referred to better jobs than were women (Schiller, 1973). The staff of a project to place black women into professional jobs felt that it only sent qualified people to apply for job openings, but those referrals were usually rejected out-of-hand because business firms did not want to hire women who could conceivably be promoted to high-echelon jobs (Derryek, 1971).

Other forms of overt discrimination were cited in additional research concerning other labor market segments. A program to assist epileptics met strong employer resistance even though the individuals involved had been given ample job preparation (Frank, 1967). The same was true of a program to help older workers find jobs (Sprague, 1966, 1966b). In fact, reemployment problems of older workers were found to be far more severe than those confronting first-time job seekers. Discrimination against offenders, drug addicts, and alcoholics were serious roadblocks to the functioning of most manpower programs seeking to enhance their labor market experiences (Friedman, 1973; Mandell, 1974; Rovner-Pieczenik, 1973).

The complex phenomenon of credentialism is also a vital part of the discrimination process. The whole purpose of training is to prepare individuals for certain job tasks. If the labor market contains artificial barriers bearing little relationship to job performance requirements—but which affect directly the opportunity to work—manpower policy goals are subverted. No matter how well training programs are conceived and administered, they will do little more than add to the frustration of the participants if appropriate jobs are put out of reach. Unfortunately, research studies reveal numerous credential requirements seemingly unrelated to job requirements. Programs to assist offenders, for instance, prove pointless if arrest and conviction records are used to screen job applicants; yet this is done frequently (Rovner-Pieczenik, 1973). Public sector employers, in particular, use a clean arrest record to judge whether a person is of "good moral character" (ibid.). Lack of a school diploma is a major obstacle to job placement for many urban black teenage women (Wallace, 1972) as well as for rural Chicanos and Indians (Abt Associates, 1971; Schneider et al., 1972). Other examples are cited in a study of the urban labor market experiences of black men and women (Harrison, 1970): the need for honorable military discharges, no record of wage garnishments, letters of reference, years of experience, aptitude test scores, seniority, and proper interview and application responses frequently influence job placement among otherwise skilled and qualified manpower program graduates. The point is *not* that such requirements are discriminatory per se. Rather, they may be used to discriminate if, in fact, they cannot be related directly to job duties.

Rural Manpower Shortcomings Persist

There is a lack of national concern for rural manpower problems and an inability to design a proper delivery system for manpower service in rural areas. In 1970, the rural population of the United States was in excess of 54 million people. The rural labor force—including people living in urban areas who worked in rural areas—amounted to 30 million workers. Rural areas contained almost 50 percent of the nation's poverty population. Yet, the limited research conducted to date on this subject indicates that rural problems have not been high on the nation's agenda.

Urban manpower problems seem to many manpower agencies to be more acute than rural problems. In particular, the U. S. Employment Service in many states has tended to reflect this bias. An interstate experimental and demonstration project to assist agricultural workers, primarily Chicanos, to settle outside of the migrant stream repeatedly met resistance from governmental agencies in most of the states that receive migrants (Abt Associates, 1971). Typically, only limited staff, meager funds, and inadequate facilities were made available by the states for the project. Little planning was done, and, in some cases, state agencies actively campaigned for the termination of the project.

The growth of the rural economy appears to be centered in the rural nonfarm sector. Research, however, shows that the expansion of this sector is not providing increased opportunities for employment for workers driven from the rapidly declining rural farm sector (Sultan and Enos, 1974). New jobs are being taken increasingly by rural women and ex-urban male workers. There is a two-way stream: ex-farm workers are leaving rural areas while ex-urban workers are finding jobs in rural areas. There is also a strong racial and ethnic group factor involved at the regional level. In the Southwest, ex-farm workers are disproportionately Chicanos (ibid.); in the Southeast, they are disproportionately black (Rogoff et al., 1972). The exodus from the farm sector, however has not been matched by a pull factor from the urban sector for ex-farm workers, causing many serious manpower problems.

Education and manpower services in rural areas are consistently described in research findings as woefully inadequate (Sultan and Enos, 1974). Part of the problem is an inability to design a delivery system for sparsely populated geographic areas (Reid and Miles, 1974). But research also indicates that a more difficult issue is present. There is strong opposition by employer groups—better organized in rural areas than are worker groups (Sultan and Enos, 1974). Employers find that programs will encourage outward mobility from rural areas by training people for urban jobs. Employers claim that farm workers do not need more training; or that those who do lack the motivation to obtain it (ibid.).

Migrant agricultural workers seem to have received a significant amount of research attention in relation to the overall rural labor force (Abt Associates, 1971; Mintz, 1968; Sultan and Enos, 1974). No doubt the explanation is that this group is more visible in its movement across state boundaries than are nonmigrant farm workers. Migrant workers have been given substantial media exposure; their situation is well known nationally. Moreover, people join the migrant stream not by choice but because of lack of alternatives (Mintz, 1968). Much less is known about the nonmigrant agricultural workers who, in fact, constitute the vast majority of the nation's farm labor force.

Manpower Policy and Programs Should Be More Receptive to the Labor Market Problems of Professional, Managerial, and Technical Workers

Regrettably, manpower policy and programs have a public image of serving only the poor and minority groups. Manpower efforts thus lack widespread popular support; the problem facing legislators who favor expansion of manpower programs come *not* so much from "overwhelming opposition" as it does from "underwhelming support" (Mandell, 1974). There are segments of the labor force in skilled white-collar jobs who could benefit from specialized manpower services. These people represent valuable investments in training and education; when this group suffers economic adversity, the value of those investments to society may be lost.

Engineers stand out in this respect. The demand for engineers is subject to both cyclical variation and changes in national priorities. Research reveals that traditional manpower agencies perceive unemployment among engineers as a problem of local origin (Bain, 1973). Hence, there is great reluctance by these organizations to commit local resources to meet their needs. The labor market for engineers is riddled with other peculiarities (ibid.). Over the years, engineering has tended to become overly specialized. There are, it seems, two entirely separate markets for employment: one involves new college graduates who are recruited directly; the other involves midcareer job changes where personal referrals are key. The labor market operations within firms employing engineers are quite unique. Many engineers are, in fact, upgraded technicians who compete with the certified engineers from universities. But when lay-offs come, it is much more difficult for these technician-engineers to find new engineering positions. Employers are reluctant to use formal channels—advertisements, public or private employment services—for hiring engineers. Conventional wisdom maintains that "good people" are found through referrals by friends and through direct applications. There is also some hesitancy about hiring unemployed engineers with advanced degrees; employers feel that such workers will not be satisfied with routine jobs.

A reasonable way to obtain expertise required to serve such a group successfully on a continuing basis would be to "piggyback" manpower services on to activities of existing professional associations. Much more needs to be learned about the ability and willingness of associations to become more deeply involved in the employment referral process. Other professional, technical, and managerial occupations could probably also benefit from a similar form of specialized manpower activity. The precise groups who might be helped and appropriate methods of service have yet to be researched.

Immigration Has Significant Impact upon Certain Segments of the Labor Force

Labor immigration has not been an area of significant research interest during most of this century. However, one recent study has been made of developments subsequent to revisions made in U. S. immigration laws in 1965 (North and Weissert, 1973). The study shows conclusively that immigrants are having "a significant impact" on the American labor market. In quantitative terms, immigrants have numbered about 400,000 a year since 1968, when the Immigration Act of 1965 took effect. About 200,000 of these people have entered the labor force directly. Thus, immigration has accounted for about 12 percent of annual labor force growth since 1968. Distribution, however, has been as important as volume. Research shows that recent immigration has more effect on cities than in the suburbs or rural areas and on certain occupations (professional, craft, and servants).

Related research shows that the labor certification requirements, supposedly designed to insure that immigration does not adversely affect prevailing labor market conditions, are a farce (North, 1971). Only about one of every 13 new immigrants is subject to certification procedures. Moreover, since certification occurs only *once*—at the time of application for immigrant status—few new immigrants actually hold jobs for which they have been certified (North and Weissert, 1973). Research also indicates that a significant number of immigrants have difficulty finding jobs for which they feel qualified. Many immigrants are downgraded from occupations they held in their native lands (North, 1971). The problem appears especially acute where vocational and professional licensing is involved. The tentative implication of research, therefore, is that the nation may be losing the talents of some immigrants due to artificial barriers that prevent them from using their full skills or to a lack of sufficient assistance for those in need of information about jobs and labor market institutions.

Related to the topic of immigration—but not specifically addressed in any major body of research—is the matter of illegal immigration. The annual flow of illegal immigrants into the United States far exceeds the legal stream; it could threaten certain sectors of the labor force, particularly low-wage earners (Abt Associates, 1971). In the near future, illegal immigration will be one of the most serious problems facing public policy in the area of employment.

Methodological Issues

This review of selected studies reveals that a full gamut of methods was used to gather and analyze research data: questionnaires, personal interviews, control groups, literature searches, participant observation, group therapy meetings, and special surveys. Given the multifaceted character of manpower and the interdisciplinary approaches necessary in exploring the subject matter, this diversity in not surprising. There is no single best way to interpret information where the conduct of human beings is involved. Nonetheless, manpower researchers—especially those dealing with practical aspects of manpower policy—must face several important methodological issues. The quality of future research in this field may be affected by these problems unless certain steps are taken.

Use of Control Groups

One of the most frequently used methods to assess the effectiveness of a manpower program is to set up a control group of individuals who are denied benefits that participants in the program receive. Efforts are made to insure that the control and the participant groups are comparable. Yet in a number of instances, serious ethical and procedural questions have arisen. Objections have been registered where health treatment is involved. Special programs to help alcoholics (Mandell, 1974) and addicts (Friedman and Zeisel, 1973) are cases in point.

With respect to the study involving addicts, the control group was extremely bitter when its members learned that they would be denied methodone maintenance while others would receive such treatment to help them return to the labor force. Beyond the obvious ethical problem, it is conceivable that the results of this study were biased by the control group's reaction to this denial of aid.

Protests have been made about control groups in other circumstances. A project to assist Indian and Chicano youths in rural settings (Reid and Miles, 1974) encountered strong opposition from school and community groups who would not allow some youths to be denied supportive services provided to others. As a result, local volunteers who were not actual peers of the program participants were used as controls. Against, this evaluation procedure raises comparability and ethical questions.

Restricting Programs to Target Groups

Programs designed to serve one specific group do so to the exclusion of other groups. While discrimination with federal funds is illegal, many programs boldly state their objectives to serve a restricted clientele. An outreach program to place black women into professional occupations in Atlanta (King, 1973) incurred the wrath of black men. By fortunate coincidence, detailed labor market data from another study were available that showed that black women were, in fact, in far worse shape than black men, helping temper the opposition.

A project to assist Indian and Chicano youth in rural areas to remain in schools (Miles and Henny, 1974) encountered resistance from school and community groups. Delays and modifications occurred because excluded needy groups demanded to be included. Outreach programs to place minority youth into apprenticeship programs in the building trades (Marshall and Briggs, 1967) have had similar problems. They have had to serve previously excluded nonminority group members seeking admission. This may be the future pattern for all such federally supported ventures, possibly reducing the feasibility of segment-oriented efforts over the long run.

Antipathy of Target Groups Toward Research

Several studies reported growing resentment among target group members toward research projects. Many groups have been the subject of studies; they are likely to be studied in the future as well. One research project conducted in Harlem and Bedford Stuyvesant to combat unemployment among black teenage women (Wallace, 1972) met open hostility. Resistance was so strong that the entire format of the study had to be abandoned and the number of participants markedly reduced. The view that "research never helps the community" was widely expressed by those who refused to cooperate.

The same obstacle was encountered in the rural Southwest in the programs to assist Indian and Chicano youngsters (Reid and Miles, 1974). Rural community groups and government officials were apparently "bitter" about being studied over and over, with researchers inevitably arriving at the same conclusion that manpower services cannot be delivered to sparsely settled areas.

Inability to Pinpoint the Reasons for Program Success or Failure

Invariably, the projects reviewed here made some effort to identify reasons for manpower program success or failure. In most instances, programs experienced some of both. Despite a desire to explain these results in terms of manipulable treatment variables, the studies commonly reflect an inability to disentangle dependency of the program on the personal characteristics of the staff (Abt Associates, 1971; Derryck, 1971; King, 1973; King and Lee, 1974; Marshall and Briggs, 1967). For example, in an extensive program to encourage migrant agricultural workers to resettle outside the migrant stream (Abt Associates), there was extreme variation in efforts made in different states. The few successful state endeavors usually were those in which the individuals on the staff were dedicated to the objectives of the program. On balance, however, the overall program did not succeed and was not refunded.

Proper Criteria for Program Evaluation

Studies of special labor force segments confront the recurring problem of determining proper criteria for program evaluation (Schramm and DeFillippi, 1973). Most manpower researchers adhere implicitly or explicitly to the principle that program objectives must be subject to measurement (Goodwin, 1971). Monetary pay-off in the labor market thus becomes, in practice, the only relevant measure (Schiller, 1973). Other gains are seldom acknowledged; spillover effects—such as added prestige, satisfaction, labor market information contacts, experience, personal confidence—are frequently mentioned but, due to quantification difficulties, seldom afforded prominence. Given the low-income clientele which most manpower programs have served to date, strict adherence to the economist's yardstick seems not only too harsh but also patently naive.

Perhaps the nature of this problem is revealed most clearly with regard to the issue of participant "creaming." If programs are to be judged in economic terms alone, project directors will invariably try to select participants who have the highest probability of benefiting from treatment. The fact that these people may be the least needy is, of course, then used to criticize the same project director for neglecting "hard core" clients. It is a classic double bind situation; frankly, program administrators often feel compelled "to cream" in order to enhance the likelihood that their programs will look good on paper (Rovner-Pieczenik, 1973). Otherwise, they argue, evaluations will be held against them. Clearly, this is a situation where the tail is wagging the dog; evaluation methods shape program operations rather than the other way around.

Interviewees Who Distort Answers or Misinterpret Questions

Obviously, the quality of research conclusions depends greatly upon the truth and accuracy of information obtained by the researcher. The reliability of subject response is a problem faced by all field researchers in the social sciences. Yet, in the studies under review, the issue was encountered a distressing number of times. For example, in one project to upgrade the skills of Puerto Rican migrant workers (Migrant Division, 1969) it was found that many participants fabricated work histories in order to qualify for the training associated with the research. In another case, a project to study the cause of high unemployment among black teenage women (Wallace, 1972), questionnaires which were to be the primary information source had to be abandoned when it appeared impossible to obtain reliable answers. In part, interviewees' resistance was due to resentment and suspicion. But, more importantly, interviewees and researchers had completely different conceptions of the purpose and content of the questionnaires. For instance, one woman listed herself as employed even though she did not have a job. She said she had a job until she decided she was not interested in working. Other participants stated that they were enrolled in school when, in fact, they had not attended classes for weeks. They felt that because they had signed up for classes, they were enrolled. Numerous other examples support the point: research based upon structured questionnaires may not allow the in-depth inquiries needed to reveal the reality of a situation. Because of the close relationship between research and public policy in the manpower area, the issue is of greater consequence than in a purely academic study. Manpower researchers need to be especially sensitive to the problem.

Policy Considerations

The Need for Precise Rather than General Labor Market Information

Where job placement was a key objective to a particular manpower program, general labor market data prove to be of little practical importance; programs need specific information pertinent to the specific labor market in which they operate. Aggregate demand information is of little use; project staff must know which firms are planning to expand and what occupations are involved. The gap between jobs in demand and job seekers who are available remains a perplexing problem. A better system of local labor market indicators still needs to be designed.

Suggestions for Future Research

Based on our sampling of OMRD research conducted on the topic of special labor market segments, several ideas about future work emerge. Some are logical extensions of what has already been learned; some are alternative lines of inquiry; and some reflect gaps in knowledge that surface only after a review of current research is completed. These research suggestions are presented in unranked list form.

The issue of the validity of a vast array of labor market credentials is in need for careful review. Do specific credentials in specific circumstances truly predict future job success or are they used simply to screen out groups less likely to possess specified requirements in only a very gross sense? The issue of minority participation in apprenticeship programs is an excellent case in point. The assumption of the apprenticeship outreach programs is that the selection tests are artificial obstacles to minority youngsters seeking access to apprenticeship. Consequently, participants receive extensive preparation in test-taking techniques, while little attention is given to basic instruction in subject matters. If the tests are irrelevent predictors, then this phase of the program well conceived. On the other hand, if testing is actually designed to determined whether the potential apprentice knows certain things, and that knowledge can be related to future job performance and long-run job retention, it may be unwise to pursue such a course.

There is a need to develop a method to recertify older workers. Such an approach must also be considered for women who have been out of the labor force for a number of years but who later seek reemployment.

The role of trade unions in shaping the course of manpower policy and programs should be examined in detail. Collective bargaining has many positive attributes. Many of the labor market segments upon whom manpower policy has focused are in the nonunion sector of the economy. Perhaps if unionization of workers in low-wage industries were increased, some of the characteristics associated with economic disadvantage would eventually disappear. On the other hand, there is a less positive thread in many research findings which indicate that trade unionism is an institutional obstacle to many of the goals of manpower policy. This is not simply because of overt discrimination of the kind practiced for years with respect to apprenticeship admissions. Rather, actual practices of collective bargaining are involved. Programs designed to upgrade certain groups of workers or to initiate affirmative action measures to change the racial or sex composition of a particular work force frequently encounter contractual restrictions that become barriers to change imposed by unions. Collective bargaining agreements often cause difficulties for programs designed to enhance opportunities for reformed addicts, offenders, and alcoholics. In some cases, the contractual provisions of informal practices are designed to protect the worker from possible loss of job rights and in other instances unions vigorously oppose efforts to change hiring standards to accommodate the needs of special groups. The desire to expand the range and availability of occupational training is often another area in which manpower programs and trade union practices have conflicted.

An effort should be made to resolve contradictions that arise in comparing manpower with equal employment opportunity research. Typically, manpower studies approach problems from an implicit human capital vantage point, and stress inadequacies in the skill and educational endowments of workers; equal employment opportunity generally attributes problems to artificial job credentials and to the limited range of jobs available to certain groups. It is unlikely that one of these approaches is correct and the other wrong. But more attention should be paid to determining the proper weight to be assigned to each view. Presently, it seems, manpower research places too little stress upon artificial dimensions of labor demand.

In a number of instances, research on low-wage markets mentions the presence of illegal aliens. The growth of such a "shadow labor force," whose numbers cannot be adquately measured or whose needs cannot be openly served, constitutes a new challenge for manpower policy. Because illegal aliens are concentrated disproportionately in certain geographic areas, they affect some labor markets more than others. As this problem is just beginning to surface and because it could become increasingly troublesome in the near future, the impact of illegal aliens on selected urban and rural labor market should be studied carefully.

Ways to provide specific labor market information at the local level need to be developed. Existing labor market data tend to be too general to be useful in many local manpower programs. Better ways need to be devised to ascertain existing job vacancies and anticipated job expansions by occupation and by precise employment enterprise. Aside from detailed demand information, there is also need for more specific labor market information regarding characteristics of the local labor supply. Local bickering over why one group is served rather than another might be reduced if up-to-date documentation were available about local labor supply characteristics. Increased responsibilities given to local Prime Sponsors under the Comprehensive Employment and Training Act of 1973 only accentuate the urgency for both demand and supply information on a more detailed basis. Local manpower planning efforts can be no better than the quality and timeliness of the labor market data vailable.

It is important for evaluation purposes to devise a method to determine the degree to which manpower results are dependent—

within a certain range—on the characteristics of program staff. Studies often indicate that staff were responsible for the success or failure of a particular program effort. At the same time, there are patterns of uniform accomplishment and failure running through many of the research findings that suggest that special staff characteristics are but marginally significant to program outcomes.

The causes for the growth of the rural nonfarm labor force need greater amplification. Existing research on this subject is contradictory as to whether ex-urban people are leaving the cities or ex-rural farm people are "stacking up" because of the absence of a "pull" force for people with limited nonfarm skills. Of course, both possibilities might be born out. The manpower implications, however, are different depending upon ultimate rural labor force composition. Moreover, there appears to be a strong racial and ethnic group dimension to the issue in the Southwest and Southeast. The rural nonfarm labor force, because of its size, deserves to be the primary focus of extensive inquiry. To date, studies have emphasized either urban or rural farm labor force activity; little comparable interest has been shown in the sizeable and growing rural nonfarm labor force.

The migrant agricultural labor force has probably received too much attention relative to its magnitude. Migrant farm workers compose only about 5 percent of the farm work force. Their economic plight is harsh, but given the extensive array of existing migrant assistance programs, it is doubtful that it is worse than the situation confronting nonmigrant farm workers. If more research is needed regarding the rural farm labor force, it should be decidedly concentrated upon the nonmigrant rural farm workers.

The significance of cultural factors upon labor force activity requires extensive study on a broad basis. The issue crops up frequently in research on a variety of labor market segments. In some instances it takes the form of negative pressures exerted by community, family, or peer groups toward participation in manpower programs. Group characteristics, such as lack of individual competitiveness, "machismo," strong family bonds, belief that individual relationships are more important than materialistic achievement, or solidarity and pride in a unique heritage, may be important in this respect. In other instances, the issue is presented in the form of lack of motivation; individuals within the group are alleged to have rather hopeless expectations about life and the future. In still other instances, research indicates precisely the opposite; there is no distinction between the aspirations of economically disadvantaged groups and those of "better-off" segments. Motivation among the disadvantaged declines only because aspirations remain unfulfilled by society.

Economists have rarely concerned themselves with the effect that cultural values of subgroups of the labor force might exert upon unemployment patterns. But the fact that this issue appears so often in research studies dictates that the contradictions and uncertainties about the labor market implication of cultural values be thoroughly examined.

Research on the influence of military service upon postmilitary service labor force patterns is scant. Available findings indicate that military experience has a decidedly favorable effect upon individuals with low educational attainment and low aptitude. Consequently, the impact of the volunteer army upon economically disadvantaged groups should be assessed. Prior research, conducted during a period of compulsory service, may have little relevance in the current setting.

Research focused on manpower programs to serve the economically disadvantaged refers frequently to health problems. Perhaps too much attention has been paid to education and training as major thrusts of manpower efforts and too little attention given to the importance of health as a key factor to successful labor market experience. It would seem that a prerequisite to participation in all manpower programs should be physical, eye, and dental examinations. The corrections of any defects uncovered should be as high a priority as the correction of education and training deficiencies. More research attention to the importance of the health dimension of manpower policy is clearly required.

Research shows that for certain labor market segments lack of English language skills is a severe obstacle to satisfactory labor force participation. Financial stipends for attendance in adult basic education, however, are not currently available. Manpower programs providing occupational preparation or work experience nature usually offer participants either stipends or wages. For some groups with linguistic difficulties, it would seem that an extension of such support to educational preparation would be a worthy undertaking. A demonstration program to test the validity of this contention would be appropriate. Even though this relates only to some groups, for them enhancing language skills would be as significant as anything else that could be done to improve economic opportunity.

Although economically disadvantaged segments of the labor force have been the primary subject of a disproportionate number of research studies, there is ample evidence, however, that significant manpower problems confront other segments. Their problems can be of national importance; and programs to assist them can be of high individual and social value. Unemployed engineers and middle-aged military retirees, for example, have received some research attention. There are perhaps other groups who could benefit from study: teachers affected by labor surplus; white-collar research workers affected by changes in federal spending or by cyclical fluctuations; lower middle-class occupations, especially clerical workers and operatives, affected by recession and inflation. If manpower policy in the United States is ever to achieve the popular acceptance that similar endeavors have in Europe, it will be necessary to broaden its base of support to a wider spectrum of the actual and potential work force. The relative isolation of manpower policy from other economic policy in the United States is also due, in part, to preoccupation with problems of the economically disadvantaged. Without suggesting that this group be abandoned, other segments of the labor force could benefit from a broader mandate in both research and policy.

After reviewing a number of research studies funded by the U.S. Department of Labor on special labor market segments, we should ask whether and to what extent the employment problems of these same segments are addressed by other federal agencies. Obviously the Department of Labor has not been alone in studying and serving these labor force segments. Yet, little if anything is known about the ways in which extensive manpower-related efforts such as vocational education and vocational rehabilitation serve groups such as veterans, racial minorities, women, ethnic groups, and immigrants. The Vocational Educational Act of 1963 created a "special need" category for people with academic, socioeconomic, or other handicaps, blocking success in regular vocational education classes. The Vocational Education Amendments of 1968 placed greater emphasis on service to these groups by earmarking a set percentage of future funding increases for them. Likewise, in 1965, administrative regulations concerning vocational rehabilitation expanded coverage in that program to include persons whose deviant social behavior results from vocational, educational, cultural, social, or environmental factors. Yet there does not seem to be research on how these changes worked out in terms of target group labor market experience. OMRD is probably precluded from evaluating per se the programs of the U. S. Department of Health, Education and Welfare, but it is obvious that the labor market segments served by these two agencies often overlap. Research on the adequacy of public policy to the needs of labor market segments should not be restricted to administratively and legislatively defined boundaries.

Concluding Observations

In the early 1970s, the strategy of approaching social and economic problems in terms of their impact upon population and subgroups came under severe political attack as a factor encouraging national divisiveness. Yet a review of Department of Labor research findings of the past decade reinforces the validity of this fundamental focus for manpower policy. Specifically, there are group characteristics that influence the employment experience of various segments of the labor force. These groups do require special attention to gain public recognition of their common plight and to serve adequately their perceived needs. Indeed, it is doubtful that manpower policy, with its focus upon efforts to enhance the earning power of individuals, could function successfully under any other mandate.

Having reaffirmed the importance of special labor market segments to the development of manpower policy, however, we must state that the research findings also carry an implicit warning against total reliance upon a segmental perspective. OMRD research to date has isolated itself from aggregate movements in the economy. The ties between manpower policy and such vital issues as business cycle fluctuations, changes in national spending priorities, proposals for welfare reform, questions of income distribution, and international economic activity are seldom mentioned. No one can presume that manpower policy functions in a vacuum. There are links between the fragmented array of manpower programs serving the specialized needs of labor market segments and aggregate economic policies; these links often exert a powerful influence upon the success or failure of individual manpower endeavors.

It is also apparent that manpower policy and manpower research in the United States have been overly restricted to problems of the economically disadvantaged segment of the labor force. As a result, manpower concerns remain largely residual to economic policy; manpower policy is often delegated the function of caring for groups missed by everything else. Not surprisingly, there is a strong client orientation in manpower program endeavors. Attention is focused upon changing the individual participant in order that he or she may become "employable." By contrast, the European manpower experience shows that it is necessary to integrate manpower policy into the operation of other economic policies (Reubens, 1970). Rather than restricting efforts predominantly to one group, services are made available to all needing assistance in adapting to changes in employment patterns. Moreover, the European approach stresses an institutional orientation geared to meeting the employment needs of employers, unions, and governmental agencies as well as those of workers. Perhaps with a wider mandate, manpower policy in this country could obtain the broad-based public support it needs to accomplish its goals for all economic strata.

Finally, a review of the OMRD research illustrates how limited existing knowledge is with regard to the proper way for policy and programs to intervene in the lives of people. Induced social change remains largely a conceptual area. Many of the projects reviewed in this paper were pioneering ventures into new areas of social policy. Many were experimental undertakings, although only a few were called such outright. In many respects, the findings of the studies serve to reaffirm the basic truism that designation and measurement of social problems remain a far easier task than the design of an appropriate social remedy.

NOTES

1. Garth Mangum, *The Emergence of Manpower Policy* (New York: Holt, Rinehart and Winston, 1969).
2. Michael Harrington, *The Other America* (Baltimore: Penguin, 1963).

3. Charles Holt et al., *The Inflation-Unemployment Dilemma: A Manpower Solution* (Washington, DC: Urban Institute, 1971).

4. Harry M. Caudill, *Night Comes to the Cumberlands* (Boston: Little, Brown, 1963); Jack Weller, *Yesterday's People* (Lexington, KY: University of Kentucky Press, 1966).

5. Kenneth Clark, *Dark Ghetto: Dilemmas of Social Power* (New York: Harper and Row, 1965); Eliot Liebow, *Tally's Corner* (Boston: Little, Brown, 1967).

6. John T. Dunlop, "Public policy and unemployment," pp. 1-16 in U. S. Congress Senate Special Committee on Unemployment Problems, *Studies in Unemployment*, 86th Congress, 2nd Session (Washington, DC: Government Printing Office, 1960).

7. Charles C. Killingsworth, "Full employment and the new economics," *Scottish Journal of Political Economy* (February 1969).

8. Caudill, op. cit., p. 365.

9. David M. Gordon, Richard C. Edwards, and Michael Reich, "Labor market segmentation in American capitalism," presented at the Conference on Labor Market Segmentation, Harvard University, March 16, 1973.

10. "An active manpower policy—its genesis and implementation," pp. 1-17 in *Manpower Report of the President: 1969* (Washington, DC: Government Printing Office, 1969).

11. "Equality of opportunity," pp. 59-69 in *Manpower Report of the President: 1968* (Washington, DC: Government Printing Office, 1968).

12. Garth L. Mangum, "Manpower Research and Manpower Policy," pp. 61-62 in *A Review of Industrial Relations Research*, Vol. 3 (Madison: Industrial Relations Research Association, 1971).

13. Ibid., p. 62.

14. Ibid.

15. Leo Grebler et al., *The Mexican-American People* (New York: Free Press, 1970), p. 439 (emphasis is supplied).

REFERENCES

Abt Associates, (1971) *An Assessment of the Experimental and Demonstration Interstate Program for South Texas Migrants: Final Report*. Cambridge, MA: Abt Associates.

BAIN, T. (1973) *Labor Market Experience for Engineers During Periods of Changing Demand*. New York: Center for Policy Research.

BEUSSE, W. E. (1974) *The Impact of Military Service on Low Aptitude Men* Alexandria, VA: Air Force Resources Laboratory.

DERRYCK, D. (1971) *Improving Retention In Apprenticeship Outreach Programs*. Waltham: Florence Heller Graduate School, Brandeis University.

FRANK, D. S. (1967) *Three Cities Job Clinic and Services System Manual*. Washington, DC: Epilepsy Foundation of America.

FRIEDMAN, L. N. and ZEISEL, H. (1973) *First Annual Research Report on Supported Employment*. New York: Vera Institute of Justice.

GILLIAM, J. L. (1969) *Final Report: Project First Chance: An Experimental and Demonstration Manpower Project*. Columbia: South Carolina Department of Corrections.

GOODWIN, L. (1971) *A Study of the Work Orientations of Welfare Recipients Participating in the Work Incentive Program*. Washington, DC: Brookings Institution.

HARRISON, B. (1970) *Education, Training and the Urban Ghetto*. Ph.D. dissertation, University of Pennsylvania.

JONES, E. B. (1967) *A Feasibility Study to Identify the Underemployed and to Examine the Labor Market Attachment of Labor Force Non Participants in a Low-Income Area*. Athens: University of Georgia Bureau of Business and Economic Research.

JONES, I. (1967) *NCCY Youth Services Project: Final Report*. Washington, DC: National Committee for Children and Youth.

JUDY, J. N. (1973) *Job Search and Economic Absorptions*. Ph.D. dissertation, Michigan State University.

KING, A. (1973) *A Pilot Project to Overcome Barriers to Employment of Minority Women in White Collar Jobs*. Austin, TX: Center for the Study of Human Resources.

_____and LEE, N. (1974) *A Pilot Project to Demonstrate Techniques for Overcoming Barriers to Employment of Minority Women in White Collar Jobs: Houston*. Austin, TX: Center for the Study of Human Resources.

KLAUSNER, S. Z. (1972) *Work Incentive Program: Making Adults Economically Independent*. Philadelphia: University of Pennsylvania.

MANDELL, W. (1974) *Retraining Problem Drinkers on the Job*. Baltimore: Johns Hopkins University School of Hygiene and Public Health.

MARSHALL, R. and BRIGGS, V. M. (1967) *The Negro and Apprenticeship*. Baltimore: Johns Hopkins University Press.

McCANN, C. W. (1966) *The Training of Migrant Farm Workers*. Denver: Graduate School of Social Work.

Migrant Division, Department of Labor, Commonwealth of Puerto Rico (1969) *Final Report on the Puerto Rican Migrant Relocation Project*. San Juan, PR: Commonwealth of Puerto Rico.

MILES, G. and HENNY, W. (1974) *An Experimental Program for Ethnic Minority Youth from the Rural Southwest*. Minneapolis: North Star Research Institute.

MINTZ, W. (1968) *A Search for A Successful Agricultural Migrant: A Study of Five Fruit Harvests on the West Coast of the United States*. New York: New York University.

NORTH. D. S. (1971) *Alien Workers: A Study of the Labor Certification Program*. Washington, DC: Trans Century Corporation.

_____and WEISSERT, W. G. (1973) *Immigrants and the American Labor Market*. Washington, DC: Trans Century Corporation.

Northside Center for Child Development and Metropolitan Applied Research Center (1973) *Adolescent Minority Females in an Urban Labor Market: A*

Demonstration Project. New York: Northside Center for Child Development and Metropolitan Applied Research Center.

OAXACA, R. (1970) *Male-Female Wage Differentials in Urban Labor Markets*. Ph.D. dissertation, Princeton University.

Operation SER (1970) *Final Report on Jobs for Progress*. Santa Monica, CA: Jobs for Progress.

PARKER, W. (1972) *Corrections Parole MDT Project*. College Park, MD: American Correctional Association.

REID, J. M. and MILES, G. H. (1974) *Final Report on An Evaluation of Three Experimental Rural Youth Projects*. Minneapolis: North Star Research Institute.

REUBENS, B. (1970) *The Hard To Employ: European Programs*. New York: Columbia University Press.

ROGOFF, B. M., SCHNEIDER, W. J., and MILES, G. H. (1972) *A Survey of Recent Literature Relevant to Optimizing the Benefits of Youth Projects for Rural Youth in Southeastern States*. Minneapolis: North Star Research and Development Institute.

ROVNER-PIECZENIK, R. (1973) *The First Decade of Experience: A Synthesis of Manpower R and D Projects in Criminal Justice and Corrections*. Cambridge, MA: Criminal Justice Research.

RYTINA, J. (1967) *The Ideology of American Stratification*. Ph.D. dissertation, Michigan State University.

SCHILLER, B. R. (1973) *The Allocation of Training Resources in the WIN Program*. College Park: University of Maryland.

SCHNEIDER, W. J., BEIDING, N., and MILES, G. H. (1972) *A Survey of the Literature Relevant to Indian Rural Youth in the Southwestern States*. Minneapolis: North Star Research and Development.

SCHRAMM, C. J. and DeFILLIPPI (1973) *Alcoholism and the American Worker: A Review of Pertinent Literature*. Baltimore: Johns Hopkins University School of Hygiene and Public Health.

SCHRAMM, D. G. (1969) *A Study of the Older Worker Who Has Attempted to Enter or Re-Enter the White Collar Labor Force Through the Assistance of Community Training Programs in Clerical Occupation*. Ph.D. dissertation, University of California at Los Angeles.

SPRAGUE, N. (1966a) *The Community In Action: Solving the Older Worker Unemployment Problems*. New York: National Council on Aging.

——— (1966b) *Final Report on Experience in Community Projects with Conclusions and Recommendations*. New York: National Council on Aging.

SULTAN, P. and ENOS, D. (1974) *Farming and Farm Labor: A Study in California*. Claremont, CA: Center for Urban and Regional Studies.

WALLACE, P. A. (1972) *Unemployment Among Black Teenage Females in Urban Poverty Neighborhoods*. New York: Metropolitan Applied Research Center.

Chapter 7

The National Longitudinal Surveys: An Interim Assessment

Herbert S. Parnes
Ohio State University

The National Longitudinal Surveys (NLS) constitute a unique research effort in the manpower field; indeed, this study is a landmark in the social sciences as a whole during the past decade. Herbert Parnes, who has directed the NLS since its inception (since 1977 Michael Borus has been Co-Director), describes the nature of the project, the types of data that have been gathered through it, the administrative aspects of the work, and some of the significant findings emerging from data analyses. Whereas the individual projects assessed by the authors of the previous chapters each tended to focus on limited problems and knowledge objectives, the NLS has been concerned with broad basic questions about individuals' employment experiences and has involved a continuing investment in a particular structure for and style of research. The NLS is a self-contained programmatic approach to inquiry; its costs and benefits are quite different from those attendant to efforts by scholars working independently—with different materials, methods, and disciplinary viewpoints—on separate aspects of an issue or topic, since their efforts may or may not eventually coalesce or be integrated in programmatic form.

Substantively, the NLS provides data on four groups in the labor force: young men and women (age 14 to 24 when the surveys began) just entering the world of work; middle-aged women (30 to 44 years old) possibly reentering the labor force; and older men (45 to 59 years old) approaching retirement. Variables included in the study

AUTHOR'S NOTE: *I am grateful for the suggestions offered for this paper by my colleagues Arvil V. Adams, Paul J. Andrisani, Carol L. Jusenius, Andrew I. Kohen, Gilbert Nestel, Edward J. O'Boyle, and Richard Shortlidge.*

cover matters of employment and unemployment; job history; health; education; training; family structure and finances; attitudes toward work; occupational aspirations; and local labor market conditions. Findings derived from the data on these and other subjects are relevant to both theoretical development in manpower and major policy concerns in the employment arena. For example, Parnes discusses NLS findings bearing upon the validity of attitudinal measures in predicting certain employment behaviors—a methodological issue; racial differences in work status and how these may or may not support theories based upon segmented labor market perspectives; and data regarding the role of health as a determinant of labor market success among workers—data that may indicate a need to link manpower policies more tightly with other realms of federal and state government activity.

The administrative requirements of a longitudinal study are far more stringent and demanding than those associated with most other sorts of inquiry. Moreover, the financial cost of longitudinal research is quite high—if only in absolute dollar terms. Parnes discusses in some depth the structure of the NLS effort, explaining reasons underlying certain organizational choices; he also considers —quite frankly—the problems, tensions, and deficiencies that have arisen within that structure.

Longitudinal research is only one of many mechanisms for generating knowledge about social events and behavior. Its advantages—at least in terms of the NLS experience—are clear: creation of a data base permitting direct and detailed examination of human development and change in the employment context; consideration of problems both theoretically and practically—in fact, encouraging a relatively close relationship between these sometimes disparate perspectives; and wide and systematic topical coverage resulting from a programmatic approach to inquiry. At the same time, longitudinal study has important disadvantages: it is expensive; there is a substantial time lag between project inception and production of initial research findings, with final results possibly emerging many years after a last interview wave; and the conceptual design of the project is not usually open to substantial modification in response to new research interests and policy demands—at least not without depreciating the longitudinal character and value of the overall effort. Parnes presents his personal appraisal of the NLS. His chapter should give the reader a basis for independent judgment about the cost-effectiveness of longitudinal research in comparison to the types of inquiry examined earlier in this volume.

This is a biography of a research project. It is an incomplete biography, because the project is still far from ended. It is a friendly biography, because it is written by one who has played a role in designing and guiding the research. It is, nevertheless, hopefully an objective biography, because its preparation has been motivated at least in part by a desire to judge whether the social investment of resources in the project, as well as the personal investment of time and effort, has been worthwhile. The biography has an even more important purpose—or at least one that is more clearly attainable—to share a fascinating research experience extending over a decade with members of the social policy and social science research communities.

The presentation is divided into five sections. The first contains a brief description of the origins of the National Longitudinal Surveys (NLS). The second describes the study as it has evolved over the years since 1965, including a discussion of the design of the samples, the nature and timing of the periodic interviews, and the types of data that have been collected. The third section relates to the administration of the study, with particular reference to the allocation of responsibility for its design and execution. In the fourth, the actual and potential "products" of the project are described in terms of (1) the variety of studies, completed or in progress, that are based upon the NLS data, (2) illustrative research findings, and (3) suggestions for additional types of research for which the data are appropriate. The fifth section draws some lessons from the experience gained in administering this type of longitudinal research.

Origins and Objectives of the Project

The National Longitudinal Surveys originated in discussions between representatives of the Department of Labor and of the Ohio State University Center for Human Resource Research in the spring of 1965. Concerned with declining labor force participation among middle-aged black men in the post-World War II period, analysts in the Manpower Administration proposed a longitudinal study aimed primarily at ascertaining the determinants of that decline. In the course of the discussions, the focus of the proposed study was broadened to include all facets of the labor market experience of men 45 to 59 years of age: the extent of labor market participation, unemployment experience, patterns of occupational and industrial affiliation, earnings, movement among jobs, and work-related attitudes. Given resource limitations, an obvious consequence of this broad orientation was that none of these topics could be investigated as intensively as would have been possible in a study with narrower boundaries.

Not long after work on the design of this study had begun, increasingly serious unemployment problems of youth and mounting sensitivity to the phenomenon of discrimination against women led to a proposal to expand the project to include three additional population groups: young men and young women 14 to 24 years of age and the cohort of women 30 to 44 years of age. Some thought was also given to studying the age group of women identical to that of the middle-aged men. On reflection, however, the 30-to-44-year-old group of women appeared to be a more appropriate choice, since it includes large proportions of labor force reentrants who face labor market problems more severe and more demanding of policy considerations than those of women somewhat older.

Each of the four age-sex groups comprising the National Longitudinal Surveys was selected because it is confronted by more or less unique labor market problems inviting the attention of policy-makers. In the case of the older group of men, these include factors such as skill obsolescence, deteriorating health, declining vigor, and age discrimination which may account for premature withdrawal from the labor force or for other manifestations of labor market difficulty. For the two groups of youth, the problems are those associated with occupational choice and with the period of early accommodation to the labor market, during which unemployment rates are high. For the older group of women, the special problems are those attending reentry to the labor force after periods of absence, during which there may have been a deterioration in both vocational and labor market skills. In addition to the specific research questions relating to the special characteristics of each of the groups, a general question concerns the ways in which the labor market allocates workers among jobs and rewards them for their productive efforts.[1]

Research Design

Before describing the NLS research design, a few words are appropriate about the nature and the unique capabilities of a longitudinal study. The essence of longitudinal research is that it is based upon characteristics of *the same group of individuals* at two or more points in time. Longitudinal analysis, therefore, involves either an examination of relationships among characteristics of these individuals in different time periods or of changes in one or more of their characteristics over time. Conceptually, a longitudinal research design does not necessitate periodic surveys; information relating to various periods in the past can be collected retrospectively in a single survey. Nevertheless, there are advantages to conducting periodic surveys, since they rely less on the fallible memories of respondents and since certain types of characteristics—especially attitudes—cannot reliably be measured retrospectively (Parnes, 1972: 13).

A longitudinal research design makes possible findings that cannot be generated in any other way (ibid.: 13-14). Perhaps the simplest and most obvious example lies in the quantification of a variety of dimensions of labor market dynamics, for example, the extent of movement into and out of the labor force, between employment and unemployment, and among firms, geographic regions, and occupations. Cross-sectional studies taken at two points in time permit a measure of the net changes that have occurred in, say, the occupational distribution, but provide no information on the magnitude of the gross flows of individuals among occupational categories that lie behind whatever change in distribution is observed.

Longitudinal data provide the only means of identifying the determining factors in developmental processes. For example, what elements in the high school experience of a young man affect the ease of accommodation to the labor market when his full-time education ends? Are there factors in a man's labor market experience during his forties and fifties that condition his retirement decision in his sixties? How does a woman's employment experience prior to marriage or birth of children affect her employment prospects when she reenters the labor market after her children are in school? Cross-sectional studies can shed little if any light on these types of questions.

Finally, longitudinal data may permit determination of the direction of causation between two correlated variables, or may make it clear that an ostensible relationship between two variables really reflects the influence of one or more variables not included in the analysis. As an example of the first of these situations, the cross-sectional relationship between health and labor force status is well known. At least for men, however, there is some ambiguity in this relationship, stemming from a suspicion that economically inactive men may be reporting health limitations in order to provide a respectable excuse for their inactivity. A longitudinal analysis can address such a suspicion, probing the extent to which the onset of a health problem in one period leads to a subsequent withdrawal from the labor force. To illustrate the case of omitted variables, consider a set of cross-sectional data showing higher wage rates for recent migrants than for nonmigrants, controlling for such variables as education, training, health, and region of residence. Such data might be used to calculate economic rates of return to migration. However, with longitudinal data one might inquire how the wage rates of migrants and nonmigrants compared, ceteris paribus, *prior to migration*. If the migrants had a wage advantage even then, it would be clear that at least part of the cross-sectional relationship reflected the fact that migration is a selective process. In other words, a part of what had been attributed to the effect of migration actually resulted from a variable not included in the analysis—for example, the greater motivation of those who migrated.[2]

The Samples

Plans for developing the samples for the surveys and for conducting the field work were discussed with representatives of the Census Bureau, which was to be responsible for these aspects of the work under a separate contract with the Department of Labor. Guided by the advice of the Bureau's statisticians, a sample of approximately 5,000 individuals was selected for each of the four age-sex categories described above. In order to permit statistically reliable estimates for blacks, the sampling ratio in predominantly black areas was to be three to four times as high as that in white areas. The samples were drawn from the 235 Primary Sampling Units (PSUs) included in the experimental

Monthly Labor Survey that was being conducted in the mid-60s to test proposed changes in the Current Population Survey (CPS) interview schedule. Thus, the sampling method was analogous to that used in the CPS. In the initial survey, each cohort was represented by a probability sample of the civilian noninstitutional population of the United States in the designated age-sex category.[3]

Two characteristics of these samples deserve special mention: First, they provided unbiased representation of their respective population groups only at the time of the initial surveys. There has been no attempt to either replace members of the samples lost through attrition or adjust the sampling weights of those remaining. Second, a very attractive aspect of the sampling design is that many of the households yielded more than one respondent, frequently across cohorts. Since households and respondents are cross-indexed, it is possible to relate to any given respondent other respondents in the same or other cohorts who were selected from the same household.

The Surveys

The original plan was to interview members of each sample annually over a five-year period. Annual interviews were in fact conducted for the two cohorts of youth: between 1966 and 1971 for the boys and between 1968 and 1973 for the girls. In the case of the older cohorts, however, biennial interviews were conducted as a cost-saving measure after 1967.[4] Interviews began at about the same time each year for the boys (October) and girls (January). Because of scheduling problems in the Census Bureau, the month in which interviews were conducted with the men and women changed during the course of the study.[5] Generally speaking, the interviewing process in any given survey extended over a two-to-three-month period.

Approximately three to four hundred interviewers were assigned to each of the NLS surveys. Since many of the procedures and labor force concepts used in the NLS were identical to those employed in the CPS, the Census Bureau used interviewers with CPS experience. A two-stage training program was developed in which supervisors from each of the Census regional offices were trained in Washington; afterwards, they trained interviewers and office clerks in their regions who were assigned to the surveys. Training materials were reviewed by the research staff of the Center for Human Resource Research and by Department of Labor personnel. Representatives of those organizations also attended many of the training sessions and accompanied interviewers during pretests.

One of the major uncertainties at the outset of the study concerned attrition in the samples over time. Attrition, however, has been low, due in large measure to the ingenuity and perseverance of the Field Division of the Census Bureau. For example, only 17 percent of the original sample of men were not interviewed in the 1971 survey, and almost half of these (8 percent) represented deaths. In other words, less than one-tenth of the men interviewed in 1966 were lost over the five-year period because of their refusal to be interviewed or the inability of Census enumerators to locate them. Attrition over the five-year period was 12 percent for the women and 14 percent for the girls. As might be expected, the attrition problem has been most pronounced among the boys because of military draft and because no attempt was made to follow subjects into the armed services. Nevertheless, about three-fourths of the original sample of boys was interviewed in 1971.

In the light of this record, and because of the widespread interest in the data generated by the NLS, officials of the Manpower Administration in 1971 suggested the possibility of continuing the surveys beyond the predetermined termination dates. In accordance with the recommendations of an interdisciplinary advisory committee that had followed the progress of the studies, the surveys were continued for an additional five years on the condition that the problem of attrition did not become unduly severe. Additional surveys were to be conducted biennially by telephone and were to be considerably shorter than those conducted during the first five years. They focused largely upon types of information which could not reliably be collected retrospectively (for example, income and number of weeks unemployed during a year). A longer face-to-face interview was scheduled at the end of the second five-year period.

The Data

It is neither feasible nor desirable to attempt a detailed catalogue of the information gathered in the National Longitudinal Surveys. It should be useful, however, to describe the conceptual framework that has guided the data collection and to delineate the major categories of variables included in the studies.

CONCEPTUAL FRAMEWORK

The general purpose of the National Longitudinal Surveys is to identify the factors accounting for variation in the labor market behavior and experience of the four age-sex subsets of the U. S. population represented by the samples. Accordingly, the theoretical structure underlying the collection of data is both broad and eclectic. An individual's status and behavior in the labor market is regarded as the product of interaction between a variety of individual and environmental characteristics. To illustrate, the length of time an unemployed person remains jobless is influenced by both personal and environmental circumstances. One set of relevant personal characteristics may influence an individual's attractiveness to potential employers, for example, education and work skills, health and physical fitness, sex, color, initiative, appearance, and age. Some of these factors may be functionally related to job performance; others may reflect employers' hiring preferences that have little or nothing to do with productivity. A second set of personal characteristics that may be influential in this context are those that determine the range of possible employers to whose attention the individual is likely to come. These include the extent and quality of labor market information, the vigor and ingenuity of job search, willingness to broaden this search outside one's area of residence and usual line of work, and the individual's hierarchy of preferences for different types of work and different kinds of economic and noneconomic rewards. Third, the unemployed individual's economic circumstances also condition the likelihood of reemployment. The extent of financial resources, the amount of income from sources other than working, and the extent of financial obligations all affect "staying power" and thus subjective requirements established for an acceptable job.

Factors external to the individual and his or her family also affect labor market experience. For any given set of personal characteristics, unemployment may be expected to be of longer duration in a depressed than in a buoyant economy. The occupational structure of job opportunities, the personnel policies of employers, and the policies of trade unions and government may also help to explain variations in the duration of unemployment. To cite just one example, the job-seeker can afford to be more selective when unemployment insurance benefits are higher; other things being equal, higher benefits will probably extend the period of unemployment.

This illustration with respect to unemployment is equally applicable to all other facets of labor market experience. Explanation for the various patterns of behavior or experience that are observed in terms of labor force participation, mobility, or occupational choice can also be sought in the relationship between individual and environmental characteristics. An individual makes choices and acts in ways that are conditioned by the total complex of personal characteristics. Behavior is also conditioned by the individual's perception of the environment; but even if environmental factors are misinterpreted or ignored, they impose real constraints upon behavior, and may produce outcomes substantially different from what the individual intended.

Obviously, no single study can hope to embrace the multitude of complex variables outlined or implied above. The National Longitudinal Surveys focus largely on the supply side of the labor market and ask the question, "What characteristics of individuals are important in accounting for variations in their labor market status and experience?" Many of the variables examined are common to all four cohorts, but some are specific to a given cohort.[6]

EMPLOYMENT AND UNEMPLOYMENT

The extent of labor market activity of each respondent is measured in several different ways. In each survey, questions are asked that permit the respondent's labor force and employment status in the preceding week[7] to be coded in precisely the same way that it is in the CPS. For the unemployed, a measure of duration is obtained, as well as a specification of methods of job search. In addition, information on number of weeks of employment and of unemployment during the preceding year, number of hours worked in the survey week, and number of hours usually worked at survey week job is obtained. A very useful measure of labor market activity that was collected in the initial survey of the women was the number of years since leaving school in which the respondent had worked for at least six months.

JOB HISTORY

The NLS survey instruments have been designed to obtain a detailed work history of each respondent over the period covered by the study, as well as a more limited history for the period prior to the initial survey. The retrospective lifetime work history questions vary among cohorts and are more intensive for the men and women than for the boys and girls. Members of each cohort were asked at least two series of questions with respect to previous jobs. For the men the questions related to the first job after leaving school and the longest job ever held; for the women the pattern of questions varied depending upon marital and child-bearing status. To illustrate, married women who had born children were asked to describe three jobs: the longest between leaving school and date of first marriage, the longest between time of first marriage and birth of first child, and the longest since birth of first child. Boys and girls were asked about their first full-time job and the job (if any) held during their last full year in high school.

In all instances, job is defined as a continuous period of service with a given employer or in a self-employed status. Information is obtained on length of service in the job and on the reason for having left it. Also, questions are asked that allow the job to be classified by occupation, industry, and class of worker.

Over the period covered by the surveys the work history obtained for each respondent is fairly detailed. In each survey respondents are asked questions, identical to those used in the CPS, which permit coding of occupation, industry, class of worker, weekly hours, and location for the current or most recent job. In addition, information is obtained on wage rate and, in some of the surveys, on union status. These data, together with information on jobs held between survey dates, permit analysis of interfirm, occupational, interindustry, and geographic mobility.

SOCIOECONOMIC AND HUMAN CAPITAL VARIABLES

A large number of characteristics relating to the socioeconomic status of respondents and to their health, education, and training have been incorporated in the study. In the initial survey of each cohort, information was obtained on a number of aspects of the early background of the respondent; for example, nationality, educational attainment of parents, and family structure when the respondent was a teenager. Data on respondents' educational attainment have been obtained for all of the cohorts, in greater detail for the two groups of youth than for the men and women. Information regarding highest year of regular school completed and type of high school curriculum has been obtained from all cohorts. In addition to this information on formal education, questions have been asked in every survey on the extent, character, and duration of training outside the regular school system.

For the youth, information on current school enrollment status has been obtained in each survey, permitting analysis of movement into, out of, and through the formal educational system over the time period covered by the study. Field of specialization in college, and amount of scholarship aid in college are illustrative of the additional types of information available for the boys and girls. Also, an index of high school quality has been constructed, based on information from questionnaires sent to the last high school attended by each respondent. Similarly, measures of the quality of higher education obtained by the respondent have been derived from a variety of published information about the college or university attended.

In the initial survey of each cohort, and periodically thereafter, the subjects were asked whether health problems or physical conditions prevented them from working or limited the amount or kind of work they could do. More detailed questions about the precise nature of these limitations were asked in the 1971 survey of each of the cohorts.

A considerable amount of information has been collected in each interview about the family characteristics of the respondent. Current marital status has been obtained in every survey; in addition, a retrospective marital history was obtained in the initial survey of the women. In each survey, questions are asked relating to all members of respondent's family who live in the household, including relationship to the respondent, age, educational attainment, and (for persons of working age) number of weeks worked during the past 12 months, usual number of hours worked per week, and occupation of longest job. Additional information relating to family members includes health condition of spouse, number of dependents, and whether parents and parents-in-law are alive. For employed women and girls with children, information has been collected on type and cost of child care arrangement. For those unemployed or out of the labor force, questions have been asked about the need for child care should the respondent find a job or decide to work outside the home. For the girls, fertility plans were explored in the 1971 and 1973 surveys.

FINANCIAL CHARACTERISTICS

Detailed information on the wealth and income of the subjects and their families has been collected over the years covered by the surveys, although the degree of detail varies somewhat among cohorts. Using the initial survey of the men as an example, questions were asked about the following assets and liabilities: home ownership, farm, business or professional practice, other real estate, automobile(s), savings or checking accounts, U. S. savings bonds, several other forms of financial assets, and several types of debt. As to income, again using the initial survey of men as an example, information was obtained on amount of income received by the respondent, his spouse, and other family members from each of the following sources: wages, salaries, commissions, and tips; net income from a business or profession; net income from operating a farm; unemployment compensation; rental income; interest or dividends or income from estates or trusts; disability benefits from a variety of sources; other social security benefits; other public assistance or welfare payments; food stamps; government pensions; and all other sources.

SOCIAL-PSYCHOLOGICAL VARIABLES

A number of social-psychological variables have been used, some uniformly in all four cohorts and others for only one or two groups. Attitudes toward current job have been explored for all four cohorts, including a measure of job satisfaction, a measure of attachment to current employer based upon response to a hypothetical job offer elsewhere, and an exploration of factors liked best and least about current job. The surveys have also attempted to tap a variety of attitudes toward work in general. For example, respondents have been asked whether they would continue to work if by some chance they were to get enough money to live comfortably without working. They have also been asked whether wages or liking the work is more important to them about a job. In each interview, nonemployed workers have been asked the circumstances under which they would take a job. For all cohorts there have been questions designed to elicit views about the propriety of labor market activity by mothers of young children. Each survey of the men has included questions relating to retirement plans and expectations.

In every survey of the boys and girls, questions have been asked concerning educational and occupational aspirations; in the initial interviews with these groups, attitudes toward school experience were explored. For these two groups, scores on mental ability tests were obtained from the last high school attended by each respondent. Each respondent in these two groups was also scored on a simple labor market information test administered in the initial survey of the boys and the 1969 survey of the girls.

An abbreviated form of the Rotter Internal-External Scale has been administered twice, over a two- or three-year interval, to each of the four samples. This scale purports to measure perceived "locus of control"—for instance, whether an individual believes that he is master of his own destiny (internal) or that what happens to him is determined largely by forces over which he has little or no control (external).

ENVIRONMENTAL VARIABLES

Although the National Longitudinal Surveys have focused largely on the supply rather than on the demand side of the labor market, the research incorporates several environmental variables developed on the basis of the characteristics of the local area in which the respondent resides. These variables, in all cases derived from sources other than the survey instruments themselves, include the population size of the local area, local area unemployment rate, an index of demand for female labor, an index of demand for teenage male labor, and the presence and type of accredited colleges in the local area.

Administration of the Project

There has been close and continuous collaboration between the Center for Human Resource Research and the Office of Manpower Research and Development (OMRD) of the Manpower Administration in the planning of the National Longitudinal Surveys and between the Center and the Bureau of the Census in their execution. From the inception of the project, Howard Rosen, Director of OMRD, has provided constant support and encouragement as well as a number of suggestions for specific research reports. Until their retirement toward the end of 1973, Stuart Garfinkle and Jacob Schiffman monitored the project for OMRD. In countless telephone and face-to-face conversations with members of the research staff of the Center they made valuable suggestions on the content of interview schedules and on policy issues to which the analysis of NLS data might be addressed. In addition, Garfinkle and Schiffman contributed substantially to the work of the Center by their thorough reviews of all research reports prior to publication.

Evolving Roles of Center and Census Bureau

The Center's interaction with the Census Bureau has been even more continuous—and also more complex. Under its contract with the Department of Labor, the Census Bureau has been responsible for selecting the samples, conducting all of the field work, coding and editing the interview schedules, preparing the data tapes, and producing the tabulations requested by the Center for Human Resource Research. The Center has been responsible for designing the content of the interview schedules, developing the coding specifications, and analyzing the data. This description, however, belies the close interaction and cooperation between the two organizations at every stage of the research. Moreover, the nature of the relationship between the Census Bureau and the Center and the functions of each organization with respect to the overall effort have changed substantially over the years.

In practice, jurisdictional lines between the Center and the Census Bureau have frequently become blurred. For example, while the content of the interview schedules is primarily the responsibility of the Center, the Census Bureau has had substantial influence in this area. For the most part this has been through valuable advice based on long experience with survey instruments, for which the research staff of the Center has been grateful. On occasion, however, the Bureau has exercised a veto power. In the early stages of the project, for instance, the Bureau steadfastly refused to administer standard psychological scales for fear of alienating respondents and possibly irritating influential members of Congress. This policy was ultimately relaxed to the extent of permitting administration of an abbreviated version of the Rotter I-E Scale in the 1969 interview schedules. The Bureau was also unwilling to use a method of collecting 12-month work histories proposed by the Center which involved coding a respondent's status in each of the months between two interview dates. Beginning with the 1970 surveys, however, the Bureau did develop a substitute scheme to produce the same kind of detail.

When the National Longitudinal Surveys began, the Census Bureau was to be solely responsible for all aspects of data processing, including the preparation of the tabulations for use by the Center in its reports to the Department of Labor. Moreover, cross-tabulations were the only type of computer output Census was prepared to produce. As it turned out, this had an important influence on the characteristics of the data tapes that Census prepared. It constructed the data files in the simplest and most expeditious manner consistent with the requirements of its table generator program, causing some problems when the tapes began to be used more widely and intensively by researchers at the Center.

It became abundantly clear over time that the NLS data could not be exploited fully through tabular analysis. Accordingly, all agreed that the Center for Human Resource Research would undertake a larger portion of data-processing activity. Once the Census Bureau had created some test tabulations requested by the Center, it would release to the Center a copy of the computer tape from which the tables had been prepared. The Center then would generate from the computer tape whatever types of data were required. This arrangement did not take full effect until the 1971 survey of the men, the 1972 survey of the women, the 1970 survey of the boys, and the 1971 survey of the girls.

The Public-Use Tapes

A second respect in which the responsibilities of the Census Bureau and the Center for Human Resource Research were significantly altered over the course of the study was in the preparation of public-use tapes. When the project began, no explicit consideration was given to making the data available to the public. As the studies and the content of the data files became known, there were numerous inquiries about how other researchers might gain access to the data. While it was clear that data collected with public funds would ultimately be in the public domain, questions arose relating to the timing and the form of the releases.

All parties agreed that the data tapes ought to be available as quickly as possible, consistent with the maintenance of adequate quality standards. The guidelines ultimately developed by mutual agreement were that the Census Bureau would prepare a public-use version of the data tapes containing all the raw information from the interview schedules as well as a selected number of constructed variables suggested by the Center.[8] It was further agreed that the Census Bureau would release these tapes approximately six months after they had become available to the Center. This time lag was intended primarily to permit the discovery and correction of errors in the data files prior to general release.

When data tapes were first received by the Center for Human Resource Research, they had a number of characteristics that made them difficult to use for anything other than the cross-tabulations for which they had originally been designed. For example, alphabetic codes had to be converted to numerics before the data file could readily be used for regression analysis, and illegal numeric codes also had to be eliminated. Moreover, since the public-use tapes supplied by Census suffered identical limitations, researchers elsewhere had to perform similar "cleansing" operations. In view of the obvious waste involved in this duplication of effort, the Center agreed in 1973 to undertake the responsibility for the public-use tapes. A conference of all known users of the NLS data files was convened during that year to consider proposed specifications for the new tapes. The Center will not only produce the public-use tapes for surveys yet to be released, but will also revise the previously prepared public-use tapes according to new specifications.[9]

Advisory Committees

On several occasions during the course of the project, advisory groups have been convened to consider issues relating to the content of the interview schedules. At the very inception of the study, a small group of consultants was invited to join Manpower Administration and Center personnel to discuss the scope of the investigation and the kinds of information that should be collected.[10] When the study of the women was being planned, a very different type of advisory group was assembled. Because members of the research staff wished to sharpen their understanding of the perceptions of poverty-group women, seven women whose names were obtained from a local welfare agency were invited to the Center as consultants for an all-day discussion of labor market problems and experiences. Although an agenda was provided for the session, the conversation was very informal, and at times the presence of members of the research staff was virtually ignored. The discussion yielded some ideas that were helpful in developing the women's interview schedule.

As the deadline approached for the preparation of the 1971 interview schedules for the men and boys, a more permanent advisory committee was established.[11] The initial meeting of this group focused on the content of what was then regarded as the final interview schedules for the two male cohorts. The committee was reconvened in May 1971 to consider the content of the "final" surveys of the women and girls. It also met in December 1972 to consider the advisability of extending the surveys beyond the initial five-year period and to make recommendations with respect to the methods of data collection (for example, mail versus telephone) and the content of the interview schedules.

Products of the National Longitudinal Surveys

The contributions of the National Longitudinal Surveys cannot at this juncture be fully assessed. This is because the study is still in progress and, most important, because complete returns are not yet in on its most unique aspect—its longitudinal nature. Nevertheless, a survey of the wide variety of purposes for which available data have been or are currently being used and an examination of some of the findings of completed studies will provide at least some indication of the potential of the data files.

Applications of the Data: Illustrative Research Projects

At the outset, it is worth noting that the Bureau of the Census has sold more than 125 copies of data tapes to some 28 researchers or research groups throughout the United States. By mid-1974 the Center had received additional orders for 41 tapes from 22 researchers. Moreover, an unknown number of "bootleg" copies of the tapes have been made and are in use.

A wide variety of research topics have been and are in the process of being investigated with the NLS data, both at Ohio State University and elsewhere.[12] A dozen volumes have been published reporting comprehensively on the data that have emerged from each wave of interviews. Three of these volumes relate to the men and are published under the general title *The Pre-Retirement Years* (Manpower Research Monograph 15, Vols. 1-3); four pertain to the boys, under the title *Career Thresholds* (Manpower Research Monograph 16, Vols. 1-4); two are based on the surveys of the women, each with the title *Dual Careers* (Manpower Research Monograph 21, Vols. 1-2); and three relate to the girls, under the title *Years for Decision* (Manpower Research Monograph 24, Vols. 1-3). In addition, there have been almost 60 studies analyzing intensively specific aspects of the data for one or more cohorts, at least 35 more studies of this kind are in process at this writing. Without attempting to be exhaustive, the range of interests reflected in research utilizing NLS data can be illustrated there.

LABOR SUPPLY AND LABOR MOBILITY

Several studies of the determinants of labor supply have been made (Egge, 1971; Fleisher et al., 1971; Fleisher and Porter, 1971; Grasso and Shea, 1972; Kim, 1972; Meyer, 1972); at least one of these has explored the effect of variations in state welfare regulations on the amount of labor services offered by poor women (Meyer, 1972). There have also been studies of a number of aspects of labor mobility. One of these has analyzed the occupational mobility of the boys to test the dual labor market hypothesis (Andrisani, 1973); another utilizes data relating to the men for substantially the same purpose (Leigh, 1976). There have also been studies of geographic moves, one of which has used data from the two male cohorts to test certain implications of human capital theory (Schwartz and Nestal, 1975) and another of which has focused on the impact of geographic movement on several aspects of the labor market status of women (Sandell and Koenig, 1978). One study used the five-year data for the men to ascertain the determinants of voluntary interfirm mobility (Parnes and Nestel, 1975).

EARNINGS AND INCOME DISTRIBUTION

A number of researchers are examining the sources of variation in earnings among individuals. Several studies have focused on the effect of variations in lifetime work experience on the earnings of women (Mincer and Polacheck, 1973; Suter, 1973; Suter and Miller, 1973); one has examined the determinants of early labor market success of young men as measured by both earnings and occupational status (Kohen, 1973). There have been several attempts to measure racial discrimination on the basis of earnings differentials (Flanagan, 1974b; Kohen, 1973), and at least two studies have investigated sex discrimination on the same basis (Odita, 1972; Kohen and Roderick, 1972). Analyses of income distribution have also been pursued on the basis of NLS data. Data for the men and the boys have been used to study the effect on income inequality of extending the accounting period beyond one year and to investigate the correlates of income instability over two- and three-year periods (Kohen, Parnes, and Shea, 1974).

EDUCATIONAL EXPERIENCE

Several aspects of the educational experience of the boys and the girls have attracted the interest of researchers. The relationship between high school curriculum and subsequent labor market success for those individuals who do not go beyond high school has been the subject of one study (Grasso, 1975). Another study is analyzing the effects of various kinds of interruption to schooling. The phenomenon of dropping out of school has been examined in at least two studies, one focusing on premature withdrawal from high school (McNally, 1977) and the other on factors associated with dropping out of college (Karnas, 1973).

WOMEN'S ROLE

A number of researchers have used data from the women's and girls' surveys to analyze women's role in both the labor market and the home. Two studies have reported on the characteristics of women in atypical occupational assignments (Roderick and Davis, 1972a, 1972b). Another, in progress, analyzes changes in women's labor force experience and work-related attitudes at different stages of the life cycle (Sandell, 1977). At least one study of fertility has been based in part on NLS data (Rosenberg, 1972). The data have also been used to examine the relationship between the amount of time a mother has spent at home (as distinguished from time spent in the labor market) and characteristics of her children in terms of mental ability and educational attainment (Fleisher, 1977).

ATTITUDES

Several researchers have emphasized some of the attitudinal measures included in the National Longitudinal Surveys. The data from the first two surveys of the men have been used to study the determinants of expected age of retirement and of changes in this expectation over a one-year period (Parnes and Nestel, 1971). There have been two studies of the correlates of job satisfaction, one among the men (Nicholson and Roderick, 1972) and the other among the girls (Nicholson and Roderick, 1973). A comprehensive study has been made of the relationships among a number of job-related attitudes in all four cohorts (Andrisani et al., 1977). There have been at least two studies of the correlates of "powerlessness" as measured by the Rotter I-E scale (Valecha, 1972; Andrisani and Nestel, 1976).

EVALUATIONS OF PUBLIC PROGRAMS

A few studies use NLS data as a means of evaluating public programs. There are at least two studies attempting to test the hypothesis that duration of unemployment is positively related to level of state unemployment insurance benefits. There is also a study of the impact of the 1967 rise in the minimum wage on the employment and unemployment experience of male youth, utilizing the data obtained in the 1966 and 1967 surveys of the boys (Egge et al., 1970). An early study based on NLS data for all the cohorts attempted a preassessment of the Nixon Administration's Family Assistance Plan by examining the characteristics of members of the samples who would have qualified under the terms of the proposed legislation (Shea and Meyer, 1972).

METHODOLOGICAL STUDIES

NLS data have been used as a basis for several methodological studies. Using a special father-son sample drawn from the data files of the men and the boys, analyses have been made of response bias in young men's reports of their fathers' education and occupation (Borus and Gilbert, 1971, forthcoming). Another piece of methodological research based on the NLS data aimed at estimating the extent to which occupational mobility registered by the longitudinal data is spurious, reflecting such factors as variation from one survey to another in wording of response or in coder's interpretations of the entries on the interview schedule (Miller, 1977).

Selected Research Findings

Given the volume and diversity of studies based upon National Longitudinal Survey data, it would be foolhardy to attempt to catalog the research findings in a chapter of this length. Nevertheless, it is possible in very general terms of illustrate some of the ways in which the surveys are helping to enhance insight into the operation of labor markets and into the determinants of individual status. Findings regarding three broad subjects are reviewed: (1) the determinants of labor market success; (2) intercolor differences in labor market experience; and (3) the predictive validity of attitudinal measures.

THE DETERMINANTS OF LABOR MARKET SUCCESS

Considerable progress has been made in identifying factors associated with variations in status in the labor market, whether status is measured in terms of occupational position, income, or wage rate. The findings strongly support the role of human capital, but have also isolated other factors that help explain relative success in the labor market.

Kohen's analysis of the average hourly earnings and the occupational status of male youth 18 to 24 years of age who were not enrolled in school at the time of the 1966 survey concluded that the strongest direct determinant of early labor market success—particularly as measured by occupational status—is number of years of school completed. However, mental ability also has an independent direct effect on both earnings and occupational status and has an indirect effect by conditioning the amount of education a young man obtains. On the basis of his data, Kohen estimates that the omission of an ability variable in measuring the relationship between years of schooling and earnings result in a 30 percent overstatement of the effect of schooling. Thus, calculations of rates of return to education are biased upward to the extent that they do not include an adequate measure of mental ability (Kohen, 1973: 137-152).

A significant relation between health condition and labor market success has also been shown. In the Kohen study, poor health was found to have an adverse effect upon both hourly wages and occupational status (ibid.: 140). Similarly, a study based on the data for the men found that poor health has an adverse effect upon annual earnings through its effect on total hours worked and on the hourly wage rate (Davis, 1972: 15).

Another variable that appears to be related to both hourly wages and occupational status is the extent of labor market information. In the case of male youth, scores on an occupational information test administered in 1966 were found to be positively related to both wage rate and occupational status in 1968, even when years of schooling, mental ability, quality of education, and socioeconomic background are held constant. Since scores on the occupational information test were positively related to amount of education, one implication of this finding is that part of the contribution of education to higher earnings occurs through the development of labor market information rather than purely through the creation of vocational skills and know-how (Parnes and Kohen, 1973: 22-23).

Formal training programs outside the regular school system appear to contribute to labor market success, although longitudinal analysis suggests that cross-sectional data tend to overstate the independent contribution of training to earnings. Arvil V. Adams found that men who received training between 1966 and 1971 enjoyed higher earnings in 1971 than those who did not, holding constant such other factors as amount of education, health, and region of residence. Moreover, the longitudinal data base permitted Adams to ascertain that those men who received training between 1966 and 1971 *already* enjoyed higher earnings in 1966 than men who did not receive such training, again controlling for other factors. Thus, some part of the apparent contribution of training to earnings reflects the fact that training is a selective process. The more productive or more highly motivated individuals are more likely to obtain training.[13]

The NLS data also attest to the importance of informal on-the-job training in conditioning earnings. For example, using age as a measure of labor market exposure, Andrisani found a significant relationship between age and 1968 wage rate among white youth (although not among black) in both the "primary" and "secondary" labor markets (Andrisani, 1973: 78-80). On-the-job training is a particularly important variable in explaining the current labor market status of women, since there is much greater variation in labor market exposure among women than among men. A relatively crude indication of the importance of this factor is provided by the NLS data on the occupational mobility of women between their first job after leaving school and the job they held when first interviewed in 1967. Among the white women, downward mobility was considerably less common and upward mobility somewhat more common among the never-married than among those who were married, despite the fact that the never-married started their careers, on the average, in occupations with higher status than those occupied by the married women (*Dual Careers* [*Manpower Research Monograph* 21] Vol. 1: 161).

Since the initial survey of women collected retrospective information on lifetime work history it is possible to develop considerably more refined measures of the influence of on-the-job training on earnings and occupational status. On the basis of these data, Larry Suter (1973) has shown a very substantial relationship between the annual earnings of women and the proportion of their working lives they have worked, controlling for years of schooling. Solomon Polachek (1973: 12) has reported that expanding the human capital model "so as to account for the additional depreciation that occurs during the periods of non-labor force participation" permits the explanation of about 50 percent of the male-female wage differential.

Evidence has also been adduced to demonstrate the effects of social-psychological variables on labor market status. For example, Andrisani (1973: 66-68) has shown that upward occupational mobility of the boys between 1966 and 1968 was related to both the occupational aspirations the youth had expressed in 1966 and the degree of internality measured by the Rotter I-E scale.[14] Similarly, for men with exactly twelve years of schooling, those above average in internality had higher average hourly earnings in 1969 than those whose internality was below average (*The Pre-Retirement Years* [*Manpower Research Monograph* 15] Vol. 3: 76).

A very interesting use of NLS attitudinal measures to explain earnings differentials is illustrated by the work of Adams and Nestel. On the basis of data from the boys' surveys, they have shown that southern black migrants to northern metropolitan areas earn more, on the average, than native northern blacks, even after controlling for differences in age, years of schooling completed, and current residence. Moreover, they provide evidence that regional differences in the attitudes of young blacks toward school and work help to explain these income differences. Young blacks who were educated in the South, irrespective of whether they migrate, have attitudes toward school and work that are more likely than those held by blacks in northern cities to lead to better-paying jobs (Adams and Nestel, 1973: 17-22).

An important question for research that has arisen in recent years is whether the determinants of labor market success operate uniformly in all segments of the labor market. According to the dual labor market theory, there is a primary market consisting of relatively attractive jobs and a secondary market consisting of jobs characterized by low wages, few fringe benefits, poor working conditions, limited channels for promotion, and high turnover. Moreover, there is little or no movement between the two markets. In the primary market, hiring and promoting correspond with the relative productivities of workers, so that the more attractive jobs go to those with the largest amounts of human capital and highest degrees of motivation. In the secondary market, on the other hand, the dual labor market view posits employers who operate as if they were allocating jobs among members of a homogeneous labor pool, so that there is little relation between the relative desirability of jobs and the characteristics of their incumbents. Paul Andrisani (1973: 83-86) has attempted to test the dual labor market hypothesis, utilizing the data from the boys' surveys from 1966 through 1968. While he found enough movement between the secondary and primary labor markets to conclude that an extreme version of the dual labor market theory is untenable, Andrisani nevertheless does show that some of the human capital variables do not operate to explain differentials in the secondary labor market as well as they do in the primary sector, and that this is particularly true among blacks.

Robert Flanagan (1974b) has also brought certain evidence to bear on the dual labor market theory. Examining racial wage differentials for the men's and the boys' cohorts, he found that for the younger group there are no significant returns to job changing, while for the older cohort such returns are positive and operate to *reduce* the white-black wage differential. Thus, his analysis provides no "support for the view that race differentials are largely the result of the restriction of blacks to low-wage, high turnover markets." While acknowledging that this is not a definitive test of the dual market theory, he asserts that "any labor market segments which may exist within an age group are not defined by differential turnover flow" (p. 50).

BLACK-WHITE DIFFERENCES

In research based on the National Longitudinal Surveys a substantial amount of attention has been devoted to comparisons between blacks and whites. Significant differences between the two color groups have been found in virtually all aspects of labor market status and labor market behavior. The data for the men serve as an illustration. As is well known from official labor force data, middle-aged black men, compared to their white counterparts, have lower labor force participation rates, higher unemployment rates, tend to be concentrated in jobs of lower socioeconomic status, and are paid lower wages. What conventional labor force data do not show is that there are also substantial attitudinal differences between blacks and whites with respect to work in general and to their jobs in particular. For example, the proportion of all middle-aged black men in the labor force who report that they would continue to work even if circumstances did not require it is somewhat lower than that among white men (*The Pre-Retirement Years* [*Manpower Research Monograph* 15] Vol. 1: 204).[15] Much larger proportions of black men than of white men regard good wages to be more important than the intrinsic qualities of the job (ibid.: 208).[16] Overall, somewhat smaller proportions of blacks than of whites (51 percent versus 58 percent) report liking their jobs very much (ibid.: 218); and, based on their responses to a hypothetical job offer, blacks are slightly more ready than whites to leave their current employers for higher wages (ibid.: 162).

From a policy point of view, it is necessary to understand the bases for such differences between blacks and whites. For example, to the extent that the lower labor force participation of black men reflects their greater desire for leisure, no particular social problem exists. On the other hand, to the extent that it reflects a greater incidence or severity of health problems or a greater "discouragement" effect resulting from unemployment, policies addressing health or antidiscrimination issues might be appropriate. As another example, if the lower wages of blacks reflects their lower productivities, increased investments in human capital or improvements in motivation would be appropriate approaches to greater equality. However, if intercolor wage differentials cannot be explained in these terms, more effective measures against labor market discrimination are in order. As a final example, understanding the basis for the attitudinal differences that prevail in the aggregate between blacks and whites is a prerequisite to providing answers to some of the questions raised above. To the extent that intercolor differences in strength of work ethic or in degree of job satisfaction and attachment merely reflect the differences between the kinds of jobs held by the two color groups, they are not "true" racial differences at all, and there is no logical basis for inferring from them possible differences in job performance. But to the extent that they reflect real cultural differences between blacks and whites, they may provide a legitimate explanation for wage differentials—even if they reflect types of discrimination that take place outside the labor market (ibid.: 240).

While there are no definitive answers to such questions at present, a number of interesting clues are revealed in some of the findings based upon the NLS data. One example is provided by the longitudinal data on the labor force participation of white and black men between 1966 and 1969. For the total cohort, the participation rates in the initial year of the study (1966) were 94.9 percent for whites and 92.2 percent for blacks, a differential of 2.7 percentage points. Between 1966 and 1969 labor force participation declined for both groups of men, but more so for blacks than for whites. As a consequence, the black-white differential had risen over the three-year period from 2.7 to 3.4 percentage points (*The Pre-Retirement Years,* Vol. 3: 17). However, when men who reported no health problems in either 1966 or 1969 are considered, the situation was quite different. Among whites the labor force participation rate declined over the three-year period by only 1 percentage point, while among blacks it actually increased by .4 of a percentage point. As a consequence, in 1969 the black participation rate was actually 1 percentage point higher than that of the whites (ibid.: 23-24). Since the proportion of men reporting no health problems in either 1966 or 1969 was identical for blacks and whites (ibid.: 5), it follows that either the severity of health problems is greater among blacks than among whites or that the labor market response to health problems of blacks is greater than that of whites. In either case, the fact that the intercolor difference tends to disappear (or even reverse) when only healthy men are considered is highly instructive.

With respect to work-related attitudes, some of the gross differences between blacks and whites tend to disappear or reverse when other factors are controlled; still, certain differences persist. In a multivariate analysis controlling for all other relevant factors, the degree of job satisfaction has been found to be at least as high among black men as among white men (Nicholson and Roderick, 1972: 21). Similarly, although the variable has not been systematically investigated, there is some evidence that when other relevant factors are controlled, black men are at least as highly committed to the work ethic as are white men. For instance, within all but three of the major occupation groups the intercolor differential in degree of work commitment is either smaller than for the cohort as a whole or is actually reversed (*The Pre-Retirement Years*, Vol. 1: 204). An another example, in a multivariate analysis of expectation of early retirement, blacks have been found to be less likely than whites to expect to retire before age 65 (Schreiner and Knutson, n.d.: 43).

In contrast, there is at least one attitudinal difference between white and black men that appears to be independent of both the amount of education the individual has and the kind of job he holds. This is the greater tendency of the blacks to attach more importance to good wages than to the intrinsic character of work. For the total sample of middle-aged men, there is a 29 percent differential between whites and blacks with respect to this question. It is true that with crude controls for type of occupation and amount of education this differential shrinks to 6 percent for those with 13 or more years of education in white-collar jobs, but it remains as high as 21 percent for blue-collar workers with 8 or less years of education (*The Pre-Retirement Years*, Vol. 1: 208).

An interesting aspect of black-white differences in labor market status involves changing behavior over time. During the first five years of NLS data for the men, there is evidence of at least a small reversal of trends apparent in the experiences of members of the sample prior to the time of the initial survey. Data collected in the initial survey showed that despite more favorable starting positions, white men were more likely than black men to move up the occupational ladder between the first job they held after leaving school and that which they occupied in 1966. In other words, the differential in occupational status between the whites and blacks became more pronounced over the course of their lifetimes (ibid.: 116-128). In contrast, between the 1966 and 1971 surveys, the relative improvement experienced by blacks was by most measures somewhat greater than that among whites, causing some shrinkage in the percentage differential between the two groups.[17] Using income as a criterion, the increase in real family income over the five-year period was 7 percent for the average white respondent and 11 percent for the average black. For those who were employed at both times, a slight but nevertheless perceptible narrowing of occupational differentials had occurred. Between 1966 and 1971 the proportion of black men who occupied white-collar jobs rose by 2.1 percent in comparison with a rise of 1.2 percent for the whites. Median hourly rate of pay for black men also rose by a larger percentage amount than that for whites, resulting in a shrinkage in the relative differential over the five-year period.

There has been at least one systematic attempt in the case of the men to ascertain to what extent wage differentials reflect labor market discrimination. Flanagan (1974b) in the study mentioned above, has attempted to ascertain how much of the 1967 wage differential between middle-aged white and black men can be attributed to characteristics that affect wage rates and how much to differences in the "prices paid for characteristics" (i.e., labor market discrimination). He found that slightly over two-thirds of the gross intercolor wage differential of 42 percent is attributable to differences in the characteristics included in his analysis (p. 45).

There has been a greater amount of work of this type done on the basis of the data for the boys. Both Andrisani (1973: 55-84) and Kogen (1973: 150-151), for example, have concluded that young black men suffer fairly substantial labor market discrimination with respect to wages and even more with respect to occupational status. Kohen (p. 92) estimates that about one-fourth of the gross difference in wage rate between whites and blacks is attributable to labor market discrimination, virtually identical to Flanagan's finding (1974b: 48), despite the fact that there are substantial differences between the two studies in the models which yield these results. Likewise, Hall and Kasten (1973: 788-789, 791-792) have produced evidence of "unequal treatment" of young black men in the labor market based on the occupational assignments of youth entering the labor market in the early sixties, controlling for "endowments" (for example, family background, highest year of school completed, and mental ability). However, their analysis concluded that by the late sixties there had been nearly complete elimination of racial bias in the way that the labor market assigned individuals to occupations, although there had been no reduction in the difference in endowments between the two groups.

Finally, one research finding giving intercolor differences with special significance from a methodological point of view is the fairly pervasive interaction found between color and other explanatory variables. That is, a number of variables have substantially different effects as between whites and blacks. As Kohen (1973: 148) has pointed out, an implication of such a finding is that "studies which represent the effects of race merely by inclusion of a dichotomous variable in the regression equation contain improperly specified models, which in turn produce inaccurate estimates of the effects of racial discrimination."

PREDICTIVE VALIDITY OF ATTITUDINAL MEASURES

From a methodological perspective, an interesting set of findings from NLS studies relates to the use of attitudinal variables as predictors of behavior. There is strong evidence that even relatively simple measures of attitudes may bear statistically significant relationships with subsequent behavior.

Both degrees of satisfaction with current job and degree of attachment to current employer as measured by an individual's response to an hypothetical job offer have been found to be related to the probability of actual interfirm movement. For example, middle-aged men who were classified as having relatively weak attachments on the basis of the hypothetical job offer question in 1966 were three times as likely to have made a voluntary job change between 1966 and 1969 as those with relatively strong attachments (17 percent versus 6 percent). Among those with long tenure—20 years or more—the differential was greater than fourfold (9 percent versus 2 percent) (*The Pre-Retirement Years*, Vol. 3: 38). Similarly, men who reported liking their 1966 job very much were less likely to have made a voluntary job change over the three-year period than those who reacted less favorably. In this case, however, differences were entirely attributable to those with less than five years of service in their 1966 job, suggesting that a lack of enthusiasm for a job causes short-tenured men in this age category to seek other alternatives, but that once substantial seniority is achieved, the absence of strong positive feelings toward the job is not sufficient to cause men to move (ibid.: 39).

Other examples of the predictive validity of attitudinal questions are provided by the data for women. Respondents who were not in the labor force in 1967 were asked what they expected to be doing five years hence. Of those who responded "working," about 30 percent were already in the labor force by 1969, in contrast to only about 12 percent of those who indicated that they would be staying home (*Dual Careers*, Vol. 2: 39). Women's attitudes toward the propriety of labor market activity on the part of mothers, as measured in 1967, helped predict actual changes in labor force participation between 1967 and 1969.[18] Among women in the labor force in 1967, those with unfavorable attitudes were more likely to withdraw between 1967 and 1969. Conversely, for those not in the labor force in 1967, women with favorable attitudes were more likely to enter (ibid.: 39-43).[19]

An Agenda for Additional Research

The data base provided by the National Longitudinal Surveys will almost certainly provide a fertile field for research for many years to come. A good portion of future research will doubtless be similar to that which has already been executed, with the advantage of additional waves of data as they become available. Despite the impressive inventory of studies already completed, most have used data for only one or two years, and no published report has yet been based upon the entire five years for which the studies were originally planned.

The extension of the project for an additional five-year period will clearly open opportunities for kinds of research that have hitherto been impossible. For example, by 1976, when the final interview with the men is scheduled to take place, about a third of the sample will be at or above the conventional retirement age of 65, and it is entirely possible that an even large proportion will have actually retired. This will permit an analysis of the relationship between retirement expectations and actual retirement behavior. With appropriate design of the final interview schedules, it will also permit an analysis of the extent and determinants of material and psychological welfare during retirement. Similarly, by the time of the final surveys of the boys and girls in 1976 and 1978, respectively, the substantial numbers (60 percent of the boys and 50 percent of the girls) who were enrolled in school at the time of the initial survey will, with very few exceptions, have left school. This will permit an exploration of the relationship between aspirations and experience while in school and subsequent labor market experience. Also, comprehensive analyses of the process of adjustment to the labor market should be possible.

LABOR MARKET DISCRIMINATION

A type of research for which the NLS data bank appears to be particularly promising is investigation into the extent and nature of labor market discrimination. As has been stated, the principal difficulty in identifying and quantifying labor market discrimination lies in being certain that all factors affecting productivity are controlled in the analysis. The social-psychological variables that exist in the NLS along with human capital measures and detailed records of labor market experience provide a better basis for doing this than most other bodies of microdata. The question of racial discrimination can, of course, be pursued within each of the cohorts, while the issue of sex discrimination can be studied on the basis of the data for the boys and the girls. In studying wage discrimination, it would seem desirable to focus on particular occupational or educational categories in order to ascertain whether there is variation in the extent of discrimination among these categories. It should also be particularly fruitful to examine changes in extent of discrimination over the ten-year period covered by the study in order to provide insight into the possible influences of the civil rights and women's liberation movements.

WORK ATTITUDES

Another promising area for research that has hardly begun to be exploited relates to attitudes toward work and jobs. More or less identical questions relating to commitment to work, factors liked and disliked about jobs, degree of job satisfaction, and degree of job attachment will have been asked of representative samples of blacks and whites in four age-sex categories over a period of ten years. This should provide a basis for some fascinating comparisons according to age, sex, and color, as well as for an examination of changes over time. The data should be particularly useful for testing empirically some of the assertions that have recently gained currency relating to the "quality of work."

FAMILY STUDIES

The substantial number of multiple-respondent households included in the NLS affords opportunities for a variety of unusual types of research. For example, there are 567 households in which there is at least one subject in the men's sample and one in the women's sample—most, of course, representing husband-wife combinations. Similarly, there are approximately 900 father-son combinations, 800 father-daughter combinations, 1,400 mother-son combinations, 1,500 mother-daughter combinations, and 1,800 brother-sister combinations. There are in excess of 300 households in which father, mother, and at least one child are included in NLS samples.

The rich research potential associated with these multiple-respondent households stems from the fact that detailed information relating to personal characteristics, labor market behavior and plans, and, most important, attitudes has been obtained directly from each individual. There is a wide variety of interesting questions that can be approached with such data. First, there are methodological studies, some of which have already been made, relating to the consistency of response to factual questions by different members of the same family. Second, there are fascinating issues relating to the consistency of various types of attitudes among family members—commitment to work, opinion about the appropriate role for married women with children, and perception of locus of control (internal-external). One rather complex analysis along such lines would be to probe the relationship between the educational aspirations of a young man and the aspirations for him expressed by his father, and the extent to which the relationship between those two sets of aspirations affects the subsequent career of the young man.[20]

Third, there is the possibility of investigating the extent to which the attitudes of one family member affect the current or subsequent behavior of other members of the family. The attitude of a man toward the propriety of labor market activity by women with children might be used as an explanatory variable in studying the labor market behavior of his wife or his daughter. As another illustration, the subsequent labor market and fertility behavior of a young women might be related to attitudes expressed by her mother when the subject was a teen-ager.

Finally, the effects of the labor market activity of one family member on the behavior of other members of the household could be investigated. Most models of labor supply assume that the behavior of individuals is guided by a desire to maximize the utility of the entire household. Nevertheless, empirical research has very rarely been able to make such a model operational because of the absence of data. The multiple-respondent household in the NLS should help eliminate this deficiency. With data for husband-wife combinations, it should be possible to explore whether and under what circumstances there are adjustments in the labor market activity of one member of the pair in response to changes in the activity of the other. One might, for example, investigate the consequences of a geographic move on the labor force participation, employment experience, occupational status, wage rate, annual earnings, and degree of job satisfaction of both the husband and the wife.

INCOME STABILITY

Another category of research needs that might be served with the National Longitudinal Survey data can be described as the dynamics of total family income. The existence of periodic data over a ten-year period will provide an unprecedented opportunity for studying the degree of stability of income, and the sources of instability. An important aspect of such research might be the degree to which various types of transfer payments contribute to family income stability over time.

Problems in Retrospect

One by-product of any research project is the experience it yields the researchers. There has probably never been a piece of research that would be redone in precisely the same way if those responsible for it could operate on the basis of hindsight. The National Longitudinal Surveys are no exception. Indeed, the very complexity of the project, as well as its longitudinal nature, have posed special problem in administration.

Certain problems stemmed from the turnover of personnel that is almost inevitable in a study stretching over a decade or more. This has made it more difficult than in other types of studies to maintain consistency in the design and execution of the research. Significantly, the writer is the only member of the NLS research staff of the Center for Human Resource Research who has been involved continuously since the project began. Moreover, substantial turnover has also occurred among personnel of the Census

Bureau involved in the NLS project. Since the inception of the study there have been three chiefs of the Demographic Surveys Division, four different heads of the Longitudinal Surveys Branch—the unit responsible for the studies at the operational level—and countless changes among such personnel as interviewers, coders, and programmers. In the Department of Labor, there have been two changes in project monitors during the first nine years.

Other problems can be attributed more to the complexity of the project than to its longitudinal nature. For example, division of staff responsibility for the four cohorts, both within the Center for Human Resource Research and within the Bureau of the Census, has made it difficult to maintain consistency of treatment among the four component studies. Moreover, the division of responsibility between the Center and the Census Bureau has created difficulties stemming largely from faulty communication.

It is impossible to know how many of the errors that have been committed during the course of the project are attributable to such factors. However, some illustrations may make the nature of the situation somewhat clearer. One of the effects of turnover on the staff of the Center has been reflected in the content of interview schedules. Frequently, a staff member pressed for including questions in an interview schedule, but left the project before the data became available. Embarrassingly there have been instances in which no current member of the staff can explain confidently why particular questions were included. In retrospect, while somewhat sterner direction may have been in order, this is difficult in a staff of professionals, particularly in an academic setting.

One of the most serious errors in the design of interview schedules cannot be attributed to turnover. In the second survey of the boys, an unfortunate error in the skip pattern of the interview schedule resulted in the failure to ask youth who had changed employers between the 1966 and 1967 surveys the reason for the job change. As a consequence, it was impossible to differentiate between voluntary and involuntary job moves. Moreover, because of the approximately two-year lag between the survey and the time the data became available, the error remained undiscovered for a substantial period and was actually repeated in several subsequent surveys for which the 1967 boys' schedule was used as a model. Needless to say, the discovery of these errors led to improved methods of reviewing the structure of interview schedules.

Some of the problems experienced in the coding of data were caused by the failure of the staff of the Center to provide Census with sufficiently explicit coding instructions. Perhaps the most serious instance concerned the coding of labor force and employment status. Specific instructions for converting the responses to the CPS series of questions on survey week activity into the officially defined categories "employed," "unemployed," and "out of the labor force" were not provided the Census Bureau by the Center. For reasons that are not entirely clear, individuals without work experience were coded as out of the labor force, irrespective of their activity in the survey week. For the two older cohorts this made no practical difference, because individuals who by that time in their careers had never worked would be very unlikely to have been looking for work in the survey week. For the boys and the girls, on the other hand, this coding had the unfortunate consequence of excluding from the unemployed those individuals who were looking for their first jobs, thereby understating unemployment and labor force participation rates. It was not until intensive analysis of the unemployment experience of young women was undertaken by a staff member of the Center that the error was discovered. The erroneous data were then correctly recoded, but only after faulty data had been published and used in a study made for the Joint Economic Committee.[21]

Of course, not all of the errors that have been discovered in the data files are attributable to inadequate communication between the Center and the Census Bureau. Most have simply resulted from programming errors surfacing after the release of the tapes by Census. Many of these are found as researchers begin to analyze the data; others have come to light as the Center's data-processing staff has prepared the public-use tapes. Most variables in which such problems are discovered can be corrected fairly readily, since the responses to the schedule items from which they have been constructed are usually on the computer tapes. In some cases, however, where there have been programming errors in the computer edit of the raw data and the Census has lost track of the preedit tape, correction has required reference to the interview schedules. To guard against the recurrence of such costly and time-consuming situations, copies of preedit tapes are now being sent to the Center for storage.

One final illustration of an undesirable outcome in project administration resulted from the failure of Center personnel to preserve consistency in the wording of interview schedules over time. The 1971 interview schedule for the men used for the first time a series of rather detailed questions on nature of disability that had been developed by the Social Security Administration for a national study of disability. It apparently escaped attention, however, that the lead-in screening question designed to ascertain whether the individual had a disability was slightly different from that which had been used in previous NLS interview schedules. This made it impossible to provide confident measures of the change in health condition of the respondents between 1969 and 1971.[22]

On the basis of such experiences, there are a number of respects in which operating procedures could be altered and tightened up if the project were to be redone. Indeed, the discovery of problems has generally led to alterations in procedures; there is clear evidence that the study, over time, has profited from its own mistakes. Whether the errors that have occurred were inordinate in number of whether they are what might have been expected for a project as complex as the NLS will be left for others to decide. Those of us in the Center for Human Resource Research and the Bureau of the Census who have been intimately involved have been inclined to recognize that in a study including four data files, each containing about four or five thousand variables for 5,000 individuals, the potential for error is very great.

Afterword

At the time the foregoing account was written the NLS had less than three additional years to run. Now, five years later, the surveys are not only still in progress but have been expanded. On the basis of responses to a questionnaire survey of all known users of the NLS data and the recommendation of an interdisciplinary panel of experts, the Department of Labor decided in 1977 to continue the surveys of the four samples for an additional five years and to begin a new longitudinal study of a national sample of youth. Relatively brief biennial telephone surveys are being conducted with each of the four original cohorts, while a longer final face-to-face interview is scheduled at the end of the fifteenth year—1981 for the two male samples and 1982 and 1983 for the older and younger group of women, respectively. The decision to continue the surveys rested in part on the remarkably low attrition rates the Census Bureau was able to achieve. In the surveys conducted in 1976, 1977, and 1978 between 69 percent and 78 percent of the original samples were interviewed. Attrition was highest among the older group of men, but half of this was attributable to deaths.

The new sample of youth consists of about 13,000 young men and young women between the ages of 14 and 21, with overrepresentation of blacks, Hispanics, poor whites, and youth in the armed services. This study, which will be based on annual interviews over a five-year period, is designed to permit a replication of much of the analysis made of the earlier cohorts of youth and also to provide a basis for evaluating the expanded employment and training programs for youth legislated by the 1977 amendments to the Comprehensive Employment and Training Act. The initial wave of interviews was conducted in early 1979. Responsibility for drawing the sample, conducting the field work, and preparing data tapes has been subcontracted by the Center for Human Resource Research to the National Opinion Research Center.

In the meantime, research based on the expanding NLS data base has burgeoned. Eighteen volumes of research findings have been published by the Department of Labor in the four series entitled *The Pre-Retirement Years, Dual Careers, Career Thresholds,* and *Years for Decision*, and four additional volumes covering the first ten years of data for each of the cohorts will appear in 1979 and 1980. In addition, there have been over 400 journal articles, theses, monographs, and working papers based on the data that have been produced by staff members of the Center for Human Resource Research and the more than 200 research groups throughout the country who have purchased the NLS public use data tapes.

There is, of course, no way of determining whether the National Longitudinal Surveys have been worth the millions of dollars they have cost. Nevertheless, the diversity of important theoretical and policy issues that NLS data have been used to explore and the strong support of the social science community for the continuation of the studies encourage a favorable appraisal. It is less difficult to decide whether the personal investment of time and effort has been worthwhile. Some aspects of the experience with the NLS project over the past 14 years have been tedious and frustrating. Moreover, there has been an occasional longing to be able to wipe the slate clean and to begin something new. Nonetheless, the creation of a unique data bank, the wealth of research findings that have been and continue to be generated, and the many close associations with other researchers that have developed are ample compensation. It has been a richly rewarding experience.

NOTES

1. Sacrificing propriety for simplicity of language, I shall henceforth refer to the four age-sex groups covered by the NIS as the "men," "women," "boys," and "girls."

2. Later portions of this paper relating to the research that has been undertaken on the basis of the NLS data will provide additional illustrations of the application of longitudinal analysis. Enough has been said at this point to set the fremework for what follows and to underscore the unique potential contributions of the kind of project that is represented by the National Longitudinal Surveys.

3. For a fuller description of sampling procedures, see *The National Longitudinal Surveys Handbook* (Columbus: Ohio State University, Center for Human Resource Research, December 1973), pp. 5-7.

4. Thus, the men were interviewed in 1966, 1967, 1969, and 1971; the women in 1967, 1969, 1971, and 1972. In 1968 a brief mailed questionnaire was sent to the members of each of these two samples, primarily to maintain contact with respondents.

5. Prior to 1969, surveys of both groups began in May; in that year and thereafter the interviews with the women began in April and those with the men began in July.

6. For a more complete listing and detailed description of the variables, see *National Longitudinal Surveys Handbook* (Columbus: Ohio State University, Center for Human Resource Research, 1973), pp. 11-24.

7. For convenience, the reference week for these questions will hereafter be referred to as the "survey week."

8. The selected variables were to be included if they were relatively difficult to construct and were judged to be of interest to a substantial number of users.

9. For a description of the characteristics of the revised public-use tapes and their documentation, see the *National Longitudinal Surveys Handbook,* op. cit., pp. 25-40.

10. Carol Brainerd of the University of Pennsylvania, Sanford Cohen of the University of New Mexico, and Gertrude Bancroft McNally of the Bureau of Labor Statistics were members of this group.

11. The membership of this group has varied somewhat over time, but has included Cynthia Fuchs Epstein (Queens College), Gerald Gurin (University of Michigan), Robert Herriott (Abt Associates; formerly, Florida State University), Ann Miller (University of Pennsylvania), and James Morgan (University of Michigan).

12. Information reported in this paper on the work that has been completed or is in progress outside the Center for Human Resource Research is doubtless incomplete. Subsequent to the NLS tape-users conference in Columbus in mid-1973, all known users of the tapes were asked to submit the titles of completed research based on NLS data as well as brief abstracts of work in progress. The responses to this inquiry were updated on the basis of additional questionnaires mailed out in February and May 1974. All references to work in progress in this section of the paper are based on abstracts provided by the researchers.

13. Arvil V. Adams, "Earnings and employment of middle-aged men: a special study of their investment in human capital," Chapter 2 in Herbert S. Parnes et al., *The Pre-Retirement Years: Five Years in the Work-Lives of Middle-Aged Men.* Manpower R&D Monograph 15, U.S. Department of Labor. Washington, DC: U.S. Government Printing Office, pp. 31-78.

14. The relationship with the I-E score was significant for the whites, but not for the blacks. Moreover, even for the whites there is some abiguity, since the Rotter test was administered in 1969, and one can therefore not be sure that the observed association did not simply reflect the effect of upward occupational movement on degree of internality.

15. It is interesting to note, in passing, that the intercolor difference in the case of women between the ages of 30 and 44 is in the opposite direction (*Dual Careers [Manpower Research Monograph 21]* Vol. 1: 174).

16. In response to the question "What would you say is the more important thing about any job—good wages or liking the kind of work you are doing," 19 percent of the white men and 48 percent of the black men responded "good wages." In this case similar, although somewhat smaller intercolor differences exist also among women (*Dual Careers,* Vol. 1: 179).

17. Herbert S. Parnes, "Introduction and overview," Chapter 1 in Parnes et al., *The Pre-Retirement Years,* Vol. 4. Manpower R&D Monograph 15, U.S. Department of Labor. Washington, DC: U.S. Government Printing Office, 1975, pp. 1-30.

18. In the initial survey there was a strong relationship between this attitudinal measure and actual labor force status. For married white women, the difference in participation rates between those with favorable attitudes and those with unfavorable attitudes was approximately 25 percent (*Dual Careers,* Vol. 1: 71).

19. The latter relationship did not prevail among blacks, however, for reasons that are not clear.

20. In the 1971 survey of the men, a question was asked relating to the amount of education the respondent wished his children to obtain.

21. See Martin S. Feldstein, *Lowering the Permanent Rate of Unemployment.* A study was prepared for the Joint Economic Committee, congress of the

United States (Washington, DC: Government Printing Office, September 18, 1973), pp. 19-20, 82, 95-96.

22. That the minor change in working of the question had an effect upon response is almost certain. Between 1966 and 1969, with identical working of the question in the two years, there was an increase in the proportion of respondents with health problems of approximately 6 percent. Between 1969 and 1971, on the other hand, the data show virtually no change in the proportion of men with health problems.

REFERENCES

An asterisk preceding an entry signifies that the report was written by a member of the staff of the Center for Human Resource Research. All citations with PB numbers are available from National Technical Information Service, U.S. Department of Commerce, 5285 Port Royal Road, Springfield, Virginia, 22151.

Comprehensive Reports

The Pre-Retirement Years (Manpower Research Monograph, No. 15)

Vol. 1 by Herbert S. Parnes, Belton M. Fleisher, Robert C. Miljus, and Ruth S. Spitz. PB 180530

Vol. 2 by Herbert S. Parnes, Karl Egge, Andrew I. Kohen, and Ronald M. Schmidt. PB 192671

Vol. 3 by Herbert S. Parnes, Gilbert Nestel, and Paul Andrisani. PB 212637

Career Thresholds (Manpower Research Monograph, No. 16)

Vol. 1 by Herbert S. Parnes, Robert C. Miljus, and Ruth S. Spitz. PB 183539

Vol. 2 by Frederick A. Zeller, John R. Shea, Andrew I. Kohen, and Jack A. Meyer. PB 201288

Vol. 3 by Andrew I. Kohen and Herbert S. Parnes. PB 201287

Vol. 4 by Andrew I. Kohen with the assistance of Paul Andrisani. PB 220734

Dual Careers (Manpower Research Monograph, No. 21)

Vol. 1 by John R. Shea, Ruth S. Spitz, and Frederick A. Zeller. PB 193239

Vol. 2 by John R. Shea, Sookon Kim, and Roger Roderick. PB 214569

Years for Decision (Manpower Research Monograph, No. 24)

Vol. 1 by John R. Shea, Roger D. Roderick, Frederick A. Zeller, and Andrew I. Kohen. PB 201289

Vol. 2 by Roger D. Roderick, with the assistance of Joseph M. Davis. PB 220735

Vol. 3 by Roger D. Roderick and Andrew I. Kohen (no PB number yet assigned)

Special Reports

*ADAMS, A. V. and NESTEL, G. (1973) "Interregional migration, education and poverty in the urban ghetto: another look at black-white earnings differentials," September.

*ANDRISANI, P. (1973) "An empirical analysis of the dual labor market theory." Columbus: Ohio State University Center for Human Resource Research.

_____, APPLEBAUM, E., KOPPEL, R., and MILJUS, R. J. (1977) *Working Attitudes and Work Experience*. New York: Frederick A. Praeger.

ANDRISANI, P. and NESTEL, G. (1976) "Internal-external control as contributor to and outcome of work experience." *Journal of Applied Psychology* 61 (March-April): 156-165.

*BORUS, M. and NESTEL, G. (1971) "Response bias in reports of father's education." *Proceedings of the Social Statistics Section of the JASA.*

_____ (forthcoming) "Response bias in reports of father's education and socioeconomic status." *Journal of the American Statistical Association.*

*DAVIS, J. M. (1972a) "Impact of health on earnings and labor market activity." *Monthly Labor Review* 95: 46-49.

_____ (1972b) "Impact of health upon earnings and labor market activity of middle-aged men." PB 210224.

_____ (1973) "Health and the education-earnings relationship." *Monthly Labor Review* 96: 61-63.

*EGGE, K. A. (1971) "Black-white differences in annual hours of work supplied by males 45-59: a progress report." PB 208428.

_____, KOHEN, A. I., SHEA, J. R., and ZELLER, F. A. (1970) "Changes in the federal minimum wage and the employment of young men, 1966-67." In *Youth Unemployment and Minimum Wages*. U. S. Department of Labor, Bureau of Labor Statistics Bulletin 1657. Washington, DC: Government Printing Office.

*FAULK, D. R. C. (1973) "Job expectations and unemployment among young women with work experience." Columbus: Ohio State University Center for Human Resource Research. PB 222738.

FLANAGAN, R. J. (1974a) "Discrimination theory, labor turnover, and racial unemployment differentials." Chapter 3 in *Labor Turnover, Racial Unemployment Differentials, and the Dual Labor Market Hypothesis*. Final Report submitted to U. S. Department of Labor, April.

_____ (1974b) "Labor force experience, job turnover, and racial wage differentials." Chapter 2 in *Labor Turnover, Racial Unemployment Differentials, and the Dual Labor Market Hypothesis*. Final Report Submitted to U. S. Department of Labor, April.

FLEISHER, B. M. (1977) "Mothers' home time and the production of child quality." *Demography* 14 (May): 197-212.

_____, PARSONS, D. O., and PORTER, R. D. (1971) "Asset adjustment and labor supply of older workers." Report 7108. Ohio State University Division for Economic Research.

*FLEISHER, B. M. and PORTER, R. D. (1970) "The labor supply of males 45-59: a preliminary report."

______(1971) "Assets, nonemployment income, and alternative models of labor supply." PB 222737.

GRASSO, J. T. (1975) "The contributions of vocational education, training, and work experience: the early career achievements of young men." Ph.D. dissertation, Ohio State University.

______and SHEA, J. R. (1972) "The effects of high school curriculum on age-earnings profiles." *Proceedings of the Social Statistical Section, American Statistical Association*.

HALL, R. E. and KASTEN, R. A. (1973) "The relative occupational success of blacks and whites." *Brookings Papers on Economic Activity* 3.

JONES, B. (1972) "Labor force participation rates of black wives." Presented at annual meeting of the Caucus of Black Economists of the American Economic Association, Toronto, Canada, December 29.

*JUSENIUS, C.L. and SANDELL, S. H. (1974) "Barriers to entry and re-entry to the labor market." Presented at Conference on Research Needed to Improve the Employment and Employability of Women, Women's Bureau, Department of Labor, Washington, DC, June 7.

KARNAS, C. (1973) "Progress through college: determinants of successful completion of each undergraduate year." Ph.D. dissertation, Ohio State University.

*KIM, S. (1972a) "Cross-substitution between husband and wife as one of the factors determining the number of hours of labor supplied by married women." PB 211648.

______(1972b) "Determinants of labor force participation of married women 30 to 44 years of age." PB 206502.

*KOHEN, A. I. (1973) "Determinants of labor market success among young men: race, ability, quantity and quality of schooling."

______and BREINICH, S. C. (1974) "Knowledge of the world of work: a test of occupational information for young men." Ohio State University Center for Human Resource Research.

*KOHEN, A. I., PARNES, H. S., and SHEA, J. R. (1974) "Income instability among young and middle-aged men." In James D. Smith (ed.), *The Personal Distribution of Income and Wealth*. New York: National Bureau of Economic Research. PB 222571.

KOHEN, A. I. and RODERICK, R. D (1972) "Causes of differentials in early labor market success among young women." Pp. 329-334 in *Proceedings of the Social Statistics Section, American Statistical Association*.

LAPHAM, V. (n.d.) "Nonresponse on assets and income in the survey of mature women." Office of Research and Development, Manpower Administration. Washington, DC: U. S. Department of Labor.

LEIGH, D. E. (1976) "Job experience and earnings among middle-aged men." *Industrial Relations* 15 (May): 130-146.

MASON, K. O. and SCHULZ, B. S. (n.d.) "Fertility, work experience, potential earnings and occupation of American women ages 30-44: evidence from survey data." Research Triangle Park, NC: Center for Population Research and Services.

McNALLY, K. (1977) "Estimation of academic attrition behavior: an analysis of predictors of high school dropout behavior in the United States." Ph.D. dissertation, Columbia University.

*MEYER, J. A. (1972) "Labor supply of women potentially eligible for family assistance." PB 213737.

*MILJUS, R. C., PARNES, H. S., SCHMIDT, R. M., and SPITZ, R. S. (1968) "Some correlates of the labor market status of male youth." Pp. 47-75 in *The Transition from School to Work*. Princeton, NJ: Princeton University Industrial Relations Section.

MILLER, A. R. (1977) "The measurement of change: a comparison of retrospective and panel surveys." Population Studies Center, University of Pennsylvania.

MINCER, J. and POLACHECK, S. (1973) "Family investment in human capital: earnings of women." Presented at Population Conference II, June 4-5, Chicago.

NAFZIGER, D. H. (1973) "A Markov chain analysis of the movement of young men using the Holland occupational classification." *Catalog of Selected Documents in Psychology* (Winter).

_____ HOLLAND, J. L., HELMS, S. T., and McPARTLAND, J. M. (1972) "Applying an occupational classification to a national representative sample of work histories of young men and women." Center for Social Organization of Schools, Report No. 132. Baltimore: The Johns Hopkins University.

*NESTEL, G. (1970) "A longitudinal study of labor market behavior—advantages and some methodological problems in analysis." *Proceedings of the Social Statistics Section of the JASA*.

*NICHOLSON, E. A. Jr. and RODERICK, R. D. (1972) "A multivariate analysis of some correlates of job satisfaction among men aged 45 to 59." PB 210925.

_____ (1973) "Correlates of job attitudes among young women." *Nebraska Journal of Economics and Business*, (Autumn): 77-89.

ODITA, F. C. U. (1972) "Differences in pay, promotion, job title, and other related factors between employed male and female college graduates as indicators of sex discrimination." Ph.D. dissertation, Ohio State University.

*PARNES, H. S. (1972) "Longitudinal surveys: prospects and problems." *Monthly Labor Review* (February): 11-15.

_____ and KOHEN, A. I. (1975) "Occupational information and labor market status: the case of young men." *Journal of Human Resources* 10 (Winter): 44-55.

*PARNES, H. S. and MEYER, J. A. (1972) "Withdrawal from the labor force by middle-aged men, 1966-1967." Pp. 63-86 in Gloria Shatto (ed.) *Employment of the Middle-Aged: Papers from Industrial Gerontology Seminars*. Springfield, IL: Charles C. Thomas.

*PARNES, H. S. and NESTEL, G. (1971) "Retirement expectations of middle-aged men." Columbus, OH: Center for Human Resource Research.

_____ (1975) "Middle-aged job changes." Pp. 79-114 in H. S. Parnes et al., *The Pre-Retirement Years*, Vol. 4. Manpower R & D Monograph 15, Department of Labor. Washington, DC: U. S. Government Printing Office.

*PARNES, H. S. and SPITZ, R. S. (1969a) "A conceptual framework for studying labor mobility." *Monthly Labor Review* (November): 55-58.

______(1969b) "Hypothetical questions as measures of labor mobility." *Proceedings*, Social Statistics Section of the American Statistical Association: 182-191.

PARSONS, D. O. (forthcoming) "Cost of school time, foregone earnings, and human capital formation." *Journal of Political Economy*.

______"Intergenerational wealth transfers and the schooling decision of male youth." Unpublished paper, Ohio State University.

PARSONS, E. (1971) "An application of Holland's vocational theory to an empirical study of occupational mobility of men age 45-59." Ph.D. dissertation, Ohio State University.

POLACHEK, S. W. (1973) "A comparison of male and female post-school investment behavior and earnings using the 1967 longitudinal survey of work experience of women 30-44 years of age." Applied Economics Workshop Paper, University of Chicago.

*RODERICK, R. D. and DAVIS, J. M. (1972a) "Atypicality of occupational assignment among young women." Presented at annual meetings of The Population Association of America, Toronto, Canada, April.

______(1972b) "Correlates of atypical occupational assignment." PB 211489.

*RODERICK, R. D. and NICHOLSON, E. A., Jr. (1972) "An analysis of some correlates of job satisfaction among men 45-59." *Proceedings of the Academy of Management*.

*ROSENBERG, H. M. (1972) "The influence of fertility strategies on the labor-force status of American wives." PB 2133743.

ROSS, S. G. (1973) "The timing and spacing of births and women's labor force participation: an economic analysis." Ph.D. dissertation, Columbia University; National Bureau of Economic Research, Working Paper No. 30.

SANDELL, S. H. (1977) "Lifetime participation in the labor force and unemployment among mature women." Presented to the Congressional Joint Committee Compendium, *American Workers in a Full Employment Economy*.

______and KOENIG, P. J. (1978) "The geographic mobility of young women and their families." Pp. 177-195 in F. L. Mott et al., *Years for Decision*, Vol. 4. Manpower R & D Monograph No. 24, U. S. Department of Labor. Washington, DC: U. S. Government Printing Office.

SAUNDERS, D. N. (1973) "Labor force behavior: a longitudinal perspective." *Review of Public Data Use* (June 30).

SCHREINER, D. F. and KNUTSON, M. (n.d.) "Women in the labor force: place of residence as it relates to labor force participation, work time supplied, and income returns." Presented at the meeting of the Mid-Continent Section of the Regional Science Association.

SCHWARTZ, A. and NESTEL, G. (1975) "Earnings of migrants in their origins and destinations." Paper No. 17. Tel Aviv: David Horowitz Institute for the Research of Developing Countries.

*SHEA, J. R. (1973) "Welfare mothers: barriers to labor force entry." *Journal of Human Resources* 8, Supplement.

______and MEYER, J. A. (1972) "Potential recipients of family assistance payments: characteristics and labor market behavior." PB 209287.

*SHEA, J. R. and WILKENS, R. A. (1972) "Determinants of educational attainment and retention in school." PB 209625.

STROMSDORFER, E. W. (n.d.) *Policy Issues and Analytical Problems in Evaluating Vocational Education*. Final Report Project No. 8-0643, Grant No. OEG-0-71-3707, U. S. DHEW, Office of Education, Office of Program Planning and Evaluation, Washington, DC.

SUTER, L. E. (1973) "Occupation, employment, and lifetime work experience of women." Presented at meetings of the American Statistical Association, New York, August 27.

______and MILLER, H. P. (1973) "Income differences between men and career women." *American Journal of Sociology* (January).

TREIMAN, D. J. (1973) "Sex differences in the process of status attainment: a comparison of working women and men." Presented at the annual meeting of the American Sociological Association, New York, August.

*VALECHA, G. K. (1972) "Construct validation of internal-external locus of control as measured by an abbreviated 11-Item I-E scale." Ph.D. dissertation, Ohio State University.

VETTER, L. and STOCKBURGER, D. W. (1974) "Career patterns of a national sample of women." Center for Vocational and Technical Education, Ohio State University.

INDEX

ABOUT THE AUTHORS AND EDITORS

PETER BARTH is Professor of Economics at the University of Connecticut. He took his Bachelor's degree from Columbia and his Ph.D. in economics from the University of Michigan. He has taught at Ohio State University and was a visiting faculty member at the Graduate School of Business, University of Chicago. He has been a Brookings Institute Economic Policy Fellow and a German Marshall Fund Fellow. In 1971-1972 he was Executive Director, National Commission on State Workmen's Compensation Laws. From 1972 to 1973 he was Director, Office of Research, ASPER, U. S. Department of Labor. From 1973 to 1978 he was chairman of the economics department at the University of Connecticut. His latest book, to be published by MIT Press in 1979, deals with occupational illness and workers' compensation programs.

VERNON BRIGGS, Jr. is Professor of Industrial and Labor Relations at Cornell University. He received his B.S. degree in economics from the University of Maryland and his M.A. and Ph.D. degrees in economics from Michigan State University. He taught at the University of Texas at Austin from 1964 to 1978. He is a member of the National Council on Employment Policy. Many of his articles and books have dealt with employment and income patterns of minority groups. Among these have been *The Negro and Apprenticeship* (coauthor), *Chicanos and Rural Poverty,* and *The Chicano Worker* (coauthor).

GLEN G. CAIN is Professor of Economics at the University of Wisconsin. Among his previous positions are those of Visiting Research Fellow, Office of Population Research, Princeton University, Economist in the Research Division of the Office of Economic Opportunity, and Associate Economist, Federal Reserve Bank of Chicago. Long active in several professional and governmental organizations, he is a member of the National Commission on Employment and Unemployment Statistics, and he has served on the National Council on Employment Policy. He is the author of several books and articles, and among his research interests are the effect of unions on labor costs in the hospital industry and evaluation research of social action programs.

DENIS F. JOHNSTON is Senior Advisor on Social Indicators, Social Indicators Office, Bureau of the Census, U.S. Department of Commerce. From July 1974 to October 1977, he was on the staff of the Statistical Policy Division, Office of Management and Budget, where he was responsible for the preparation of *Social Indicators 1976,* issued by the Government Printing Office in December 1977. During that period, he also served as U.S. Representative to the Working Party on Social Indicators of the Organization for Economic Cooperation and Development (OECD) in Paris. He holds a Ph.D. degree in sociology from the American University (1961) and has taught a number of courses at universities in the Washington, D.C. area. He is the author of numerous articles on such topics as labor projections, manpower development, social forecasting methods, and social indicators.

RAY MARSHALL is the nation's 16th Secretary of Labor. He received a B.A. from Millsaps College, an M.A. from Louisiana State University, and a Ph.D. in economics from the University of California at Berkeley. Before entering government service, he was director of the Center for the Study of Human Resources at the University of Texas. He also taught economics at Texas and was chairman of the economics department there from 1970-1972. Earlier, he taught economics at the University of Mississippi, Louisiana State University, and the University of Kentucky. Long active in numerous professional and academic organizations, he has served as president of the Industrial Relations Research Association and the National Rural Center. He was chairman of the Federal Committee on Apprenticeship and director of the Task Force on Southern Rural Development. He has published numerous books and articles in the fields of economics, labor-management relations, rural economics, apprenticeship, and trade unionism.

JON MICHAELSON is an attorney, practicing with the firm of Hopkins & Carley in Palo Alto, California. He received a B.A. from Pomona College, an M.A. from the Lyndon B. Johnson School of Public Affairs, University of Texas at Austin, and the degree of Juris Doctor from the University of California at Berkeley (Boalt Hall). He was a VISTA volunteer, supervised the VISTA program in New Orleans, Louisiana, and was a member of the staff of the Assembly of Behavioral and Social Sciences, National Academy of Sciences, where he served as study director for the Committee on Department of Labor Manpower R & D. He is a former editor of *Industrial Relations Law Journal.*

HERBERT S. PARNES is Professor of Economics and Chairperson of the Faculty of Labor and Human Resources at Ohio State University. He received his B.A. and M.A. degrees at the University of Pittsburgh and his Ph.D. at Ohio State. During leaves of absence from Ohio State University since 1950 he has served as Visiting Associate Professor of Economics at Princeton University, Visiting Professor of Business Administration at the University of Minnesota, and Consultant to the Organization for Economic Cooperation and Development in Paris. His writings include *Research on Labor Mobility* and *The Pre-Retirement Years* (coauthor). Since 1965, he has served as project director (more recently codirector) of the National Longitudinal Surveys of Labor Market Behavior, the subject of his contribution to this volume.

MICHAEL J. PIORE is a member of the faculty in the Department of Economics at the Massachusetts Institute of Technology, where he has held an appointment since 1966. He is a member of the National Council on Employment Policy and a Consultant to Action. He has made numerous contributions to the literature on employment and training policy and specifically to issues involving internal labor markets, dual labor markets, and economic segmentation. New lines of inquiry include international comparisons of labor-management relations and economic performance.

GORDON I. SWANSON is a member of the faculty of the Department of Vocational Education at the University of Minnesota. He is a member of the Advisory Committee to the Education and Work Group of the National Institute of Education, and he served on the National Academy of Science, National Research Council's Committees on Experimental Manpower Laboratories as well as on the Committee on Vocational Education Research and Development. Contributions to the literature have embraced leadership development, entrepreneurial training, and educational planning.